WITHDRAWN

WITHDRAWN

HEGEL'S CIRCULAR
EPISTEMOLOGY

*Studies in Phenomenology and
Existential Philosophy*

GENERAL EDITOR
JAMES M. EDIE

CONSULTING EDITORS

David Carr
Edward S. Casey
Stanley Cavell
Roderick M. Chisholm
Hubert L. Dreyfus
William Earle
J. N. Findlay
Dagfinn Føllesdal
Marjorie Grene
Dieter Henrich
Don Ihde
Emmanuel Levinas
Alphonso Lingis

William L. McBride
J. N. Mohanty
Maurice Natanson
Frederick Olafson
Paul Ricoeur
John Sallis
George Schrader
Calvin O. Schrag
Robert Sokolowski
Herbert Spiegelberg
Charles Taylor
Samuel J. Todes
Bruce W. Wilshire

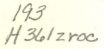

HEGEL'S CIRCULAR EPISTEMOLOGY

Tom Rockmore

INDIANA UNIVERSITY PRESS • Bloomington

This book was brought to publication with the aid of a grant
from the Andrew W. Mellon Foundation.

© 1986 by Tom Rockmore

All rights reserved

No part of this book may be reproduced or utilized in any form or by any
means, electronic or mechanical, including photocopying and recording, or
by any information storage and retrieval system, without permission in
writing from the publisher. The Association of American University Presses'
Resolution on Permissions constitutes the only exception to this prohibition.

Manufactured in the United States of America

Library of Congress Cataloging in Publication Data

Rockmore, Tom, 1942–
Hegel's circular epistemology.

(Studies in phenomenology and existential philosophy)
Includes index.
1. Hegel, Georg Wilhelm Friedrich, 1770–1831—
Contributions in theory of knowledge.   I. Title.
II. Series.
B2949.K5R6   1986   121'.092'4   85-45037
ISBN 0-253-32713-X
1 2 3 4 5   90 89 88 87 86

CONTENTS

86-6415

ALLEGHENY COLLEGE LIBRARY

INTRODUCTION

This book concerns a basic concept in Hegel's thought. Hegel often has been held not to be interested in, or to have gone beyond, epistemology. Although it is correct that he was not interested in a certain form of epistemology, most widely represented in modern philosophy after Descartes and prior to Kant and more recently in contemporary analytic thought, it would be hasty to conclude that he was not interested in epistemology.

On the contrary, Hegel was deeply concerned with the problem of knowledge, which he approached through his frequently mentioned, rarely studied, and poorly understood doctrine of circularity. Accordingly, the aim of this work is to study this Hegelian doctrine, its relation to Hegel's understanding of the problem of knowledge, and, beyond Hegel, its importance for epistemology in general. Even were circularity not a central concept in Hegel's thought, it would be important to elucidate it as part of the general task of comprehending and evaluating a major philosophical theory.

The importance of the concept of circular epistemology for Hegel's thought, although not yet for the problem of knowledge in general, is grasped more easily than is his understanding of it. Although his writings provide numerous allusions to circularity, he never discussed the problem in detail. Not only for this reason has there been little attention devoted to this aspect of his thought. In order to discuss it, it is necessary to infer the general outlines of the doctrine, the problem for which it is intended, its relation to that problem, and its usefulness to that end. But even prior to such discussion, it is not difficult to indicate the importance of circularity within Hegel's position. For if, as Hegel suggests, philosophy is intrinsically circular, then his entire position can be said to rest upon this concept, which accordingly is central to it.

In order to develop this point, I will discuss in some detail the doctrine of circularity everywhere presupposed, but only imperfectly described, in Hegel's writings. However, the aim of this study is not confined to elucidating or evaluating this doctrine, as important as that task may be. It is, rather, a means to a further, more significant end, which is to utilize this aspect of Hegel's thought to illuminate the wider problem of knowledge. Whatever interest there might be in a study of Hegel's position for its own sake clearly is outweighed by the manner in which it can be said to surpass the boundaries of its own historical moment through its continuing relevance.

This inquiry differs from much of the current Hegel discussion in that it focuses on a particular concern. In practice, that means that although, as Hegel would have it, the truth is the whole, I do not intend to consider the entire Hegelian position, surely an enormous task. Yet that is not necessarily a handicap, nor is it unfair to Hegel to apply to his own position those standards which he routinely reserved for others. For only in rare instances did he approach other views in detail, and he frequently focused his attention on one or another facet of the position under review.

Thus, the present study is not intended as yet another massive tome on the entire Hegelian corpus. It does not concentrate on one of the major writings in order to produce a detailed commentary, nor will it provide a detailed analysis of selected early manuscripts. In addition, there will be little of the quasi-philological study of a single text or manuscript, or even a fragment thereof, which has become increasingly popular. Instead, all the relevant techniques will be applied in a manner appropriate to the task at hand.

Another departure from the usual practice is the degree of attention to the historical background. The reason for that is both general and specific to Hegel's view. Ever since the inception of the philosophical tradition, it has been urged that genuine thought is somehow automatically protected from the ravages of time, in which it occurs but by which it is not limited. This belief is more an instance of philosophical hope than a description of what obtains. More recently, this belief has taken the form of a distinction between historical and systematic forms of discussion. A typical instance is Quine's reported distinction between those persons interested in the history of philosophy and those interested in philosophy.[1] The implicit conclusion, widely accepted in contemporary thought, is that if only we can begin afresh in total abstraction from, and even bereft of knowledge regarding, the history of philosophy, we can avoid its errors.

This suggestion is unacceptable, since the appeal to system as the criterion cannot be defended without reference to the history of philosophy in respect to which the concept of system is meaningful. It should further be noted that the distinction between system and history has its own history, which tends to undermine the allusion to merely systematic forms of thought. Kant, who drew this distinction clearly (see B864), also clearly failed to respect it in his own position, which depended upon his reading of other views. This distinction would be justified only if a position or doctrine could reasonably be grasped and evaluated without reference to the discussion in which it emerges and in terms of whose problems it is meaningful. But thought is never independent of social being, if only because ideas inevitably are intended to respond to concerns already raised by others, in relations to which they must be assessed.

The following is predicated upon the belief that philosophy and its history cannot be disjoined. This point can be sharpened with respect to Hegel, whose thought, more than that of any other philosopher since Aristotle, is the product of a conscious desire to come to grips with preceding philosophy in all its forms. It would not be necessary to recall this well-known Hegelian point here if it were not, to use Hegelian terminology, more often recognized than grasped.

Even were it not the case on other grounds, a rigid distinction between historical and systematic approaches is obviously uncongenial to Hegel's own position, which expressly is meant to combine them in a way which forbids their being dissevered. The rarely acknowledged practical consequence is that study of his position must necessarily, and not only incidentally, make use of his reception of other views in order to understand the intent, nature, and significance of his thought. For the system that Hegel constructed on the basis of his reading of other positions cannot be studied fairly in isolation from them.

In order to understand the Hegelian doctrine of circularity and the reason for which it is introduced, it will be necessary to consider in some detail the relation of Hegel's thought to modern German philosophy. It is not known widely enough that Hegel's original position arose not in relation to the Greek philosophical tradition, to which it only later was extended, but through meditation on the post-Kantian philosophical moment. In particular, Hegel's concept of circularity was the result of his interest in the ongoing concern to reformulate the critical philosophy in fully systematic form. This endeavor, which was of signal importance for the evolution of the entire post-Kantian idealist movement in German philosophy, is now largely ignored. Certainly, a number of its major participants have since receded into the history of philosophy. But these thinkers were well known to Hegel, who often responded in some detail to views which influenced the elaboration of his own, especially as concerns circularity.

In order to understand the intent of that doctrine, it will be necessary to reconstruct in some detail this facet of the reception of the
critical philosophy. Indeed, this reconstruction is unavoidable; the
pre-Hegelian background of this doctrine is significant in itself, certainly significant for Hegel's thought, and largely unknown. Anything
less than a detailed treatment of this period would fail to provide an
element essential for the appreciation of Hegel's doctrine of circularity and of wider use for the study of the position as a whole.

In practice, there will be some close discussion of a number of
figures in the history of philosophy, not all of whom are usually
mentioned in accounts of Hegel. His own thought, of course, depends
on extensive knowledge of the entire history of philosophy. Not surprisingly, students of Hegel rarely approach his command of historical sources. In part for this reason, discussion of his position, when it
refers to others, most often concerns a selected group of major
philosophers, including Kant, Aristotle, and Schelling.

On the contrary, the present discussion will stress Kant, Reinhold,
to a lesser extent Bardili, and certainly Fichte. With the exception of
Kant and Fichte, these names do not figure prominently in the Hegel
literature, and are not of basic importance in the history of philosophy. But if we recall that the doctrine of circularity was formulated in
response to the restatement of the critical philosophy in the form of a
grounded system, the need to dwell on these particular, often minor,
figures, is apparent: Reinhold initiated the discussion in question; the
form of his position to which Hegel responded arose under the
influence of Bardili; and Fichte provided the first clear formulation in
the German idealist tradition of the doctrine of epistemological circularity, although not its first formulation, in a form Hegel made his
own.

Discussion of Hegel's position will follow the proposed reconstruction of its background. Such discussion depends for its success upon
the proper choice of texts. Interestingly, consideration of Hegel's
thought in different languages and literatures tends to consider different sources as primary. Romance- and English-language discussions have concerned themselves mainly with the *Phenomenology of
Spirit,* with some attention to the *Science of Logic.* German-language
discussions have for some time emphasized the latter, turning only
more recently to early manuscripts, including the *Jenaer Schriften* and
the *Philosophy of Right.* Although these choices can be defended in
various ways, for present purposes it will be useful to focus our
inquiry on the *Differenzschrift* and the *Encyclopedia of the Philosophical
Sciences.*

The appropriateness of the *Differenzschrift* is almost self-evident. It is Hegel's initial philosophical publication, and the place in his corpus where the doctrine of circularity is initially formulated. The relevance of the *Encyclopedia* is equally evident; since Hegel explicitly designated this work as the official statement of his thought and provided no fewer than three versions of it, there is no reasonable alternative to it as the source of the mature view, including the mature doctrine of circularity.

A word also should be said about terminology. Hegel's doctrine of circularity leads to an antifoundationalist epistemology. The use of the terms *foundationalism* and *antifoundationalism* may appear out of place, even an egregious projection of contemporary terminology onto an older theory. It would seem that the latter term has emerged only within the last decade in analytic philosophy. But despite the analytic emphasis on language, ideas frequently precede the terms in which they are described. However much analytic philosophy and Hegel's thought differ, they share in part, with phenomenology, as well, the concern to resolve the form of the problem of knowledge bequeathed by Descartes to the later philosophical tradition.

This shared concern justifies the description of Hegel's thought through terminology which emerges only later in the modern tradition. Such terminology also provides an indication of a family resemblance, despite differences due to a change in perspective, between Hegel's own rejection of foundationalist epistemology and later forms of phenomenology and analytic thought. The use of such terminology in the present context is helpful in that, by calling attention to the relation of Hegel's epistemological view to later epistemological theories, it suggests a standard for the evaluation of the Hegelian approach.

ACKNOWLEDGMENTS

If I rarely refer in this book to others whose writing has been helpful to me, it is because no one I have read accomplishes, or even undertakes, what I have tried to do here. In that sense, my discussion here builds upon both all of the views of the philosophers with whom I have come into contact and none of them.

It is a pleasure to express my gratitude to colleagues, friends, and institutions who were helpful to me in the preparation of this study. An anonymous reader for Indiana University Press made careful, useful comments on an earlier version of the manuscript. Edward Casey, John E. Smith, and Maurice Natanson were helpful in various ways, either by suggesting the project to me, through remarks on an earlier version of the manuscript, or in conversation productive of useful insight.

Special thanks must go to the Alexander von Humboldt-Stiftung, whose generous award of a research fellowship [Forschungsstipendium] made it possible for me to spend the academic year 1981–1982 in Tübingen, West Germany, where the first draft was written. The entire Philosophisches Seminar welcomed me there with grace and good will, collectively and individually. I am especially indebted to Klaus Hartmann for stimulating discussion, warm personal contact, and every possible courtesy during my stay in Tübingen.

For an equally important form of generosity, required for the successful completion of this project, I would be remiss not to thank my wife and children.

A Note on Sources

For a study of this kind, the problem of whether to use available translations or to make one's own must be faced. One also must choose among the currently available editions of Hegel and other authors. In practice, I have employed the available English translations with some modifications. In all but rare instances, references are given both to the original and to an available translation.

The following abbreviations will be used in notes cited in the text:

A or B = Immanuel Kant's *Critique of Pure Reason,* trans. Norman Kemp Smith, 1st, or 2d ed.
SL = Hegel's *Science of Logic,* trans. A. V. Miller
PM = Hegel's *Philosophy of Mind,* trans. William Wallace
E = *The Logic of Hegel,* trans. William Wallace
PR = Hegel's *Philosophy of Right,* trans. T. M. Knox
PH = Hegel's *Philosophy of History,* trans. J. Sibree
HP = Hegel's *Lectures on the History of Philosophy,* 3 vol., trans. E. S. Haldane
FN = *Faith and Knowledge,* trans. Walter Cerf and H. S. Harris
D = *The Difference between Fichte's and Schelling's System of Philosophy,* trans. H. S. Harris and Walter Cerf.
PN = Hegel's *Philosophy of Nature,* trans. A. V. Miller
P = Hegel's *Phenomenology of Spirit,* trans. A. V. Miller

Unless otherwise indicated, all references to Hegel's writings will be given in the text in parentheses and will include an available English translation, if any, and the volume and page number of the recent edition: *G.W.F. Hegel: Werke in Zwanzig Banden* (Frankfurt a.M.: Suhrkamp Verlag, 1971).

HEGEL'S CIRCULAR
EPISTEMOLOGY

I

CIRCULARITY AS A PROBLEM IN HEGEL'S THOUGHT

This introductory chapter explains in a preliminary way why an analysis of Hegel's doctrine of circularity is necessary, and it provides the context for such an analysis. For even if, according to Hegel, the proper way to begin is to begin, several tasks require attention prior to direct study of the concept of circularity. And although such tasks indeed belong to the inquiry itself, from which they cannot be isolated as transcendental conditions thereof, they nevertheless must be attended to as conditions of the discussion to follow.

Four preliminary tasks are prerequisites for the study of the Hegelian view of circularity. The first is the establishment of a preliminary understanding of the term *circularity*. Second, an account is needed of the nature and extent of Hegel's concern with this concept. Third, a sketch must be provided of its prior discussion in the Hegel literature. Finally, the historical background must be reconstructed against which Hegel was led to formulate his doctrine of circularity. In view of its length and complexity, the fourth task will be taken up separately in chapter 2.

1

An obvious way to define *circularity* is by an appeal to geometry. Clearly, the concept has a geometrical source. It is equally well known that *circle* can be defined as "that plane figure for which every point on its circumference is equidistant from its center." But even if circularity indeed is invoked in these and similar terms by many writers, including Hegel, the philosophical interest of this concept certainly is not limited to its possible mathematical role. For this specific geometrical figure often has been invoked in an epistemological context to justify claims to know.[1]

The association of geometry and epistemology is obvious. At least since Plato's definition of philosophy as the science of sciences, geometry has enjoyed a special role within philosophy, disproportionate to its intrinsic mathematical importance. From the geometrical perspective, circularity and linearity can be contrasted as two major forms of epistemological justification; that is, arguments can be said to be either circular or linear.

Both forms of argument are well represented in the history of philosophy.[2] An example of a linear form of argument is Descartes's position. Its linear character is apparent in the claim that an Archimedean point can be identified, whose truth can be established without recourse to presuppositions, and which is rich enough to permit the deduction of all further true propositions. This argument and others like it are linear, since propositions which occur later in the chain of justification are regarded as true in virtue of their relation to preceding propositions, and not conversely. Such an argument can be said to be "linear" regardless of whether it can be held to meet strict mathematical criteria of linearity.

Circular arguments differ from linear in that an argument can be said to be "circular" if earlier propositions in the chain of reasoning are justified by their relation to later propositions, which in some sense follow from them. Such an argument can be said to be "circular" whether or not it can be held to meet strict mathematical criteria of circularity.

In the sense understood here, circular arguments are widely represented in the history of philosophy, virtually since the origins of the tradition in ancient Greece. Heraclitus mentions circularity repeatedly, for instance in Fragment 60, where the way up and the way down are described as the same,[3] and in Fragment 103, where it is said that on the circumference of the circle the beginning and the end come together.[4] It is unclear whether a clearly epistemological function can be attributed to circularity in Heraclitus's thought. But the beginnings of an argument of this kind are associated early on with claims for knowledge by other contemporary pre-Socratics. An example is the association of a view of circularity with the doctrine that like knows like. In Parmenides' poem, the way of truth is described as circular, and the way of opinion is characterized as linear. The result is to ascribe epistemological functions to circularity and linearity, which are correlated with knowledge and opinion.

A similar view is restated by Plato in the *Timaeus*.[5] Plato there suggests that the sphere is the most perfect of all figures (33 B-C), that the world is spherical, and that the soul comes to know through circular motion (37 A-C), in short through what may be called the correspondence of epistemological circularity to cosmological circularity.

As concerns circular and linear forms of justification, a turning point occurs in Aristotle's thought. Aristotle maintains the cosmological view of circularity even as he rejects the associated epistemological claim. He praises the circle as the most perfect geometrical form (Meta. V, 6, 1016b 17–18) and, it is widely known, emphasizes circular motion in his doctrine of the unmoved mover. But he forcefully criticizes circular thought on at least two occasions (Prior. Ana. 57b 18, and Post. Ana. I, 3, 72b 25–73a 20). He also specifically attacks the Platonic view of the soul as developed in the *Timaeus*.[6]

In virtue of Aristotle's criticism, later thinkers appeal less frequently to circular than to linear forms of justification. But circularity is by no means absent in the post-Aristotelian philosophical tradition. It is represented in the skeptical tradition by several thinkers, including Carneades.[7] It is especially prominent in neo-Platonic thought, e.g., in Proclus.[8] It later appears in St. Thomas's view of reflection.[9] A restatement of the Greek doctrine that like knows like occurs in the idealist view that we know only what we make, anticipated by Vico [10] and present in the writings of Kant,[11] Fichte, and Marx.[12] Circularity is further present in Nietzsche's reaction against idealism, and in later Italian neo-Hegelianism,[13] especially in the positions of Gentile and Croce. And it is prominent in recent hermeneutical philosophy in the views of Dilthey, Heidegger, Gadamer, and others.

2

The discussion so far has shown that circularity and linearity are two forms of epistemological justification well represented in the history of philosophy. What now must be determined is the manner in which this concept is present in Hegel's position. This phase of the discussion will include three segments: a brief mention of Hegel's terminology, a sketch of his appeal to circularity in his writings, and a brief examination of an epistemological appeal to this concept in the context of the justification of claims to know. Although the terminology Hegel employs supports the approach to this doctrine as basically epistemological, inspection of his writings reveals its occurrence in a wide variety of forms and contexts, some of which clearly are unrelated to the problem of knowledge.

Even before we sketch the range of allusions to circularity in
Hegel's writings, it will be useful to glance at his terminology for a clue
as to his understanding of the concept. It is Hegel's practice not to
forge a series of neologisms or to create his own special terms, but
rather to rely on the standard German language, which he employs
with a precision and consistency unsurpassed by other German
thinkers. Although German is rich in vocabulary, in particular in
synonyms and near-synonyms, it should be noted that Hegel consistently employs only one of the available ordinary German words to
refer to circularity, which, in consequence, takes on the status of a
technical term in his writings. It seems likely, in the absence of contrary indications, that his consistent utilization of the word *circle*
[Kreis] reflects a deliberate choice to isolate that word in the German
language which best reflects the meaning he wished thereby to isolate.

Other words, with closely related meanings, were available to Hegel
had he wished to make use of them. Perhaps the closest synonyms are
provided by the terms *Zirkel* and *Ring,* each of which, as does *Kreis,*
has a plurality of meanings associated with it. If, to simplify, we
restrict ourselves merely to the main denotations, the difference between these terms is easily specified. *Ring* primarily denotes "a round
or spiral form, as for instance a ring." The primary meaning of *Zirkel*
is "the instrument with which circles are drawn, namely a compass."
The word *Kreis* is defined as "a curved line, especially as the geometrical figure of the circle." Since the denotations of these words
have not shifted notably over the past two centuries, Hegel's insistence
on the word *Kreis* suggests that in the first instance he had in mind the
geometrical figure, that is, a curved line which departs in terms of its
curvature from linearity and which further curves back upon itself.

This point is helpful in the present discussion. Hegel's choice of
terminology would seem to suggest that he appeals to the concept of
circularity in the context of the rejection of linearity as an appropriate
form of argument. From this same perspective, it further could be
inferred that Hegel's appeal to circularity is meant to recall the pre-
Socratic doctrine that like knows like. For circular thought is precisely
adapted to know its object, since it mimics the motion of the real,
which is itself circular in form. But when we turn our attention from
Hegel's choice of terminology to the range of allusions to circularity in
his writings, we find that although they are a persistent theme
throughout his thought, they occur in numerous ways and in different contexts, some of which, such as the discussion of Newton's
sling, are unconcerned with epistemological justification.

The earliest allusion to circularity that I have been able to discover antedates the recognizable philosophical formulation of a specific doctrine in a systematic context, which does not occur before the *Differenzschrift (= The Difference between Fichte's and Schelling's System of Philosophy).* The allusion occurs in the so-called "Systemfragment von 1800," a small portion of a larger manuscript presumably completed towards the middle of September of that year. Hegel, or possibly Schelling, there differentiates between religion, which is concerned with the elevation of man from the finite to the infinite life, and reflection, which, on a lower plane, is occupied with the transition from the finite to the infinite. He then describes the activity of reason as being directed towards a middle point [einen objektiven Mittelpunkt] (II, 423) before adding, in Kantian language, which perhaps reflects the influence of Schiller, that pure spatial activity can be thought of as providing a similar point of union [Vereinigungspunkt] (II, 424).

The doctrine towards which Hegel was groping here is an early form of the concept of the absolute, which still bears the imprint of Schelling's thought, in which a point of rest [Ruhepunkt] is attained through the union of the finite and the infinite in a central point, especially as provided in the work of art. In the *Habilitationsschrift, De orbitis planetarum,* there are several passages in which Hegel specifically discusses the alleged geometrical circularity of planetary orbits in connection with the analysis of Kepler's laws, for instance in the following passage: "In circolo formali aequalis distantiae notio a puncto peripheriam efficit: et primitivus ejus character est, ut neque ulla diameter neque ullus peripheriae locus reliquis infinite multis excellat."[14]

As noted, this theme initially occurs in a systematic philosophic context in the *Differenzschrift,* where Hegel attempts to take the measure of contemporary German philosophy, in the course of his account of Reinhold's effort to preserve the systematic claim of the critical philosophy through a reduction of philosophy to logic. In a passage which will be analyzed in detail below, Hegel objects to the endeavor to ground knowledge in an initial principle for the reason that a philosophic system constitutes a whole in which every element is equidistant from the center.

From this text onwards, the theme of circularity becomes a permanent feature of Hegel's discussion. It recurs in *Faith and Knowledge* in the discussion of Jacobi, who is considered in relation to Reinhold. At nearly the same time, Hegel provides specific discussion of circularity in a historical context in an article on skepticism published in the *Kritisches Journal der Philosophie,* entitled "Relation of Skepticism to

Philosophy: Presentation of Its Different Modifications and Comparison of the Newest with the Old" ("Verhältnis des Skepticismus zur Philosophie. Darstellung seiner verschiedener Modifikationen und Vergleichung des neuesten mit dem alten," 1802). Although circularity is mentioned there explicitly in the account of the skeptical tropes, there is no mention of Hegel's own doctrine. Finally, one can note a passage in Hegel's "Wastebook" (1803–1806) where he restates the view, already alluded to in connection with the account of circularity in the *Differenzschrift*, that the fundamental principle of a position is its result, not its beginning (II, 550).

In the later writings, beginning with the *Phenomenology*, the view of circularity is in constant evidence, both in the works published by Hegel and in the series of notes edited by others after his death. Within the *Phenomenology*, this theme occurs on several distinct planes, including the criticism of dogmatism as exemplified in mathematics in the famous preface, and in the body of the work in relation to truth (P 71, 465; III 98, 559), spirit (P 464; III, 558), the concept (P 488: III, 585), and human activity within the context of the discussion of reason (P 218–220, 237, 240; III, 272–73, 293–94, 297). Especially noteworthy in the latter account of human activity is the manner in which Hegel follows Aristotle's view (Meta. Theta, 1048b 18–35) in insisting that human development is a teleological process in which the difference between subjectivity and objectivity is ultimately a distinction within unity. Circularity lies in the relation between the subject as potential, which acts upon the object in order to realize itself, and the subject as fully actual.

In the *Science of Logic* (*Wissenschaft der Logik*, 1812, 1816), this theme occurs often. Examples include the description of the whole of science as a circle (SL 71; V, 70), the discussion of scientific progress as circular (SL 71–72; V, 71), the image of the true infinity (SL 148; V, 163–64), the mention of the geometrical circle (SL 205; V, 234), and reference to the circle as the symbol of true eternity (SL 215; V, 247–48). In the second volume, this concept occurs above all in the discussion of absolute knowledge, in which forward progress is described as a return to the beginning (SL 838, 841; VI, 567, 570), and in the characterization of philosophy as the circle of circles (SL 842; VI, 571).

In the *Encyclopedia of the Philosophical Sciences* (*Enzyklopädie der philosophischen Wissenschaften*), the circle is a persistent theme throughout. Allusions to circularity can be detected in more than 20 of the 577 numbered paragraphs. If we follow the division of the book, the distribution of the references to circularity by numbered paragraph is as follows: In the introduction, philosophy in general is described as a circle of circles (15) and as presuppositionless since it returns into itself (17). In the *Logic,* the initial part of the account of philosophy, there are references to the circle in the discussions of the essence [Wesen] and the concept [Begriff]. In the former, attention is drawn to the distinction between a circle and its concept (119); and the circle which, Hegel pretends, arises from the interrelation of cause and effect (154). In the discussion of the concept, we are told that syllogistic conclusions follow from a circle in which opposing elements are mediated; and the speculative idea, which, Hegel suggests, follows syllogistically, is described as circular (235).

In the second part of the work, the "Philosophy of Nature," the circle arises in several, less clearly philosophical contexts. In the discussion of mechanics, mention is made of the circular movement of the sling in Newton's analysis of forces (266), and of Newton's rejection of the circle in favor of the ellipse in his account of planetary motion (ibid.). In the account of physics, chemical processes in general are described as a circle of particular processes (329). And in the account of organic physics, which in contemporary terminology would fall under the heading of biology, the development of the body is characterized as a circular process related to itself (337, 346). There is further an allusion to the surrounding [Umkreis] provided by general inorganic nature (361).

Finally, in the "Philosophy of Spirit," the last main division of the *Encyclopedia,* in the account of subjective spirit we learn that development is a circular process which occurs only on the individual level (387). In the discussion of the absolute idea, the three main divisions of philosophy (logic, nature, and spirit) are held to be interrelated in circular fashion through a series of syllogistic conclusions, in which each is the conclusion provided by the employment of the other two as respectively major and minor premises (574–577).

A similar concern with circularity is also in evidence in those writings which appeared only posthumously. In the *Lectures on the Philosophy of History (Vorlesungen über die Philosophie der Geschichte),* the development of nature is characterized as circular (XII, 74). In the *Lectures on Aesthetics (Vorlesungen über die Aesthetik),* all parts of science are described as constituting a circle which moves both backwards and forwards (XIII, 43), and the circle is evoked as the image of eternity (XIII, 395); in the second volume, the relation between linearity and circularity is mentioned (XIV, 312), and the use of circularity in Romantic architecture is evoked (XIV, 335). In the *Lectures on the*

Philosophy of Religion (Vorlesungen über die Philosophie der Religion), we
are told that the relation of the natural and spiritual realms to religion
forms a circle (XVI, 108).

Finally, in the *Lectures on the History of Philosophy (Vorlesungen über die
Geschichte der Philosophie),* there are a number of references to cir-
cularity. They include the circular development of spirit (HP I, 27;
XVIII, 51), another evocation of the circle as the symbol of eternity
(HP I, 88; XVIII, 109), and again in reference to nature as forming a
circle in a discussion of Heraclitus (HP I, 289; XVIII, 333), and the
further allusion to ideas as circular (HP I, 346; XVIII, 400). In the
second volume, there is further reference to circularity in the *Timaeus*
(HP II, 78; XIX, 93), and to the concept of essence as circular in
Aristotle's thought (HP II, 145; XIX, 160 ff.)

That ends our brief survey of the discussion of circularity in Hegel's
wider corpus. The aim of this survey was to point to a persistent
interest in this concept throughout the entire Hegelian corpus, including the *Nachlass,* as well as to indicate the different forms and
situations in which it appears. It is apparent even from this rapid
consideration that in many cases Hegel's references to circularity
either are not clearly epistemological or are even clearly non-
epistemological. An example of the latter kind is the allusion to
Romantic architecture in the discussion of aesthetics. Since there is
more than one kind of circularity at work in Hegel's thought, it would
be interesting to explore the relation among the various forms. But I
shall resist this temptation, in order to turn now to the relation
between the concept of circularity and epistemological justification
suggested by Hegel's choice of terminology.

The relation of epistemological circularity to epistemological justification in Hegel's thought could be explored in several ways, including through a study of his view of knowledge or of a series of passages
in different writings in order to determine the use to which circularity
is put. But it would be premature to discuss in detail the role of this
concept within the theory of knowledge before a relation to it has
been established. I shall now establish this relation through the analysis of a single passage in which circularity plays an epistemological
role. Although other texts could have been chosen, it will be sufficient
to concentrate on a passage in the *Phenomenology* in which Hegel
criticizes mathematical reasoning as a form of dogmatism.

In the preface to the *Phenomenology,* immediately after his discussion
of consciousness, Hegel examines the relation of truth and falsity,
which are described as belonging to particular, motionless thought
(P 22; III, 40). In that regard, dogmatism is described as the convic-

tion that truth can be captured in a permanent result or directly known (P 23; III, 41). This insight then is applied to mathematics (P 24–27; III, 42–46). The results of mathematics in the form of a theorem are, Hegel says, merely a true insight, which relates to the subject, yet which in virtue of its generality is unrelated to the object. "In mathematical cognition, "Hegel writes, "insight is an activity external to the thing" (P 25; II, 43).

In his criticism of mathematics, Hegel has two related points in mind. On the one hand, he wants to show the intrinsic limits of mathematics as a possible source of knowledge. On the other, he desires to indicate the superiority of philosophy to mathematics as an epistemological source. Both points rest on the deeper claim that mathematics, in virtue of its generality, is unable to grasp the truth of reality in motion. "The True," Hegel now states in a felicitous phrase, "is thus the Bacchanalian revel in which no member is not drunk" (P 27; III, 46).

It seems unnecessary here to undertake a defense of Hegel's controversial view of mathematics. But it would be a mistake to argue that if that view can be refuted, which has not been shown, the position as a whole could be rejected. For whatever the fate of the critique of mathematics, it is no more than an illustration of the more general point that a form of thought which is divorced from the movement of reality, and hence feeds only on itself, is necessarily one-sided and abstract, or linear.

The criticism of the linear character of abstract, mathematical thought points towards a more adequate, circular standard, a form of philosophy that Hegel here describes as "the process which begets [erzeugt] and traverses its own moments, and this whole movement constitutes what is positive and its truth" (P 27; III, 46). In other words, in order for thought to know reality that, as alive, is in movement, it must be like its object.

Accordingly, Hegel describes the process of understanding, that great power of the negative which so impressed Marx, as "the circle [Kreis], that remains self-enclosed, and like substance, holds its moments. . . . " (P 18; III, 36). Truth is similarly described as circular: "It [i.e., the True—T.R.] is the process of its own becoming, the circle that presupposes the end as its goal, has it at its beginning, and is only actual through development and through its end" (P 10; III, 23). And thought is further described as circular: "Through this movement the pure thoughts become Notions [Begriffe] and are only then what they are in truth, self-movement, circles, what its substance is, spiritual essence" (P 20; III, 37).

It is evident that Hegel regards the circularity of thought, which grasps the circular movement of reality, as an acceptable alternative to that form of dogmatism illustrated by mathematics. The latter, as deductive and abstract, or linear, fails to relate to any object. This criticism recalls the pre-Socratic doctrine of the adequacy of thought to its object, in which each is circular, as a condition of knowledge. But there is another, specifically modern dimension to Hegel's discussion, which is presupposed here, and which is not apparent without reference to the modern philosophical tradition. It would not be useful to indicate in detail that aspect of Hegel's position before an account of the discussion to which it responds. But it will be helpful at least to make a general point about the implications for knowledge of Hegel's rejection here of linear modes of thought in favor of circularity.

This point can be made in terms of alternative epistemological strategies for the relation of thought to being. Three general strategies can be distinguished, which can be designated as the Greek intuitionist approach, modern Cartesian rationalism, and the circular form of theory associated here with Hegel. In the Greek approach, employed, for example, by Plato at the highest level of the divided line, knowledge in the full sense is based on direct intuition of reality. But this strategy must be abandoned as soon as the naive Greek view of ontology is denied. In modern philosophy, beginning with Descartes, there is a return to the mathematical model indicated in the discussion of the divided line, with the important difference that the initial principle from which the theory follows, in quasi-geometrical fashion, is known to be true. The claim for knowledge depends, then, on the deductive relation of the remainder of the theory to an initial principle whose truth is known.

Hegel's specific rejection of the latter form of argument commits him to the search for an epistemological alternative. The strategy he proposes, and which builds upon an antecedent in the post-Kantian tradition, can fairly be regarded as an inversion of the rationalist model. In his denial that an initial principle, in virtue of its relation to the theory that follows from it, can be demonstrated a priori, Hegel is obligated to demonstrate it in another manner. In his alternative analysis, the initial point of the theory is demonstrable only a posteriori in terms of the explanatory capacity of the framework to which it gives rise, in fact the relation of thought to its object, or being. Clearly this kind of epistemological strategy is circular, although not in a vicious sense, since the appropriateness of the beginning of the explanatory framework, and accordingly the claim to know, is demonstrated in terms of the result upon which it then depends, instead of making the result depend on its relation to the starting point of the theory.

This circular form of epistemological argument can be regarded as an alternative to the linear strategy widespread in the post-Aristotelian tradition in the form of a qualified return to the pre-Socratic approach. The presence in Hegel's position of a theory of knowledge based on a doctrine of circularity is of evident interest, both for its own sake and because it often has been suggested that he is not concerned with epistemology and that his own view of knowledge is at best naive. If Hegel does propose a theory of knowledge, it is important to determine its nature and limits.

3

It seems useful now to survey, albeit briefly, previous discussion of circularity in the Hegel literature. There is precedent for this kind of survey, for instance in Fulda's helpful summary of the relevant prior discussion in his own inquiry into the problem of the beginning of the *Science of Logic*.[15] More generally, a survey of this kind is indicated since if each commentator is not to start anew, the present inquiry, if it is necessary at all, must build upon and justify itself in terms of the earlier discussion.

It is not, of course, possible to survey here the entire Hegel literature; nor is it clear that such a survey is still possible. Certainly its dimensions now would seem to preclude more than a selective acquaintance by even the most industrious scholar. Fortunately, an exhaustive account is not necessary. A selective, brief review of some items among the current Hegel bibliography will suffice to indicate that there is at present no adequate study of this concept, especially its epistemological variant.

It is no secret that, in this age of the computer search, bibliographic research has made rapid progress. The single most complete bibliography of the international reception of Hegel's thought of which I am aware lists more than 12,000 titles in the time span 1802–1975 in all languages.[16] It is significant that in the keyword index [Stichwortregister], which encompasses more than 120 closely printed, double-column pages, there is not a single reference to a study of any kind of Hegel's view of circularity. Now, even if one cannot expect this enormous bibliography to be exhaustive, it is nonetheless plausible to presume that it represents an adequate indication of the present state of the Hegel discussion, at least in that period to which it refers. Accordingly, the complete lack of allusion to this aspect of Hegel's thought is indicative of the degree of attention it has received in the Hegel literature.

One ought not, however, to attribute too much importance to any bibliography, since a mere list of titles or series of comments never can replace direct acquaintance with the works enumerated. Most studies of Hegel either mention in passing or fail entirely to evoke his doctrine of circularity. To take just one representative instance, Nicolai Hartmann's older work, *Die Philosophie des deutschen Idealismus, II Teil. Hegel,* [17] which appeared more than half a century ago, remains one of the better general surveys of the entire position. Yet it contains only three rapid references to circularity in more than 330 closely printed pages, in which the author alludes to, but does not demonstrate, the manner in which the system forms a circle (410), which can begin at any point (427) and which terminates in the concept of essence (455).

A similar tendency either to omit all reference to circularity or at best to mention this concept only in passing is characteristic even in the more recent Hegel discussion.[18] Several exceptions should be noted. To turn first to the English-language discussion, Walter Kaufmann cites several passages in which Hegel mentions circularity, and also furnishes a diagram, following Müller, in order to indicate that the Hegelian system was intended to form a circle.[19] More helpful is a remark by Charles Taylor in the course of a discussion of the entire Hegelian corpus.[20] After noting that Hegel's aim is to reconcile the finite with the infinite, Taylor indicates that for Hegel the proper image of infinity is a circle (115). The merit of this suggestion is to imply that for Hegel both reality and the science adequate to know it are akin to the movement of Aristotle's God, thereby relating Hegel's thought to the preceding philosophical tradition through the concept of circularity. Regrettably, Taylor does not develop this topic further.

A slightly fuller, but still unfocused account of circularity is available in Stanley Rosen's recent study.[21] Like Taylor, Rosen notes that the Hegelian absolute is circular in virtue of its presuppositionlessness. But unfortunately, the nature of this fundamental Hegelian claim is not examined, nor does Rosen endeavor to bring together his scattered comments on circularity within the boundaries of a single, unified account.

In view of the relatively recent development of interest in Hegel within the English-language discussion, one ought not to make immoderate claims on its behalf. The European debate began earlier, during Hegel's lifetime. But although continental scholars continue to maintain close contact with the sources of Hegel's thought, and are often closer to the original texts, several examples will suffice to show that not enough has been done in even the continental discussion to understand Hegel's doctrine of circularity.

There are only three works of which I am aware in the French-language Hegel discussion that even mention circularity. Hyppolite makes a single allusion to this concept, not in his masterly study of the *Phenomenology* but in a collection of studies on Marx and Hegel.[22] More interesting is a series of allusions made by Alexandre Kojève in his well-known work on the *Phenomenology*.[23] Hegel's doctrine of circularity is described here as his single new epistemological element (287ff.). But the result is a vicious circle (468ff.), because of the impossibility of determining the end of history, which Kojève holds is Hegel's aim, even if circularity is the sole criterion of truth (486ff.) and of philosophy (530ff.). From a very different perspective, Pierre-Jean Labarrière returns to this theme to understand the *Phenomenology*, whose specificity as a system depends on circularity.[24]

The German-language discussion of this concept is more frequent, but not necessarily more adequate. Theodor Litt suggests in passing that according to Hegel, philosophy is a circular process that realizes itself in the form of linear progress in time.[25] Walter Schulz twice has attacked the circle as a fundamental aporia in Hegel's system.[26] He has been answered in part by Klaus Harlander, who suggests (incorrectly, I believe) that circularity has no decisive function in Hegel's position.[27] In a response to Fulda's study, Horst Henning Ottmann draws a distinction between critical rationalism, hermeneutics which relies on circular reasoning, and *Letzbegründung*.[28] In the course of his work, Ottmann often alludes to, but does not develop, the concept of circularity.

Others have given attention to the historical roots of Hegel's view. In an excellent study of forms of thought, Hans Leisegang suggests that the origin of Hegel's view of science as the circle of circles lies in Scotus Eriugena.[29] Lacking is an indication of how or why Hegel's thought is related to this source. More recently, Klaus Düsing has usefully drawn attention to the relation of Hegel's doctrine of circularity to Fichte's early thought, although he does not develop this point.[30]

With the exception of Ottmann, none of the writers mentioned so far in relation to the German-language discussion provides more than occasional mention of circularity in Hegel's position. Two exceptions should now be discussed. W. R. Beyer has devoted a short monograph to the idea of circularity in the views of Hegel and Lenin.[31] According to Beyer, both Hegel and Lenin defend reflection theories of knowledge [Abbild-Begriffe der Erkenntnis], which is surely false as con-

cerns the former. Nor is it correct as regards Hegel that neither
employs the image of the circle for systematic purposes. And it is
further doubtful that Lenin's own theory is merely a restatement of
Hegel's own concept of circularity in materialistic form.

As concerns Hegel's position, the single most extensive discussion of
circularity of which I am aware is Friedrich Kümmel's study of Plato
and Hegel.[32] This book is part of a never-completed larger study of
the problem of epistemological circularity. According to the author,
the positive evaluation of the hermeneutic circle, which occurs only in
the nineteenth century, rests on the more general problem, ap-
prehended in various ways in the history of philosophy, of the relation
of the part and the whole. This problem, which initially arose under
the heading of the one and the many, must be resolved in order to
overcome skepticism.

The book includes a historical introduction, followed by two nearly
unrelated discussions, entitled respectively "The Platonic Diaeresis
and Its Ontological Presuppositions" and "Hegel's Dialectic of Freedom as Objective Mediation." The discussion of Plato makes use of a
single hint in the *Philebus* to consider the entire corpus, with special
attention to the later dialogues. At 15 C, Plato suggests that the *aporia*
in the relation of the one and the many must be transformed into a
euporia. Kümmel in turn proposes that this passage can be linked to
others, including one in the *Theaetetus* at 209 D-E, in which the
question of specific difference is posed. He remarks in this connection: "This definition includes all the aspects of a positive grounding
of knowledge which can be grasped only in connection with its possible *aporia* (and the circle itself as such is the central *aporia* of sophistic
logic and dialectic)."[33] But although it is possible to construe the
Platonic concern with the problem of the one and the many as a form
of epistemological circularity, it is far more likely that the latter doctrine is the consequence of centuries of philosophical meditation on
the limitations of the Platonic view of knowledge.

Kümmel's discussion of Hegel is intended to meet an objection
raised by Schulz concerning the intrinsic dualism in Hegel's thought.
Following Schulz, Kümmel regards the question of critical reflection
as Hegel's central problem. More precisely, if the absolute subject is to
preserve a relation to objective being, the manner of the relation
needs to be understood if thought is not to move on the plane of an
unthinkable reality or on the level of the emptiness of negative self-
reflection. In response, Kümmel suggests that if Hegel does not
provide an answer, he at least provides a framework for its successful
formulation. In other words, according to Kümmel Hegel was aware

of the problem, and there are resources adequate within his position to resolve the ambiguity to which Schulz refers.

The positive achievement of Kümmel's book is that it represents an effort to provide a study of aspects of the concept of circularity in Hegel's position. But in this respect, Kümmel's discussion is at best a mere beginning. Like the authors of so many other works on Hegel, Kümmel confines himself mainly to sympathetic exposition of the texts. There is no attempt to understand Hegel's doctrine of circularity against the historical background and within the framework of the system as a whole. Nor, finally, despite Kümmel's expressed optimism about the resources of the position, is there any effort to meet the criticisms raised against it, especially Schulz's point, which, although apparently conceded by Kümmel, is fatal to the position.

The modest intent of this chapter was not to furnish an analysis of Hegel's doctrine of circularity but to begin to clear the way for this analysis to be carried out. It was necessary to provide an initial characterization of this concept, to survey its treatment in Hegel's corpus, and to summarize its reception in the Hegel literature.

The results of this discussion can be stated quickly. It has been shown that circularity and linearity are alternative approaches, well represented within the history of philosophy, to justify claims to know. It further has been shown that Hegel appeals to circularity, which he understands by analogy with the geometrical figure, and rejects linearity, for the same epistemological purpose, in writings from all portions of his corpus. It finally has been shown that although this concept is mentioned in the Hegel literature, perhaps most often with respect to the *Phenomenology*, there is as yet no adequate study of it within the Hegelian position. Indeed, to strengthen this latter point, there is at present no detailed account either of Hegel's view of circularity or of its role within his theory of knowledge, which is the topic of the present study.

ALLEGHENY COLLEGE LIBRARY

II

EPISTEMOLOGICAL JUSTIFICATION

SYSTEM, FOUNDATION, AND CIRCULARITY

This chapter inquires into the immediate context in which the concept of epistemological circularity appeared in German idealism and in Hegel's thought. This doctrine arose within the debate about the reformulation of the critical philosophy in systematic form. Although this debate has been little studied and is very complex, a reconstruction seems in order of the conceptual context in which Hegel's view of circularity took form. Such a step is needed because, although that context is largely unknown, it was known to Hegel in detail, and determined the formation of his own view, especially as concerns circularity.

It often has been said that the period from Kant to Hegel is one of the two richest in the history of philosophy. But although the positions in that period have been examined frequently, the relation between them, the intrinsic dialectic of that moment of the philosophical tradition, is poorly known at best.

Different reasons can be adduced for our comparative ignorance of the evolution of thought in this period. To begin with, there is the interest in systematic thought rather than a historical approach. The former tendency certainly has contributed to a general neglect of the historical side of philosophy. Second there is the correlative stress on positions in isolation from each other, although it would seem that a thorough understanding of any thinker conscious of the discussion of his historical moment cannot be achieved merely through study of the position in isolation from others belonging to its intellectual context. Then there is the distorting influence exercised by the Hegelian concept of the history of philosophy upon the comprehension of the thought of Hegel's own time. In practice, that has meant that even those favorably disposed towards an understanding of the interrelation of the views of this period tend to assume without scrutiny an interpretative model which arguably not only fails to do justice to, but indeed significantly distorts, the positions in question.

This stress on the Hegelian view of the history of philosophy is unfortunately also in evidence in the study of Hegel's position. For although the genesis of his thought has been examined with great care, especially the early manuscripts, there has been insufficient attention to the problems to which Hegel was reacting in the contemporary debate.

The evolution of the post-Kantian discussion can be described in numerous ways. Since there is more than one strand in this complicated debate, obviously there is no single dimension whose description will present the entire controversy. But in view of the present concern with Hegel's concept of epistemological circularity, it seems wise to forego any attempt at a wider account of the evolution of post-Kantian thought in order to concentrate on a single, significant aspect. Since the appeal to circularity occurs in relation to the critical philosophy, it will be useful to focus the discussion on the debate in this period relative to systematic philosophy as it developed following the publication of the *Critique of Pure Reason*. The aim is to illustrate the emergence of a positive form of circularity in Hegel's thought as a novel solution to the problem then under discussion.

Prior to an account of the post-Kantian discussion, it is important to emphasize a change in the function of the concept of system within the history of philosophy. Beyond the evident overlap between ancient and modern thought on this as well as other topics, two broad attitudes can be distinguished: the concept of system is invoked primarily either to interrelate the parts of a wider position or, on the contrary, with the express purpose of justifying the claims to philosophical knowledge. Although there are numerous exceptions, it would seem in general that earlier views of systematicity are concerned mainly with the former, whereas more recent thought, especially in the post-Kantian discussion, stresses the latter.

In fact, that is an oversimplification, as are most historical generalizations. But it is clear that the problem of epistemological justification is specifically modern, despite the presence early in the philosophical tradition of various forms of skepticism. That the relation of system and justification has not been studied more frequently is not

surprising. Since the problem of system in post-Kantian thought has
attracted little notice, it might be expected that even less attention has
been accorded to this problem as concerns the history of philosophy.[1]

In order to appreciate the response to the critical philosophy, as
concerns the problem of system, it will be necessary to address Kant's
position briefly. Let us now rapidly sketch the reaction to the publication of the *Critique of Pure Reason* solely in terms of the problem of
systematicity. It should be noted immediately that there is more than
one concept of system in the philosophical tradition. In fact, at the
time Kant wrote, there were two different views of system competing
for his attention. These two different concepts of system, associated
with Wolff and Lambert, provide a conceptual framework for an
understanding of Kant's own grasp of systematicity.

Wolff and Lambert insisted respectively on the unity provided by
the deductive relation between the elements of the theory and the
need to establish a foundation, or basic proposition, for it. Wolff
especially stressed the deductive interrelation of the individual propositions which are the expression of systematic truth.[2] The result is a
congeries of interrelated propositions.[3] Lambert, on the contrary,
emphasized the ultimate principle from which the system was to be
derived in an explicit reference to the quasi-rationalist concept of the
foundation of a building.[4]

Although they clearly are different, it is less clear that the views of
Wolff and Lambert are incompatible. Lambert's emphasis on a foundation [Grundlage] is at least implicitly present in Wolff's own concept
of system, for instance when he writes:[5] "Qui multas veritates inter se
connectere et procul remotas ex principiis e longinquo petendis con-
tinuo ratiocinorum filo deducere valet." The idea of a prior concept
does not exclude that of an ultimate ground. Conversely, the interest
in the fundamental principle on which the system rests does not
exclude the deductive interrelation of its parts. In that sense, the
concepts of system defended by Wolff and Lambert are merely one-
sided emphases on the rationalist concept of philosophy as the deductive elaboration of the consequences of an initial, demonstrably true
principle (for instance, as noted in the Cartesian view of the cogito as
an Archimedean point). But it is also evident that the emphasis on
either deductive interrelation or a ground to the exclusion of the
other perspective results in a vastly different concept of system.

The opposition between these two concepts of system has been used
on occasion as a framework to appreciate Kant's own position and to
understand those of his successors. It has been suggested in this
respect that Kant is dependent mainly on Wolff, but also on Lambert.[6]

It further has been suggested that Kant's successors can be regarded mainly as the conceptual stepchildren of Lambert.

The implication, then, is that since Kant and his successors follow different views of systematic thought, the post-Kantian concern to systematize the critical philosophy was inconsistent with its own inspiration. But although in part correct, this judgment is also an oversimplification, since Kant's own writings reveal a certain ambiguity with regard to the concept of system. Nor is it accurate to regard the post-Kantian thinkers in general, especially Fichte and Hegel, as concerned with the concept of a final ground to thought at the expense of the deductive interrelation of the elements of their respective views, or certainly, as concerns Fichte, at the expense of the discussion of the concept of system as such.

The problem of system is addressed repeatedly by Kant in the writings of the critical period, and occasionally before that time. In the *Critique of Pure Reason,* Kant mentions the problem of systematicity in several places, most explicitly in "The Transcendental Doctrine of Method," in the section entitled "The Architectonic of Pure Reason." Here Kant defines *architectonic* as the "art of system" before specifying his conception of knowledge under the rule of reason as "not a mere rhapsody" (B 860). Rather, as a "system," it is "the unity of the manifold modes of knowledge under one idea" (ibid.).

Kant's understanding of the concept of systematic unity is made clear in the next sentence, when he describes it as "the concept provided by reason [Vernunftbegriff]—of the form of a whole—in so far as the concept determines *a priori* not only the scope of its manifold content, but also the positions which the parts occupy relatively to one another" (B 860). The parts of the theory form a unity under a single idea, in terms of which they cohere, against which each appears as a necessary element able to be inferred in its absence from the others, and which as a whole is articulated and not a mere aggregate. Conversely, the governing idea requires development on an a priori basis according to the principle of purpose which limits the multiplicity and the interrelation of the parts.

It is significant that Kant insists here on the unity of the elements under an idea, under the unity of purpose or the interest of reason, and not on an absolute foundation in the rationalist sense. In consequence, he remains close on this point to Wolff, despite his criticism elsewhere of the latter's dogmatism. Wolff also did not pretend to deduce the grounds of the system, but rather to deduce the system from its grounds as a whole. By the same token, Kant remains close to his own precritical thought. In an early text, "Principiorum Primorum

Cognitionis Metaphysicae Nova Dilucidatio" ("Neue Erhellung der ersten Grundsätze metaphysischer Erkenntnis," 1755), Kant objects to the endeavor of Leibniz to found knowledge on the principle of noncontradiction on the grounds that there can be no initial principle from which all knowledge can be deduced.[7]

Kant's treatment of the concept of system, as summarized here, suggests that the organization of the elements under an idea is merely subjective according to the interests of reason, that is, purpose. From this perspective, the concept of system as such appears as a regulative idea, but not as constitutive. But in his restatement of the concept of the fundamental principle [Grundsatz] mentioned in connection with the "Nova Dilucidatio," Kant appears to take a somewhat different line, and in effect to evoke the possibility of an objectively grounded system of thought.

In the *Critique of Pure Reason,* in accordance with the overall investigation, the concept of the fundamental principle is defined as a concept which is not susceptible to being grounded in higher and more general knowledge, and which serves to guarantee, on the basis of its subjective source, the possibility of the knowledge of objects in general as given in experience (see B 188). The fundamental principles, hence, function, as Kant specifies in a passage added in the second edition, as "principles *a priori* of the possibility of experience" (B 294), indeed as the only possible basis of all a priori synthetic propositions. But surprisingly, in the afterword to the "Transcendental Dialectic," concerning "The Regulative Employment of the Ideas of Pure Reason," Kant further holds out at least the possibility of a nonsubjective, objective, indeed transcendental foundational principle (see B 676).

The difficulty in specifying the precise outline of Kant's view of systematicity is due mainly to two factors: the essential ambiguity of the original position described in the *Critique of Pure Reason,* and its later modification in accordance with the evolution of his thought. On the one hand, there is a tension at this time between two different, perhaps not fully consistent perspectives, that is, that associated with the subjective unification under an interest of reason and that related to an objective, transcendental ground. On the other hand, the outlines of Kant's concept of systematic thought are further blurred by the later evolution of his understanding of the unity of reason.

The relation between the unity of reason and systematicity is clear, since the latter depends on the former. In the *Metaphysical Foundations of Natural Science (Metaphysische Anfangsgründe der Naturwissenschaften,* 1786), Kant defines science as a system which "should be a whole of knowledge according to principles."[8] This view is nearly identical with that in the *Critique of Pure Reason*, with the emphasis on system as regulative, not constitutive. Slightly earlier, in the *Fundamental Principles of the Metaphysics of Morals* (1785), he stresses the unity of pure practical reason with its speculative counterpart, which is differentiated only in practice, since there is only one reason which is differentiated in application.[9]

In the *Critique of Practical Reason* (1788), however, Kant again raises the prospect (already noted in the *Critique of Pure Reason*) that the theoretical and practical capacities of reason can be united so that everything can be deduced from a single principle in order to achieve full satisfaction.[10] But in the *Critique of Judgment* (1790, 1793, 1799), he adopts a significantly weaker view when he distinguishes two basically different domains: theoretical philosophy, dependent for its possibility on the concept of nature [Naturbegriffe], which presupposes for its possibility the concept of freedom.[11]

Even beyond the ambiguity in Kant's understanding of system, a further difficulty is posed by the presence of a concept of a transcendental ground [transcendentaler Grundsatz] in his writings. In even evoking the possibility of a final epistemological ground in a quasi-rationalist sense, it would seem that Kant enters into contradiction with at least the spirit, if not the letter, of his critical philosophy. For the very idea of the critical philosophy, in particular the insistence on the limitation of the sphere of the legitimate employment of reason, and hence the attendant limitation on the scope and nature of knowledge, apparently excludes such a concept. That is further the thrust of the precritical "Nova Dilucidatio." In other words, since knowledge cannot surpass the phenomenal plane, neither can knowledge on that level be grounded through reason.

Kant's suggestion that a rationalist ground might be possible, although he did not provide one, is highly significant for the later evolution of German idealism. For whether or not this goal is wholly consistent with Kant's position, a series of later thinkers, beginning with Reinhold, held that without a systematic structure, which in this context was interpreted to mean "an initial principle, or final ground, from which the entire system could be deduced," the critical philosophy was lacking the form which alone would enable it to guarantee its scientific character and provide adequate justification for the claim to knowledge.

In other words, these writers took seriously Kant's claims in the *Critique of Pure Reason* that "*philosophy* is the system of all philosophical knowledge" (B 866), or again that we need to determine the "complete system of pure reason" (B 736), or still again that "the philosophy of pure reason is either a *propadeutic* (preparation) . . . and is entitled *criticism,* or secondly it is the system of pure reason. . . ." (B 869). But they also held that Kant's claim to provide a systematic formulation of his system was largely illusory.[12] In order to be true to the spirit of Kant's position as it was then understood, it therefore appeared necessary to reconstitute the critical philosophy in the form of the system which Kant discussed but did not provide.

The desire to reconstitute the critical philosophy in fully systematic form gave rise to a spirited debate. This discussion involved at different times defenders and critics of Kant, simple exegetes and highly talented philosophers, thinkers whose principal importance consisted merely in their participation in the ongoing discussion and others whose writings were of intrinsic importance apart from the context in which they appeared. Among the most important participants, we find the names of Reinhold and Schulze, Maimon and Fichte, Schelling and Hegel.

A good summary of this situation is provided by the young Schelling, then a convinced Fichtean. In one of his earliest writings, in a passage reacting to Schulze's skeptical attack on Reinhold's position, Schelling expresses his conviction that the latter's theory of the capacity of representation [Theorie des Vorstellungsvermögens] soon could be reformulated in a manner which would answer the crucial questions of the relation of form and content that must precede all science in a manner exempt from further skeptical attack.[13]

This passage is helpful as an indication of the nature and scope of the discussion in German idealism after the appearance of the critical philosophy. In the course of his own endeavor to contribute to the problem of the form of philosophy as such, and hence to its possibility in general, Schelling usefully refers to the other main protagonists in the discussion, including Reinhold and Schulze, Fichte and Maimon. Particularly interesting is the paradoxical assertion that Reinhold's contribution to the resolution of the problem of the form of philosophy ultimately can withstand the skeptical objections earlier brought against it by Schulze, although the needed restatement must, following the position proposed in the *Critique of Pure Reason,* avoid the appeal to a final principle of all form.

The paradox obviously lies in the suggestion that Reinhold's position can resist the criticism directed against it only through the adoption of a strategy directly opposed to that employed in it, as indicated by Fichte (on whom Schelling is here heavily dependent) and Maimon. But Schelling's observation is nonetheless valuable, because it offers an essentially correct assessment of the importance of Reinhold's discussion of the problem of system, or form, in the wake of Kant's position, as well as in its insistence on the non-Reinholdian manner in which this difficulty was temporarily resolved in Fichte's thought.

In order to follow the complicated debate concerning the reconstruction of the critical philosophy in systematic form, it will be helpful to concentrate on a recurrent central concept. I have chosen the image of the circle, since, to a variable degree, this image is constantly present throughout the discussion in which it functions as a *Leitfaden,* through the association of circularity and epistemological justification. Circularity, to be sure, by no means is confined to the debate concerning the critical philosophy, but is widespread in the entire nineteenth-century German philosophical tradition. Mendelssohn, for instance, appeals to circularity as an indication of his inability to grasp Jacobi's view.[14] Similarly, Schelling uses this image to indicate conceptual difficulty.[15] Nietzsche appeals to circularity in relation to his concept of the eternal return of the same[16] and as the image of science and life.[17]

If we concentrate merely on the critical philosophy and the discussion to which it gave rise, we can note an interesting shift in the epistemological grasp of circularity. In Kant's writings, circularity appears in several guises. Following a number of writers since Aristotle, there are numerous passages in which Kant stigmatizes circular reasoning as in principle mistaken, e.g., in the *Critique of Pure Reason,* earlier in the *Inaugural Dissertation,* and later in the *Introduction to Logic.* But Kant also refers to circularity in other, nonnegative ways. In the *Critique of Pure Reason* alone, there are references to the circle of experience (A 4), the relation of the radius to the circle (B 508), the orbits of the comets (B 690), and, in a remarkable passage which anticipates Hegel's view, the suggestion that it is intrinsic to reason itself to seek completion in a system of knowledge through "completion of its circle [Vollendung ihres Kreises]" (B 825).

A similar ambiguity about circularity is also present in the post-Kantian discussion about the systematic reconstruction of the critical philosophy. In general terms, there is an important difference to be noted between the appeal to circularity as designating that avoidable mistake in reasoning known as the petitio principii, and as a positive feature necessarily constitutive of all forms of epistemology. Indeed, even before the second edition of the *Critique of Pure Reason* appeared, the objection of the intrinsic circularity of the critical philosophy was raised. Herder, for instance, suggested almost immediately that the

concept of reason which is self-critical is self-contradictory, because it
is circular.[18]

The alternation between negative and positive forms of epistemological circularity, the change in polarity of the sign affixed to
this concept, is the single most important epistemological aspect of the
discussion concerning the reconstruction of the critical philosophy in
systematic form. In this discussion, Reinhold played an exceptional
role in comparison with the modest intrinsic value of his position, or
rather series of positions.

In the present reconstruction of the debate concerning the systematic reconstruction of the critical philosophy, four reasons justify
close attention to the views of this modest thinker. In the first place,
Reinhold figures in the debate as a pioneer, a conceptual explorer
who discovers but fails to describe to any degree a new continent of
thought. Second, he was warmly accepted by Kant as an expositor of
the critical philosophy. Kant's desire to recognize Reinhold's contribution in this regard is hardly surprising in view of the mainly negative
reviews of his own major work. It is indeed well known that his
exasperation over the joint review by Garve and Feder led him to write
the *Prolegomena*. Third, Reinhold, not surprisingly, as the result of his
endorsement by Kant, was widely recognized by contemporaries as
proposing a nearly identical doctrine.[19] Finally, since Reinhold begins
the debate in question, the entire later discussion 's composed either
directly or indirectly of a series of responses to his own endeavor to
reconstruct the critical philosophy.

Reinhold's theory of elementary philosophy was developed in a
series of stages, prior to its abandonment by its author. During this
period, Reinhold's views are inseparable from his interpretation, defense, and revision of the critical philosophy. His discussion of Kant's
thought began in a series of *Letters on the Kantian Philosophy (Briefe über
die Kantische Philosophie)*, which appeared in 1786–87 in journal form,
and later in a second edition in a book published in 1790. Reinhold's
intention here is to protect Kant's critical theory against the meta-
criticism leveled against it by Herder. In a letter to Herder, Reinhold
indicates in dramatic terms his desire to be one of the "voices in the
desert" to "prepare the way" for the "second Immanuel."[20] It is for
this reason not surprising that Schopenhauer compared him to the
first apostle. We also can note Kant's uncharacteristically warm response, in a letter, to views he regarded as precisely identical with his
own.[21]

On the basis of his new-found recognition, secure through the
publication of his work on Kant, Reinhold became professor of phi-

losophy in Jena. During this period, he tempered his initial enthusiasm for Kant's thought by the recognition of the imperfect manner in which it was stated, which in turn led to the formulation of his own elementary philosophy. As early as the *Attempt at a New Theory of the Human Capacity for Representation (Versuch einer neuen Theorie des menschlichen Vorstellungsvermögens,* 1789), he was concerned with the systematic identification, explanation, and justification of the premises of the critical philosophy, through the introduction of a new theory of the capacity of representation [Vorstellungsvermögen].

This view was further developed in the *Contributions to the Correction of Previous Misunderstandings of Philosophers (Beyträge zur Berichtigung bisheriger Missverständnisse der Philosophen),* published in two volumes (1790, 1794). In the first volume of this work, entitled *Concerning the Foundation of the Elementary Philosophy (Das Fundament der Elementarphilosophie betreffend),* Reinhold formulated his Principle of Representation, the basic concept of his position, as follows:[22] "In consciousness, the representation [Vorstellung] is distinguished from both subject and object, and related to both." Slightly later, he published a short précis of his position, *On the Foundation of Philosophical Knowledge (Über das Fundament des philosophischen Wissens,* 1791).

Reinhold's concern to ground Kant's critical philosophy further played a determining part in the thought of this period, as witness his exchange of letters with Jacobi, Fichte, and Maimon. But Reinhold's own position underwent rapid evolution. In 1794 he left Jena for Kiel, at the same time as his thought began to evolve in another direction. In 1797 he abandoned his elementary philosophy and became a disciple of Fichte,[23] who was himself earlier influenced by Reinhold.[24] Finally, after a short period in which he was a follower of F. H. Jacobi,[25] in 1800 his allegiance shifted to C. G. Bardili.[26]

This brief account of Reinhold's changing series of philosophical allegiances is useful to gain a general awareness of the rapidly developing character of the discussion concerning the systematic reconstruction of the critical philosophy. For although the discussion itself was set in motion by the formulation of the elementary philosophy, this position no longer was held, even by its author, as early as a decade after its inception. And when Hegel, less than a generation later, began to write, in response to the continuing discussion of Kant's thought, the form of Reinhold's view to which he reacted was no longer its early, more significant phase but rather its distant, nearly unrelated successor, formulated under the influence of Bardili. But through his reception by Hegel, even after the abandonment of his most interesting stage of a philosophical position which was never of more than modest intrinsic importance, Reinhold continued to play the role of a conceptual catalyst in the evolution of the post-Kantian discussion.

The elementary philosophy is described by Reinhold in more than one text. In order to outline this position, it will be convenient to take as our source his discussion *On the Foundation of Philosophical Knowledge,* which has the advantage both of being relatively condensed and of presenting a mature form of this most protean position. As early as the preface, Reinhold raises the question of the form appropriate to science in order to justify the elementary philosophy. He remarks that neither logic, metaphysics, ethics, natural theology, nor the *Critique of Pure Reason,* nor any other empirical science, insofar as it presupposes philosophy, possesses "secure, recognized, generally valid foundations. . . ."[27] And he further remarks that the necessary foundation will continue to be lacking until a fundamental philosophy is elaborated, which he defines as "a science of the common principles of all particular philosophical sciences. . . ."[28] Otherwise stated, the elementary philosophy is the science which contains those principles presupposed but necessary to ground any and all forms of philosophical science.

This definition of elementary philosophy corresponds to, and is justified in the body of the text by, Reinhold's reading of the modern philosophical tradition. Following Kant and others, Reinhold here employs the concept of circularity in a negative fashion, in order to refute the epistemological pretensions of the major positions in the modern philosophical tradition, including that of Kant. As Reinhold reads this period, its main members are Locke and Leibniz, Hume and Kant.

Both Locke's empiricism and Leibniz's rationalism are precritical, since they simply assume their respective presuppositions without any attempt to justify them. And the theories are demonstrated by their adherents only through a circular, and hence inadmissible, form of reasoning, Further, if Hume has demonstrated that these presuppositions are effectively false, Kant has performed the same service for the presuppositions of dogmatic skepticism. But Kant's critical theory is itself based on a simple presupposition incapable of demonstration. For as concerns the fundamental proposition of the critical philosophy, Reinhold writes: "Its meaning can be explained only through its application, but in no way can it be developed or justified without a circle."[29]

On consideration, it is evident that the "critical" reading of the modern philosophical tradition here proposed presupposes a normative standard, largely rationalist, for thought as such. Knowledge can be based only on a form of Archimedean point, in this case the Principle of Representation. The problem of knowledge, analyzed in this fashion, consists in the determination of the proper epistemological ground, which Reinhold believes he has discovered in his analysis of the capacity of representaion. This principle, which arises as a fact in consciousness, is described by him as indemonstrable but self-evidently true. On this basis, Reinhold thinks that he is able to provide an unshakable foundation for the elementary philosophy which, in closely Kantian fashion, he regards as the condition of the possibility of all science, and accordingly as the source of all knowledge.

Reinhold's proposed solution, in allegedly Kantian manner, of the problem of knowledge quickly provoked heated debate. At least four main criticisms were formulated in the ensuing discussion. In the first place, it was argued that the critical philosophy, as already complete in its original formulation, did not require a reconstruction, either of the type suggested by Reinhold or in general. Second, the elementary philosophy was submitted to a searching examination in order to uncover and to criticize its own presuppositions. There was further an attempt made to reformulate Reinhold's Principle of Representation in another form adequate to meet the objections raised against it, in order ostensibly to carry out the task undertaken in the elementary philosophy, but which in fact resulted in a nearly complete refutation of it. Finally, by a wave of the conceptual magic wand, as it were, circularity, which until that time had been regarded as an epistemological liability, was transformed into a necessary ingredient for the solution of the problem of knowledge. These reactions called forth either directly or indirectly by the elementary philosophy are associated respectively with the names of Maimon and Schulze, Fichte and Hegel.

Of the two skeptical thinkers, Maimon and Schulze, the former is by far the more important as concerns the intrinsic interest of his position, even if the latter is more influential in the debate concerning the reconstruction of Kant's position. Maimon's preeminence in the discussion, in which every participant routinely raised the claim to a unique but wholly satisfactory comprehension of the critical philosophy, is attested to by none other than its author. In a letter discussing critically and in detail the manuscript of the *Attempt at Transcendental Philosophy (Versuch über die Transzendentalphilosophie)*, Kant clearly states that Maimon's reading of the critical philosophy is unrivaled among his opponents and for its grasp of the main problem.[30]

Maimon's reaction to Reinhold is available in an exchange of letters between the two thinkers which he later collected and published with an accompanying philosophical manifesto. In addition to its evident philosophical interest, this book has a personal nature rare in the normally arid literature of professional philosophy. The letters reveal Maimon's increasing frustration at Reinhold's refusal to engage in serious discussion on the grounds that he finds the other view incomprehensible.

In this context, we can understand Maimon's judgment of Reinhold, which, although particularly harsh, is not wholly false, and is relevant to other thinkers, as well. According to Maimon, Reinhold belongs to that class of writers who think through concepts without concerning themselves sufficiently about the objective reality of ideas, which underlie their proofs but which, in the case of Reinhold, are mainly false.[31]

The importance of this passage, which surpasses its personal nature, is to establish that Maimon's verdict on Reinhold's view presupposes its relation to Kant's, and hence presupposes as well a prior and independent interpretation of the critical philosophy. Although critical of Kant's views, as Kant himself acknowledged, Maimon held that the critical philosophy already was fully developed from a theoretical point of view.[32] The reconstructions of it proposed in the post-Kantian period, according to Maimon, were more apt to lower than to raise the level of Kant's position.

The significance of this claim in the midst of the discussion of the critical philosophy is almost self-evident. Maimon is not suggesting that Kant's thought is beyond amelioration, for instance from a stylistic perspective. But as concerns the intrinsic subject matter, there is no further progress to be made on precisely the same terrain. The clear implication is that the entire discussion set in motion by Reinhold, and not only his own view as such, is without purpose, since it cannot serve to perfect Kant's thought. Nor is this claim wholly false, since although the results of the debate were certainly philosophically useful, to the extent that it gave rise to such major positions as those of Fichte and Hegel, none of the later thinkers merely eludicated ideas already contained in the critical philosophy despite repeated assertions to that effect.

Maimon's judgement of the elementary philosophy is a function of its claim to found thought in an initial principle. Although Maimon concedes that Reinhold's "law of consciousness" expresses a fact (which no one would deny), he holds that other than through a confusion, neither a transcendental, nor a psychological deduction can show that this principle [Satz] is an ultimately primitive fact [ursprüngliches Faktum] without falling prey to circular reasoning [ohne einen Zirkel zu begehn].[33]

In a word, although Maimon allows the purely factual nature of Reinhold's principle of representation, he disallows the further claim made on its behalf. In effect, he raises against Reinhold the same sort of objection that the latter had brought previously against the four major positions identified in the modern philosophical tradition. It follows that despite Reinhold's strategy of appealing to a factual resolution of the conceptual impasse he had identified in order to circumvent the inability of theory to ground itself without falling into circular reasoning, the strategy employed is unsuccesful: it leads to a similar result.

The importance of Maimon's objection to Reinhold's position far transcends the latter. Despite Kant's contrary belief, it is but another example of the inability to resolve theoretical problems on a practical level. And there is further a more specific consequence concerning Fichte's position. For to the extent that it follows a strategy similar to that employed by Reinhold, it must be vulnerable to a form of Maimon's objection.

Maimon's criticism, if granted, successfully disposes of Reinhold's specific strategy to provide an ultimate justification of knowledge by grounding the capacity of representation in a fact. Maimon then goes beyond specific criticism in order to make a more general point. It is, he concedes, neither possible nor necessary to demonstrate the truth of initial principles. We are concerned with neither the reality, possibility, or actuality of such principles. Rather, we are interested in their capacity to permit the deduction of a science in the form of a systematic unity. For instance, in the realms of higher mathematics and physics, the principles invoked have the status of mere fictions adequate to explain a given phenomenon [Erscheinung], the condition of the possibility of a form of experience. But other than that they remain merely hypothetical. And although principles on occasion may appear self-evident, at best one can and indeed must demonstrate the need to utilize the principles in question, but not their veracity as such.[34]

It is not necessary here to discuss the quasi-operationalist form of philosophy of science which Maimon suggests. We can, however, note that the extraordinary interest of Maimon's criticism by no means is limited to the immediate context. His point is that the entire post-Kantian discussion of the systematic reformulation of the critical philosophy is superfluous, since knowledge as such neither requires nor admits of ultimate justification. He thus both surpasses the foundationalist approach in German philosophy to which Reinhold and many who reacted to him gave voice, and anticipates the contemporary concern with ungrounded forms of epistemology. Long before Nietzsche, and in a more precise form, Maimon can be said to have raised the fundamental objection against the need for and possibility of philosophical system. But as is often the case in philosophy, the more profound thinkers are not heard rapidly, if indeed they are heard at all. Therefore, it should not come as a surprise that the rather more systematic, but superficial, critique of Reinhold advanced by Schulze was also more influential in this debate.

Schulze intervened in the discussion in his book, the full title of which reads *Aenesidemus, or on the Bases of the Elementary Philosophy Proposed by Professor Reinhold in Jena: Together with a Defense of Skepticism against the Presumptions of Rational Critique.*[35] Schulze's critique of Reinhold, which appeared anonymously under the pseudonym Aenesidemus, needs to be viewed against the background of his own position, whose outlines are already apparent in the complicated title of this book.

Schulze is above all a skeptical thinker, as is evident in the choice of the pseudonym. Aenesidemus was a leading Greek skeptic, who renewed the teachings of Pyrrhonism in Alexandria in the first century B.C. Skepticism, as Schulze understands it, sets itself in opposition to any unrestricted claim to know of whatever sort. For this reason, Schulze's discussion of Reinhold is not an end in itself. Although much of the discussion in this work in fact is concerned directly with Reinhold, Schulze's interest is not in the position as such, but rather with it as representative of the critical philosophy.

There is, according to Schulze, an opposition between critical reason [Vernunftkritik] and skepticism.[36] Although Reinhold's intention is to carry out the task begun by Kant, according to Schulze skepticism is unaffected either by the critical philosophy or by Reinhold's restatement of it. For skepticism cannot accept the claim to either the certainty or the universality of the basic propositions [Grundsätze], or premises, on which the critical philosophy is based.[37]

Schulze is correct in perceiving an opposition between the critical philosophy and skepticism, although not in the simplistic fashion suggested here. Kant's view of skepticism avoids a simple opposition through the introduction of an important distinction between the skeptical method and skepticism. Skepticism as such is intended to defeat any claim to knowledge, as a "principle of technical and scientific ignorance . . . which strives in all possible ways to destroy its reliability and steadfastness" (B 451).

On the contrary, the skeptical method concerns itself with the resolution of disputes arising within understanding. It aims precisely at "certainty" [Gewissheit] through the discovery of "the point of misunderstanding in the case of disputes which are sincerely and competently conducted by both sides. . . ." (B 452) As so defined, the skeptical method is fully in accord with, and in fact indispensable for, Kant's position, as he himself stresses, above all for the account of the antinomies of reason. But skepticism as such, as Kant notes, is to be rejected. For lack of knowledge can never be an end point of the discussion, but is rather the cause of its beginning (see B 786).

To put the point in another way, in the process of the development of pure reason, despite the importance of skepticism as a counter to the claims of dogmatism, it must cede before the critique of reason (see B 788–89). It follows that there is a basic disagreement between Schulze and Kant: Schulze holds that it is sufficient merely to endeavor to refute any and all claims to know, as he here tries to do; on the contrary, Kant believes that the task of criticism of other views is not merely a necessary preparation to the formulation of a truly critical position.

The simplistic fashion in which Schulze opposes, in non-Kantian fashion, skepticism and critical philosophy determines the entirely negative, philosophically jejune manner in which he criticizes Reinhold's thought. The lack of nuance in Schulze's appreciation can be shown through a comparison between his and Maimon's discussion of the elementary philosophy. The point of contact is, not surprisingly, the problem of the kind of demonstration to which first principles are susceptible, already evoked in Maimon's critique of Reinhold. In a portion of the book written in the form of a pseudoletter addressed by Aenesidemus, the skeptic, to Hermias, a critical thinker, the former suggests that the claim that truth is to be encountered in awareness of experience can be adopted as a hypothesis able to resist the attacks of rationalism and empiricism; but despite the demand raised by the critical philosophy to do so, neither it nor the elementary philosophy can demonstrate its basic ideas, although they are believed to yield apodictic truth.[38]

If we examine this criticism, we can note that it is generally similar to Maimon's reading of Reinhold. As skeptics, both Schulze and Maimon criticize the appeal to a basic principle. But it is evident that Maimon's discussion possesses a finesse largely absent in Schulze's writing. The latter's insensitivity to philosophical nuance is apparent in two main differences concerning the respective treatment of the problem posed by an initial epistemological principle.

In the first place, perhaps because his ultimate target is not Reinhold but Kant, Schulze is less concerned than his fellow skeptic with inquiring into the extent to which the spirit of the elementary philosophy is consonant with that of the critical philosophy. Now, it is not difficult to grasp why an opponent of the critical philosophy would feel it necessary to engage in a discussion with an important commentator pretending to extend Kant's position. But it follows neither that the claim to complete the critical philosophy need be granted, nor that agreement of the effort itself with the spirit and letter of Kant's thought need be acknowledged without the kind of detailed examination which is lacking here. Certainly the effect of Maimon's examination of the concept of an initial principle calls into question the consistency of Reinhold's endeavor, apart from any indication of the extent of its success, with the spirit of the critical philosophy.

Second, it should be noted that Schulze's failure to inquire into the relation between the positions of Reinhold and Kant gives rise to a less than perspicuous treatment of the problem of the initial principle. Maimon's suggestion that such principles need not be demonstrated is doubly significant. It enables Maimon to hint that the intent of the elementary philosophy to achieve certainty is in fact inimical to the critical philosophy; and it further enables him to maintain, on another level, a sophisticated form of skepticism, based on a subtle interpretation of the thing-in-itself, largely in accord with the critical philosophy. For in this respect, the Kantian position is itself skeptical, since it clearly denies knowledge of things-in-themselves.

In this sense, Maimon's reception of the critical philosophy is not a simple rejection of it but rather an interesting elaboration of one of its intrinsic consequences. Schulze's skepticism, on the contrary, is in comparison more simplistic, since its aim is merely to infirm any claim to establish certain principles. Just as Aenesidemus had established a series of skeptical tropes questioning the veracity of sense perception, so Schulze now extends this perspective to the level of conceptual principles. By the same token, he explicitly excludes the hypothetical status of such principles as incompatible with knowledge, a clear difference from Maimon's view, and perhaps from Kant's, as well. But regardless of whether, if Schulze's argument can be established, it will infirm Kant's position, there can be no such doubt with respect to the elementary philosophy.

Schulze's strategy, commensurate with his view of skepticism as the constant reestablishment of doubt, is to show that although Reinhold seeks to ground all the principles of the critical philosophy in the proposition of consciousness [Satz des Bewusstseins], this proposition is not demonstrated.[39] The discussion is developed under the heading of the "Fundamental Teaching of the Elementary Philosophy" ("Fundamentale Lehre der Elementar-Philosophy") in nine sections, each of which provides the detailed examination of one or more allegedly central theses. The most important portion of the discussion is contained in the first two sections, concerning respectively the proposition of consciousness (pp. 44–58) and the "Underlying Concept of Representation" [Der ursprüngliche Begriff der Vorstellung"] (pp. 59–69).

In comparison with each other, the discussions in the three main sections are at best uneven. Schulze offers three main criticisms of the proposition of consciousness: it is "not a basic proposition" (p. 45); it is not "throughout limited by itself" (p. 48); and it does not express either "a generally valid proposition [or] . . . a fact which is not bound to any definite experience or certain reasoning" (p. 53). But these criticisms, although not without merit, are formulated mainly without consideration of the intent of Reinhold's view, and hence are not always relevant to it.

The first criticism is based on the assumption, current in philosophy since Aristotle, that the absolutely fundamental law of thought is the law of noncontradiction. This assumption leads Schulze to suggest that Reinhold cannot demonstrate the primacy of the law of consciousness without engaging in circular reasoning.[40] But since Schulze merely asserts, but fails here to establish the truth of, this claim, upon which the accusation of circularity rests, the refutation cannot be said to hold, at least not in the form in which it is stated. Nor is the criticism as such obviously relevant. For Reinhold is concerned not with the intrinsic order of principles which must be presupposed for rational discourse, but rather with the conditions of the possible justification of the claim to derive knowledge from experience. A similar point also can be made with respect to the last criticism, since according to the critical philosophy, which Reinhold follows at this time, no meaning can be attached to a claim of knowledge apart from that for a subject of possible experience.

The other criticism, as concerns the imprecision in Reinhold's statement of his basic concept, is relevant and important. Schulze develops this point in the second part of his discussion concerning the concept of representation [Vorstellung]. After initial clarification of the mean-

ing of the terms *representation, subject,* and *object,* he remarks, concerning their relation, that if the representation is to be thought of
only as that, it must be considered not insofar as it is related to subject
and object but as it can be thought of in relation to both subject and
object.[41] This subtle correction of Reinhold's understanding of the
relation in question is highly significant, since it grounds the possibility of knowledge of the object through its representation. Such
knowledge otherwise would be excluded, if the same representation
did not relate to both subjective and objective epistemological poles.
This observation was further influential in the immediate philosophical discussion. Fichte's recognition of the importance of Schulze's
reformulation of Reinhold's concept of representation was an important step in the formulation of his own position.

Although both Maimon and Schulze were reacting to Reinhold's
endeavor to endow the critical philosophy with systematic form in
terms of an initial principle, the differences in their respective approaches could scarcely be greater. I have been unable to find any
evidence of Schulze's reaction to Maimon; but the latter was fully
aware of the lack of agreement between their views. In a letter to
Reinhold, he describes this difference as of "celestial dimensions"
[himmelweit].[42]

Fichte is the author of the fourth and last position to be considered
in relation to the attempt, initiated by Reinhold, to provide a systematic reconstruction of the critical philosophy. In this context, to an
extent equaled only by Reinhold's view, Fichte's view literally is
brought into being in order to resolve the discussion concerning the
restatement of Kant's thought. But unlike Reinhold's position, which
is significant only in relation to this debate, Fichte's is a major philosophical landmark, whose importance in no way is limited to the
occasion to which it responds.

In view of the scope of Fichte's thought, it will be necessary to
restrict consideration here merely to its relation to the discussion
initiated by Reinhold. In this respect, there is an important difference
which opposes Fichte's view to its predecessors in a manner that
renders it useful for the constitution of Hegel's own position. Like his
predecessors, Fichte also makes use of the concept of circularity in the
course of his attempt to formulate a theory of philosophical system on
the basis of a single concept. But there is a remarkable change within
his thought on the crucial point of the relation of circularity to
systematicity. For in the course of his consideration of this problem,
Fichte gradually rethinks the concept of circularity, so that it functions

no longer negatively, as a reason to reject a suggested form of theory, but positively, as a constitutive element of theory as such.

As is often the case in an ongoing discussion, the relation between the participants (in this case Fichte and his predecessors) is both clear and hardly so. Although it is clear that Fichte was aware of and even influenced in his thinking by the views of the other participants, the precise nature of that influence, and even the relation of Fichte's view to Kant's, are open to question. In part, this uncertainty is due to the fact that although Fichte was a polemical writer, unlike Maimon and Schulze, who provide detailed expositions of their grasp of other views, Fichte's corpus does not contain more than occasional, often misleading hints about its relation to the positions of Kant and the other post-Kantians.

Any account of the relation of Fichte's position to its predecessors does well to begin with Kant. There can be little doubt that Fichte consciously intended his position to bring to a successful conclusion the philosophical revolution inaugurated by Kant. But although an analogous claim was made routinely by other participants in this discussion, in Fichte's thought, for a variety of reasons, it acquired increased credibility. Certainly one factor was the unusual personal identification with Kant. The details of this identification—including Fichte's trip to Königsberg, where he was rebuffed by Kant, and the accidentally anonymous publication of his first book, the *Critique of All Revelation* (*Kritik aller Offenbarung*, 1792), which initially was regarded as the long-awaited Kantian work on religion—are too well known to require discussion here.

Also interesting is Fichte's belief that Kant's position was based on the former's fundamental principles.[43] The excessive nature of this assertion is diminished when we remember that Kant had made a similar claim to understand Plato better than he understood himself (B 370), and that similar claims were made by others, including Schelling.[44] Now, Kant, to be sure, was unwilling to recognize Fichte's claim with respect to the critical philosophy. Kant's criticism is formulated in a single sentence, in which he stigmatizes Fichte's alleged concern to deduce a real object from pure logic.[45] Fichte reacted to this criticism in a letter to Schelling, where he attempted to dismiss the objection as a mere verbal quibble.[46] Whether it is, in fact, a mere quibble is a question of judgment, although it should be noted that there is a deeper question implicit here—that is, the sense that can be given to any claim to be the legitimate representative of a given perspective. But it is of interest to note that Fichte's assertion that he

alone was the legitimate successor to Kant, despite numerous rival
claims, was given special weight by his contemporaries.

Fichte's specific understanding of Kant's position determined both
his attitude towards other post-Kantians and the direction in which
his own thought later developed. His grasp of Kant and the post-
Kantians is perhaps most easily accessible in his correspondence. In a
draft of an early letter, Fichte remarks that he is aware of the critical
philosophy as an impenetrable fortress which neither Kant nor
Reinhold has successfully constructed.[47] This letter permits two inferences to be drawn: that Kant's position, if not the form in which it is
stated, cannot be surpassed, and that the critical philosophy has never
yet been successfully formulated. Fichte confirms the first inference in
another letter, where he states that the critical philosophy is correct
with respect to its results, but not its basic principles.[48]

In view of his opinion of Kant's thought, Fichte's dissatisfaction with
Reinhold's attempted reformulation of the critical philosophy made a
successful completion of this task a matter of the highest philosophical
priority. A correct appreciation of Fichte's relation to the post-Kantian
thinkers is necessary to grasp the nature of the view he advanced in
order to complete the critical philosophy. In general terms, Fichte's
thought can be understood as including four interrelated elements,
which together gave rise to the initial form of his position.

To begin with, Reinhold's conception of the initial principle is inadequate as it stands. On this point, Fichte seems to be reflecting prior
knowledge of the critique leveled against Reinhold by Schulze when
he writes, in a letter to Reinhold concerning the latter's *Foundation of
Philosophical Knowledge,* that even before reading Reinhold he accepted the latter's principle of consciousness, although it must be
derived from still-deeper principles.[49]

Second, despite the tactful (for Fichte) manner in which the demur
is stated, it is clear that Fichte has been influenced by Schulze. The
dimensions of this influence, which had the effect of overturning
Fichte's prior acceptance of Reinhold's specific criticism but not the
reliance upon the general approach to philosophical system in terms
of an initial principle, is reflected in two letters of similar tenor. In the
earlier letter, he states that Aenesidemus has convinced him that
neither Kant nor Reinhold has been successful in providing a scientific form of philosophy, and accordingly has shaken his own view,
which can be restructured only in terms of a single principle.[50] We
can, then, understand Fichte's admission, in the initial sentence of his
early metatheoretical text "On the Concept of the Science of Knowledge" ("Über den Begriff der Wissenschaftslehre," 1974), that he has

become convinced through his reading of Schulze and Maimon that despite the efforts of the most intelligent writers, philosophy has yet to reach the status of an evident science.[51] Here Fichte merely extends his appreciation of the critique of Reinhold advanced by Schulze to include Maimon, as well.

Finally, despite the evident failure of Reinhold's endeavor, Fichte believes he has discovered a way in which to develop a system based on a single principle, and hence to carry out in satisfactory fashion the reconstruction of the critical philosophy in full systematic form. The claim in quesiton, if not its execution, is clearly suggested in the next sentence of this text, where Fichte states that he believes himself to have discovered the proper manner to respond satisfactorily to the well-justified objections raised by the skeptics against the critical philosophy.[52]

The position which Fichte elaborates is influenced greatly by Kant and the post-Kantians already mentioned. As already noted, Fichte, like Reinhold, accepts Kant's results, but he rejects the manner in which they are formulated, even as he declines Reinhold's attempted restatement of them.[53] He is influenced in different ways by both Maimon and Schulze. His appreciation of Maimon as a thinker of the first magnitude, spelled out in a letter to Reinhold [54] after the publication of the *Foundation of the Entire Science of Knowledge* (*Grundlage der gesamten Wissenschaftslehre*, 1794), when Fichte already had laid claim to the title of the leading philosopher of the age, is highly significant, and is reflected in the reworking of themes from Maimon throughout that work.[55] But although Maimon's influence on the constitution of Fichte's thought in general should not be neglected, as concerns his treatment of Reinhold's problem of system based on a single principle, a greater, indeed decisive, importance must be accorded to Schulze's influence.

Important philosophical positions usually are overdetermined by numerous factors, and hence are not explicable in terms of a single influence. But although such is also the case for Fichte's view, to an unusual extent it took shape in a single occasion, namely, his extremely sober and thoughtful review of Schulze's polemical attack on Reinhold's elementary philosophy.[56] Fichte's approach, which determines his own later thought, consists in the partial acceptance of Schulze's critique. More precisely, he adopts the attitude, presumably under Maimon's influence, that Schulze ought not to have questioned the correctness of Reinhold's principle of representation. But he concedes Schulze's major point, that is, that the principle is inadequate as formulated. Fichte's twofold response consists in the endeavor to formulate an adequate version of Reinhold's principle, and further to rethink the function of this principle for the problem of knowledge.

As concerns the form of the principle, Fichte accepts without question Schulze's criticism, which he restates as a basic element of his own thought. In the discussion of Schulze's book, Fichte quotes a passage, noted above, in which he proposes a reformulation of Reinhold's principle, before reformulating Schulze's suggestion as the claim that the representation is related to the object as the effect to its cause, and to the subject as an accident to substance.[57]

The significance of this new formulation, which is by no means merely a linguistic change, is, as Fichte points out to defend Reinhold's original principle against the skeptical attack launched on it by Schulze. But Fichte objects to Schulze's own restatement of this principle, since the appeal to a causal relation between an object and its representation is inconsistent with the claim that prior to the latter, the former is unknown. The intent, then, of Fichte's own formulation of Reinhold's principle, as restated by Schulze, is to provide a version of it which makes plain the parallel between the ontological and the causal relations.

More important than an adequate restatement of Reinhold's principle, in the light of Schulze's objections and attempted reformulation, is the fashion in which Fichte rethinks its philosophical function. Although he does not embrace skepticism, as is evident in his replacement of Schulze's language by his own, he is also unwilling to admit that theory can be grounded, as Reinhold desires. For even if a theory can be shown to derive from a single, prior principle, as Reinhold intends, Fichte denies, as Reinhold also intends, that the initial principle itself can be demonstrated within the theory.

In a passage of great importance, Fichte responds to those, such as Reinhold, who seek to ground the critical philosophy, as well as those, such as Schulze, who believe that an adequate ground for it has yet to be found. Fichte's argument, which is conducted on the quasi-Kantian terrain of ethical freedom, provides a rejection on general epistemological grounds of the possibility of a foundation to knowledge. In his claim that the critical attitude consists precisely in the rejection of the demand to found the autonomy of the subject, because of the primacy of practical reason over its theoretical counterpart, Fichte asserts that the role of philosophy in general consists in demonstration on the basis of the consciousness of the subject. The purpose of philosophy is to explain the content of consciousnes from a point within it; and the result is a necessary circle which cannot be surpassed and which provides for us the innermost relation of knowledge.[58]

Fichte's examination of the concept of circularity is an aspect of his position which so far seems not to have received more than passing notice, but which is important both in respect to his own thought and for the grasp of Hegel's position. On inspection, we can perceive here a transformation of the function of this concept from the negative designation of a failure in the reasoning process, as already indicated everywhere present in the discussion prompted by the critical philosophy, to a positive description of an ineliminable element of thought itself, hence devoid of negative signification.

The full significance of this reinterpretation of circularity, both for Hegel's own position and for thought itself, will emerge only in later chapters. It may, however, be indicated here that Fichte's reinterpretation of circularity has several immediate consequences. To begin with, there is the neutralization of the identification of circularity within a given theory as indicative of a failure in the reasoning process. Second, there is an apparent rejection of the quasi-linear approach to knowledge present in the philosophical tradition since Aristotle, especially in modern philosophy since Descartes, which subtends the objection based on the identification of circularity. Finally, there is a qualified return to an older, circular approach to knowledge, from the critical perspective inaugurated by Kant.

In Fichte's position, the revised concept of circularity emerges in the course of his meditation on the conditions of the justification of knowledge, the problem with which Kant and the post-Kantians are centrally concerned. His earliest published writings betray the usual negative appeal to the concept of circularity for purposes of criticism.

In the *Critique of All Revelation,* for instance, he attacks the argument for the supernaturalist view, "which is without doubt a circular proof [Cirkel im Beweisen]."[59] In the aforementioned review of Schulze's book, circularity is evoked in three passages. Besides that already mentioned, there are references to the capacity of representation and to the concept of the thing-in-itself. In reference to the former, Fichte indicates that there is an intrinsic circularity in the concept of representation, in which the understanding is enclosed, since this capacity exists for and through itself.[60] That is another form of the idea contained in the passage on circularity already referred to in the review of Schulze.

In a later passage concerning Leibniz, Fichte attributes without apparent reason the discovery of the necessary circularity of the understanding to Kant.[61] And slightly later, in the *Contribution to the Correction of Judgments of the Public on the French Revolution (Beitrag zur Berichtigung der Urtheile des Publikums über die französische Revolution,*

1793), in a discussion of the different ways in which a person can relate to different segments of society, he remarks that the concept of the social contract is also circular.[62]

Conscious of the importance of his discussion of circularity, Fichte developed it further in other texts of this period: in the first sketch of the position, in the *Foundation of the Entire Science of Knowledge (Grundlage der gesamten Wissenschaftslehre)*, and in the metatheoretical discussion "On the Concept of the Science of Knowledge" ("Über den Begriff der Wissenschaftslehre"). Here it will be sufficient to note that there are few discernible differences in the many references to circularity in these three sources. And it further can be noted that such differences as can be observed are due not to a development of the analysis of circularity in this relatively short time, but rather to the particular character of the texts in question.

The initial sketch of Fichte's transcendental position, the *Own Meditations on Elementary Philosophy (Eigne Meditationen über Elementarphilosophie)*, probably was written at the same time as the review of Schulze's book. But it was not published by Fichte, and it first appeared in the recent complete edition of his works in a volume published in 1971. Here there are numerous references to circularity, especially in the beginning portions entitled "Logic of the Elementary Philosophy" and "Logical Rules."

Fichte appeals to circularity as concerns the defense of Reinhold's theory against skeptical criticism, its relevance for his own naissant theory, and as such. These are all aspects of a wider view of circularity which is constantly presupposed, occasionally hinted at, but never developed in this text. In relation to Reinhold, for example, Fichte concedes Schulze's objection that the elementary philosophy presupposes logic,[63] and further identifies a series of other instances in which circularity appears in what will become his own view, such as the domains of quantity and reality,[64] reality and activity,[65] thought and necessity.[66] These are merely special instances of the circularity, which results in the need to demonstrate the necessity of all things through a philosophy built on a single fact.[67] But the critical edge of the accusation of circularity is disarmed, since, as Fichte states, if it is necessary it cannot be a criticism.[68] For this reason, Fichte feels justified in referring to the necessary circle of our mind.[69] Although there may be a problem as concerns the relevance of circularity at a given point in the theory, Fichte is clear that his own system is circular,[70] and further clear that it is difficult [schwer] to avoid circularity in explanation.[71]

The key claim which here emerges, in common with the review of

Schulze's book, is that circularity is unavoidable, so that mere recognition of its presence is not sufficient to identify an error in the reasoning process. A similar point is also made in the two other texts mentioned from this period.

"On the Concept of the Science of Knowledge" is, as its title makes clear, basically a metatheoretical study of the conditions of the possibility and nature of theory in general. The few allusions to circularity suffice, however, to carry the argument further from a metatheoretical plane in a single, crucial respect. Here for the first time, Fichte explicitly works out in detail the quasi-rationalist concept of system in terms of an initial premise, already present in Reinhold's position, according to which a rigorously developed science can rest on one and only one fundamental proposition. It follows, by implication, that an important, indeed central, task confronting any view which lays claim to the status of science is to determine the initial principle which alone can permit it to assume wholly systematic form.

The other text from this period, the *Foundation of the Entire Science of Knowledge,* contains a number of direct references to circularity. At this point, Fichte is clear in his insistence that thought as such is ineliminably circular. Accordingly, with a directness not present earlier, he proceeds to identify numerous instances of circularity in his own position. A partial list of such instances would include that following from the concept of the act [Tathandlung],[72] in the relation of the principles of identity and opposition,[73] in the relation between the I [Ich] and the manifested,[74] in the relation of product and activity,[75] and in the relation of the real and the ideal.[76]

Perhaps more interesting is the further development of the point that philosophy needs to determine its initial principle, already implicit in the metatheoretical text. Fichte makes this explicit claim as early as the first sentence of the first paragraph of the work, when he describes his task as the determination of the absolutely unlimited, fundamental principle [Grundsatz] of human knowledge.[77] But he immediately adds in the next sentence that if this principle is to be truly basic, it can be neither proven nor limited.[78] This assertion, which is the direct consequence of the quasi-rationalist, but antifoundationalist, concept of systematic theory which Fichte here defends, is extremely significant. For it follows that the process of the development of theory is in principle an endless task. Every theory needs to seek its origins as a necessary element in the process of its own self-justification. But in virtue of its original, and hence wholly independent, character, dependent on nothing else within the theory, the original proposition is not itself subject to demonstration. In other words, the process of theoretical justification is always and necessarily incomplete.

Despite the absence of a detailed, or even more than tangential, treatment of epistemological circularity as such in the texts of this period, it is obvious that Fichte is aware of the importance of this concept. It is further apparent that he has a general, although never clearly stated, doctrine in mind. This doctrine can be paraphrased succinctly as the claim that because of its very structure, knowledge is circular and hence does not permit a linear justification in terms of its initial principle, known to be true.

The temptation to follow the evolution of this doctrine in Fichte's later writings must be resisted here for two reasons. On the one hand, the present aim is not to understand Fichte's thought as such, but only as it contributes to the constitution of Hegel's own position. And although there is abundant evidence of rapid evolution in Fichte's thought, as well as at least some evidence of Hegel's awareness of several later writings, there is reason to believe that he was neither closely familiar with them nor aware of the evolution of the position.

Nor is it possible at this point in the discussion to examine the general significance of the claim for circularity, since its role in Hegel's view has not yet been studied. But the significance of Fichte's suggestion, in the context of the discussion initiated by the publication of the *Critique of Pure Reason,* is difficult to exaggerate.

In the discussion of German idealism, it long has been the practice to stress the continuity between the positions of Reinhold and Fichte. Fries, for instance, remarks that Fichte merely develops Reinhold's basic concepts, falling more deeply into his errors.[79] Fries is certainly correct that Reinhold's reception of the critical philosophy was a formative influence on the evolution of the debate concerning its systematic reconstruction. But the enormous difference should be noted between Reinhold's intent, which Fichte shares, and the disagreement as to whether, to put the point in Kantian language, the goal in mind is constitutive of philosophy or merely a regulative idea. This difference of opinion, which concerns the intrinsic nature of philosophy, can usefully serve here to summarize the results of the debate concerning the reconstruction of the critical philosophy.

The result is a clear opposition. Reinhold's proposed reformulation of the critical philosophy is intended to justify the possibility of knowledge by transforming Kant's position into a system which derives from a single principle. The aim is to transform a theory which only claims to be science into one that in fact is science, through the justification of all its constituent elements. In a word, for Reinhold the only manner in which the possibility of knowledge can be secured is through a linear form of argument which avoids any hint of circularity, which can only vitiate the claim to know.

Fichte certainly shares Reinhold's acceptance of the basic rationalist model of system in terms of an initial principle. But in consequence of his rejection of the view that this principle can be established as correct, Fichte makes the very circularity, which Reinhold sought to avoid as a mistake in reasoning, constitutive of the process of knowledge. It follows that circularity cannot be avoided, but rather must be acknowledged. And it further follows that the claim to knowledge must forever remain hypothetical, since it necessarily is limited by the relation of a theory to its indemonstrable, initial principle. For although Reinhold and Fichte both claim allegiance to Kant, their respective efforts to reconstruct the critical philosophy as systematic science result in a radical opposition as concerns the linear or circular character of knowledge.

The significance of this result for the grasp of Hegel's position can be quickly anticipated. Hegel was aware of this debate, and of the views of Reinhold and Fichte. As will now be shown through discussion of Hegel's initial philosophical publication, in his reaction to this debate Hegel accepts against Reinhold Fichte's point that knowledge is an essentially circular process. But he denies the resultant inference that the outcome of the process is in any way less than the full form of knowledge which always has been sought in the philosophical tradition. From the perspective of the endeavor to reconstruct the critical philosophy, Hegel's attempt to demonstrate that knowledge in the full sense can be attained through a system which is circular can be regarded as a third argument, alongside those of Fichte and Reinhold. And it further can be regarded as an effort to attain the goal fixed by Reinhold by means of the counterargument advanced by Fichte, which would seem precisely to foreclose this possibility.

III

CIRCULARITY, SYSTEM, AND ANTIFOUNDATIONALISM
THE *DIFFERENZSCHRIFT*

The preceding chapter was concerned with the gradual emergence of the concept of circular epistemology in the discussion subsequent to the publication of the *Critique of Pure Reason.* This chapter will study Hegel's reaction to that discussion in the *Differenzschrift,* his earliest philosophical publication. In that text, Hegel responds to the opposing lines of epistemological argument concerning the reconstruction of the critical philosophy, as developed by Fichte and Reinhold. His response may be fairly described as a Fichtean-inspired critique of Reinhold's foundationalist approach to knowledge, for which he substitutes his own antifoundationalist, circular view of philosophy as system.

In order to understand Hegel's own view, we need to grasp his critique of Reinhold, which occurs in the course of a reading of contemporary German philosophy, in terms of a normative concept of that discipline. It accordingly will be necessary to consider both the normative concept of philosophy Hegel proposes and his reading of contemporary German thought. But since Reinhold's protean position was, at the time Hegel considered it, heavily influenced by Bardili's, if we are to understand the view which Hegel criticized, we also must address its relation to Bardili's thought.

We can begin with a consideration of Bardili's influence on the form of Reinhold's thought to which Hegel responds. C. G. Bardili was a minor anti-Kantian, whose own thought tended towards a pre-Kantian form of objective realism, opposed to any subjective contamination of knowledge. He sought to achieve this result through the appeal to logic as the ground of all philosophy. Today Bardili is nearly unknown, and he was certainly of little influence on the contemporary discussion. But he was well known to, although not better thought of by, Hegel in his capacity as preceptor in the Tübinger Stift during Hegel's student years there, prior to a later appointment to a professorship in Stuttgart.

The relation between Reinhold and Bardili is difficult to elucidate. Bardili was considerably younger than Reinhold, and may well have been influenced by him, as Fichte later claimed. The converse relation is demonstrated more easily. Certainly the interest in Bardili's concept of representation is a central theme in Reinhold's position, both prior to and after their encounter. In a volume of letters between them, which he later edited, Reinhold notes in the preface that his review of Bardili was the first to appear.[1]

He begins the first letter in typically enthusiastic fashion, with the statement that for nine weeks he has been studying Bardili with an enthusiasm he never has known for any book.[2] And he credits Bardili at the same time with the solution to the question preoccupying him, which was posed first by Leibniz, that is, philosophy as science.[3] Again scarcely a month later, he writes of the book and of Bardili's answering letter that he has been occupied daily with continued study of Bardili's thought and of its new formulation.[4] Indeed, already Reinhold is planning to incorporate Bardili's thought as part of his own plan to revise Fichte's position through a proposed "coalition" of Bardilean logic and transcendental philosophy.[5] Yet only a few months later, the initial enthusiasm already has run its course, when Reinhold, in another letter to Bardili, admits that his initial enthusiasm for the latter's view is based largely on its conflation with Jacobi's.[6]

In fact, here as elsewhere, Reinhold's interpretation of the history of philosophy is largely suspect, as a single example will show. In a letter to Bardili (January 1800) noted above, Reinhold further cites his own letter to Fichte, in which he in part suggests that Bardili's theory is not, as he believes, opposed to Fichte's, but rather is a wholly new exposition of the latter transcendental idealism.[7]

There is, to be sure, a certain similarity between Fichte's view of absolute activity and Bardili's idea of unlimited repetition. And it is possible, as Reinhold asserts, that Bardili's knowledge of Fichte is largely derivative. But beyond this limited analogy, there is a basic dissimilarity apparently ignored by Reinhold. For Fichte follows Kant in making objective knowledge depend on subjective activity. As Bardili correctly realized, for Fichte, to employ the latter's terminology, the absolute ego is merely an abstraction from the finite ego, or real human being. Indeed, that is the basis of Bardili's own criticism of Fichte's position. But in his refusal to permit the copresence of subjec-

tivity and objectivity in epistemology, in his decision to make the claim
for epistemological objectivity directly dependent on the absence of
any subjective contamination, Bardili in effect makes a qualified return to a pre-Kantian perspective, the alleged inadequacy of which
was the basic reason for the Copernican turn. That Reinhold, the
Kantian, failed to grasp the basic difference concerning this cardinal
point between Fichte, who followed Kant, and Bardili, who opposed
the critical philosophy, is evidence for the superficial nature of his
understanding of the contemporary debate.

In retrospect, it is not surprising that the book which so interested
Reinhold, Bardili's *Sketch of the First Logic* (1800),[8] since it set itself
against the critical philosophy, failed to excite interest in philosophical
circles. It is in ways a typical work by a young scholar, since it prom-
ises, as the full title makes clear, to provide a fully purified version of
logic devoid of the errors of preceding thought. The book is further
replete with the kind of pseudoscientific formulae affected by Schelling in his philosophy of nature, which makes it highly tedious reading.

Bardili's fundamental anti-Kantianism is apparent in the opening
lines of the preface, where he quotes Kant's famous critique of Fichte,
cited above, in order to turn it against the critical philosophy. Kant, of
course, wanted to denounce what he regarded as an attempt to deduce the world as given in experience from pure thought. Bardili,
however, is less interested in the reproach addressed to Fichte than in
the apparent factual nature of Kant's view of logic. Misinterpreting
the point which Kant urges against Fichte's view, that is, that the
material world cannot be deduced from logical principles, Bardili
suggests that that in fact must be carried out if knowledge is to be
possible.

The initial obscurity in Bardili's endeavor to relate logic to knowledge and the concept of the ground is dissipated immediately if we
realize that his aim is not a theory of logic as such. Rather, he is
concerned with the logical conditions of the possibility of knowledge
in a quasi-Kantian sense. The point seems to be that Kant has shown
us that knowledge depends on its possibility in general. But neither
Kant nor anyone else so far has demonstrated the deduction of the
real objects which in fact are known from the pure logic by which they
are conditioned. Accordingly, Bardili's understanding of his task is
twofold: to show the limitations of previous logic, or other efforts to
secure the possibility of knowledge; and to demonstrate how real
knowledge is grounded in the pure conditions of its possibility.

Bardili's analysis of previous logic is superficial and hasty. With the exception of some critical study of the views of even more minor contemporary thinkers, such as the Kantians Käsewetter and Maass, prior logic merely is dismissed through an argument from authority odd in virtue of Bardili's "critical" stance. Previous logical views may well contain true propositions, although in virtue of their contamination of pure form with content, the strength of their conclusions has merely inductive validity. That is because they depend on the critical philosophy, from whose perspective such errors could not have been foreseen.[9] Kant, to be sure, in a well-known passage to which Bardili refers, writes that since Aristotle it is abundantly clear from its results that logic need not step back from where it was (see B vii–viii). But the absence of a contingent need to modify a logical doctrine is not a demonstration of its logical validity.

Bardili's discussion of Kant's position, necessary to bolster his point that Kant recognized the weakness of previous logic, although he did not remedy it, is considerably more detailed, but not more satisfying. Confining himself mainly to the *Critique of Pure Reason,* a restriction justifiable in view of the concern with the theoretical conditions of knowledge as such, Bardili criticizes various aspects of the critical philosophy, including the impurity of the categories (84ff.), an alleged confusion between constitutive and regulative ideas as concerns the concept of the supreme being (94 ff.), the problematic concept of critical realism in the thought of Kant and Fichte (98ff.), and the relation of actuality and possibility (144). Bardili's general point, which he urges in various forms against particular aspects of the critical philosophy, is that although in principle knowledge is confined to appearance, Kant constantly seeks knowledge beyond the limits so defined.[10]

In order to understand Bardili's position, it is useful here to distinguish between the criticism as stated and its significance for his own thought. It would take us too far afield to discuss in detail the various points he raises against Kant, some of which are not without merit. Certainly his suggestion that Kant's transcendental analysis of knowledge in terms of subjectivity is circular, since it presupposes what it expects to demonstrate, ought not to be taken lightly. And he is correct to note that Kant seeks to discover whether we possess the capacity to know through a train of reasoning which precisely presupposes that capacity. But the more general point concerning Kant's violation of the limits set by his theory cannot be conceded as formulated, even if that is occasionally the case. For as early as the introduction to his treatise, Kant is careful to specify that although knowledge begins with experience, it is not limited to experience. There is accordingly no tension in Kant's view if, as Bardili points out, the domain in which speculative reason functions lies beyond the possibility of sensory intuition. But on the contrary, even if the criticism is unsuccessful, it is not difficult to grasp Bardili's preference to ground knowledge in an a priori analysis.

Bardili's own position is a radical version of the concern of the critical philosophy to guarantee the possibility of knowledge, in the direction of pre-Kantian thought, through appeal to the quasi-Leibnizian view of the principle of noncontradiction. The argument is formulated in a diffuse fashion, which can be summarized as follows: The task of philosophy is to demonstrate the conditions of the possibility of knowledge as derived from experience of objects. Now, the prior condition of sensory experience of objects is their real possibility. But only those objects are possible which are free of contradiction, by which Bardili means that they "can be repeatedly observed as belonging to the essence of thought."[11] It follows that the ultimate ground, or in Bardili's terminology the *Prius kat'exochen*, of knowledge in general lies in the a priori ascertainment of noncontradiction through repeatability in consciousness.[12]

It is evident that Bardili's position is problematic. He seems to be reasoning *ab posse ad esse*. Even if the inference from actuality to possibility is permissible, the converse line of reasoning, from possibility to actuality, is fallacious. But although Bardili's effort to reduce philosophy to logic may appear misguided, his intent to understand the possibility of knowledge in terms of its ultimate ground influenced Reinhold's thought, and through it Hegel's view.

The essay by Reinhold to which Hegel responded, written under the influence of Bardili, is entitled *Contributions to the Easy Survey of Philosophy at the Beginning of the Nineteenth Century*.[13] It is, in fact, the initial installment of a work in three parts, the first of which was completed on November 23, 1800, and which appeared in three successive years beginning in 1801.

The initial installment is subdivided further into historical and systematic portions, preceded by an introduction. Here Reinhold's view is described as including a normative concept of philosophy, a judgment concerning its intrinsic capacity to advance beyond its present state on the philosophical path taken by idealism, and a suggestion for an alternative course. The view itself can be summarized in terms of three interrelated statements: (1) Although the evolution of the philosophical revolution begun by Kant and continued by the later idealists has disconfirmed all views about its course, it is clear that a new turn [Wendung] is now required in order to carry out the transformation of philosophy into science, initiated by Plato; (2) In Kant's and in succeeding forms of transcendental philosophy, the central concept is active subjectivity; but on this basis, philosophy cannot become science, so that all such claims made for it, including those made earlier by Reinhold, must be rejected; and (3) The goal of philosophy to become science can be reached only through Bardili's view of logic, that is, his concept of thought as thought [des Denkens als Denkens].

In the remaining portion of the essay, Reinhold develops the points summarily stated in the introduction. He begins with a brief historical discussion of philosophy from Bacon to Kant. This account, which is not deeper than any which can now be found in a reasonably detailed contemporary history of philosophy, was interesting at the time for Reinhold's emphasis—a point later repeatedly stressed by Hegel—on the sense in which similar problems are addressed in different ways by successive philosophers. According to Reinhold, the basic task of all philosophy is to ground the reality of knowledge.[14] Beginning with Bacon, whom Reinhold regards as that thinker who initially broke with the Middle Ages in his concern to establish the conditions of authentic science, Reinhold traces this concept through its various forms in later thought, from Descartes to Hume, ending in this essay with German eclecticism, supplemented with occasional remarks on later thinkers.

In a rapid shifting of philosophical gears, Reinhold turns immediately from historical to systematic considerations. In amplification of his earlier normative claim, he suggests that philosophy is an effort to ground knowledge as such.[15] Now, the manner in which that can be accomplished is to establish a deductive relation between true facts and the prior ground from which they follow, which implies that knowledge as such depends on the appeal to an absolute ground.[16] In this regard, the problem with Kant's position is that it harbors an unresolved dualism of empirical knowledge and absolute conscience.[17] Fichte, to be sure, has surpassed Kant in his insistence on self-objectivating activity as the principle, not only for practical philosophy but for philosophy as such.[18] And Schelling has helped us to grasp the immanence of the infinite in his view of the absolute as subject/object.[19] But the conceptual movement begun by Kant and continued by his successors ends in an impasse, according to Reinhold, since idealism leads to materialism, and both lead to skepticism.[20]

Reinhold's view is not independent of a normative conception of philosophy. He makes this dependency clear in the discussion of the

teaching of reason [Vernunftlehre]. Since philosophy can be science
only if the true follows from the primordially true, its task consists in
the analysis of the application of thought as thought.[21] But if we seek
to determine the nature of thought as thought, an answer, according
to Reinhold, cannot be forthcoming on the plane of theory, but rather
only in the display or utilization of this capacity.

Prior philosophy has failed so far to grasp the nature of thought,
which is, however, exhibited in mathematical reasoning. That is defined here in various ways, all of which are held to be equivalent to
absolute self-identity.[22] But since the point of appealing to mathematical reasoning was to identify an instance of the application of
thought as such, Reinhold is justified in his suggestion that the essence, or inner character, of thought consists in unending repetition,
or pure identity.[23]

As it stands, Reinhold's discussion is clearly fragmentary. His
awareness of this fact was certainly one of the reasons which impelled
him to develop his analysis of Bardili's concept of thought as such in
the second installment of his work. This topic can safely be omitted,
since it was not available to Hegel when the *Differenzschrift* was being
written and did not influence his view later. But it is doubly puzzling
why no prior philosopher can be said to have analyzed thought as
such, since that was certainly a primary goal of the *Critique of Pure
Reason,* on one reading of that work. Indeed, the concept of mathematical reasoning which Reinhold obscurely suggests here seems
clearly derivative from Kant's view in that treatise. Further, the view of
identity which Reinhold identifies as the essence of thought as
thought is no more than a restatement, in other terms, of the position
taken by Fichte in the *Foundations of the Entire Science of Knowledge,* as
Reinhold was certainly aware.

Despite the residual obscurity of Reinhold's view, the general intent
is not difficult to perceive. Since Reinhold, like Hegel and Schelling,
regarded Fichte as having carried the critical philosophy beyond
Kant, it is not surprising that he situates his own view in relation to
Fichte's. That occurs in two open letters [Sendschreiben], both addressed to Fichte, where Reinhold asserts that he formerly believed
Fichte's principle of identity and Bardili's analysis of thought as such
to be the same.[24] But he now understands that there is a basic
distinction between the former's transcendental idealism, which as
subjective cannot aspire to objectivity,[25] and the latter's rational realism, in terms of which the intrinsic goal of idealism can be attained on
an objective basis.[26]

Reinhold's entire essay is an extended argument for his own reading of German idealism. But perhaps the most interesting dimension of his argument is revealed only in his brief account of "The Natural History of Pure Egology, Called Pure Reason," in which he focuses on the concept of subjectivity. As concerns Kant's distinction between pure knowing and pure doing, Reinhold suggests that both Fichte and Schelling direct attention to the concept of pure activity,[27] in terms of which the pure ego is to be understood in isolation from the human individual.[28] But in point of fact, there only are real, empirical human beings, even if the emphasis on philosophical abstraction tends to conceal this point. Reinhold, accordingly, asserts that the import of his essay is to have shown that abstraction is subtended by the real, empirical subject.[29]

Hegel's response to Reinhold is contained, as noted, in the *Differenzschrift*. In a historical moment such as the present, when items of limited interest routinely receive extended treatment in a burgeoning secondary literature, the lack of concern with this text is indeed surprising. This essay, which is Hegel's initial philosophical publication, is significant not only for Hegel's view of epistemological circularity but for his wider position. Unlike so many first publications, it is, however, neither a brief notice nor a tentative comment on a matter of current concern. It is a well-thought-out statement, of considerable amplitude and surprising maturity, concerning other thinkers and the nature of philosophy. In the course of the discussion, there are both systematic and historical comments, remarks which constitute the armature of a theory of philosophy as necessarily assuming systematic form arising from Hegel's reading of recent philosophy, and a polemical, but deeply insightful, interpretation of the status of recent thought. The exceptional interest of this text is only heightened when it is realized that here as elsewhere Hegel is faithful to his practice of long reflection prior to the statement of a doctrine which almost never is modified as to essentials in later writings.

The text itself is in fact a long article which appeared in the *Critical Journal of Philosophy*. The idea of a journal of this type already had been raised by Fichte in a letter to Schiller (December 2, 1800), although he did not in fact found one. However, Fichte's suggestion was put into practice by Schelling, who was already well known as a Fichtean adherent, at a point at which he was in the process of loosening his Fichtean ties. He founded the *Journal* in collaboration with Hegel, who at the time was still unknown.[30] Its stated aim was defined in the initial declaration of intent (apparently of Hegelian inspiration, although even that is controversial) as the critical separation of philosophy from unphilosophy in terms of the standard of the

Idea. Hegel's *Differenzschrift*, which appeared as an article in the issue dated September 1801, was occasional, as can be seen from its full title: *The Difference between Fichte's and Schelling's System of Philosophy in connection with the first fascicle of Reinhold's contributions to a more convenient survey of the state of philosophy at the beginning of the nineteenth century.*[31]

The occasional status of the article has been the topic of some comment. The suggestion has been made that it is based on a mere pretext, because of a clear distortion, in which Hegel is manifestly unfair to Reinhold.[32] But although it is not difficult to understand the desire to defend Fichte against Hegel's reading of his position,[33] the proposed reduction of the intrinsic importance of the *Differenzschrift* merely to an occasion which Hegel unfairly exploited would, even if it were true, represent at best an incomplete account. For the crucial problem of epistemological circularity, upon which Hegel's reception of Reinhold turns, is not mentioned.

It would certainly be an error to overlook the occasional element in this text, its relation to its historical moment. But that is not the point at issue. Hegel, it seems clear, would be the first to concede the occasional status of his text, or indeed any other since, as he never tires of observing, it is the nature of the case that thought itself is basically inseparable from its historical moment. The problem, then, is whether one can be reduced to the other—in other words, whether thought is nothing but a reaction to its historical context.

As concerns the present text, that kind of inference should be resisted on several grounds. Although Hegel did seize upon the publication by Reinhold as the occasion to reply to a well-known contemporary writer, it would seem that work on this text had been underway for some time, prior to Reinhold's own discussion.[34] Further, it was to be expected that Hegel would begin to publish in order to make a name for himself as other than an associate of Schelling. Nor is there any evidence, in spite of the occasion upon which Hegel seized, that the essay itself is merely occasional in nature. Although Hegel does avail himself of the occasion provided by Reinhold, his treatment of the latter's thought is by no means occasional; rather, it is an integral part of a more general theory of philosophy, in particular of its latest stage.

In this respect, the discussion of Reinhold offers an outstanding example of what Hegel here characterizes as unphilosophy, that form of philosophy which is of merely occasional importance. Finally, it should be noted that in his response to Reinhold, Hegel surpasses a merely negative comment on the latter's thought. In fact, Hegel's response is of great significance, both for his own position and for philosophy in general. Rather than a mere misunderstanding, or an evasion of the issue raised by Reinhold, Hegel's response offers a doctrine intended to resolve—on quasi-Fichtean grounds, hence in philosophically substantive fashion—Reinhold's problem of the systematic reconstruction of the critical philosophy.

If we turn now to the text of the *Differenzschrift*, we can note that it is relatively short (approximately 115 pages, depending on the edition), especially in comparison with the massive tomes published at that time. The work itself is divided into a preface and three main divisions, plus an additional division added by the editor. Here we find a normative view of the nature of philosophy as such, where Hegel discusses a series of related topics in the process of giving shape to a general idea of the nature of philosophy. This discussion is followed by an application of that idea as a standard for the interpretation of the contemporary philosophical discussion, especially as concerns the views of Fichte, Schelling, and Reinhold, leading representatives of philosophy and unphilosophy.

The complex nature of the argument Hegel will develop in detail is already apparent in the preface. There Hegel states that his immediate purpose is to provide a correct interpretation of the positions of Fichte and Schelling, which Reinhold unfairly has conflated, more than to react to the latter's "revolution of bringing philosophy back to logic" (D 79; II, 9). Differentiating between the spirit and the letter of the Kantian philosophy, in accordance with a distinction drawn by Kant and later employed by Fichte as a standard for the proper interpretation of philosophical texts,[35] Hegel suggests that Fichte, as he himself claimed, was true to the spirit of Kant's thought.

Fichte's position is in fact a genuine idealism, since, as concerns the deduction of the categories, it exhibits a speculative identity of subject and object, in particular through the concept of pure thinking that thinks itself in the identity of subject and object conceived as ego equals ego. But just as in Kant's position, in which pure reason has finally no legitimate function, so Fichte's establishment of the pure concept of reason and speculation, which renders philosophy possible, ultimately is undermined by his identification of reason with consciousness, a merely finite form. Yet Reinhold has failed to perceive either a specific contribution due to Fichte's thought or the sense in which Schelling's view differs from it.

This summary of Hegel's initial statement of purpose should not be mistaken for a demonstration of his argument. It is merely an indication of the point Hegel plans to develop in the text. But although our overriding concern with this text is as it relates to Hegel's criticism of

Reinhold, even at this stage it is clear that his rejection of the latter's philosophy cannot be considered in isolation from the remainder of the discussion. For Hegel's critique of Reinhold is dependent upon a prior interpretation of the distinction between what he regards as the only two contemporary forms of philosophy. Now, since the endeavor to grasp the relevant distinction between the views of Fichte and Schelling is itself the result of the application of a normative concept of philosophy, it seems difficult to avoid at least some attention to this phase of Hegel's discussion. For it is only when we have grasped what Hegel thinks philosophy to be and how this concept is exemplified in its only genuine contemporary system that we shall be able to understand his reasons for the rejection of Reinhold's thought as non-philosophy.

The discussion of the "Various Forms Occurring in Contemporary Philosophizing" is curiously named, although in part it is an adequate reflection of Hegel's view. It is, in the first instance, inadequate as a characterization of what Hegel does in this section. For it suggests a descriptive account of kinds of contemporary philosophy, which appears only later in the discussion of the positions of Fichte, Schelling, and Reinhold. On the contrary, the title makes by implication a profound point upon which Hegel insists in this essay and elsewhere, and upon which his interpretation of his contemporaries turns. For implicit in the concept of forms of present philosophizing is the view that philosophy, which at any given moment assumes different shapes, is in fact necessarily one.

The section as a whole is subdivided into eight paragraphs in which Hegel treats related topics. He immediately turns to the concept of the univocal character of philosophy as such in his account of the "Historical Character of Philosophical Systems." There he makes three observations whose importance is evident, even prior to their subsequent development in his thought. Philosophy is, to begin with, the search for knowledge. But every philosophy is capable of being assimilated and dealt with in historical fashion. Second, from a historical perspective, the originality in different positions lies not in their content, which they have in common, but rather in their form. In this respect, Hegel notes that Fichte's view is original as concerns the particular form of his system, while Reinhold's originality lies in the tendency of founding and grounding [Ergründungs- und Begründungstendenz] philosophy. Finally, Hegel observes, here providing the framework for the claim that different positions have a common content, that reason is speculative only when it takes cognizance of itself and entrusts itself to the Absolute which is its object. Speculation is defined as the activity of the one and universal reason upon itself.

Taken together, the significance of these three observations lies in the manner in which they provide an intellectual matrix in terms of which Hegel draws a double distinction. On the one hand, he distinguishes different forms of philosophy, which reasonably can be regarded as providing a successively more adequate grasp of their common content. On the other hand, he differentiates between true philosophy, which is by definition speculative, and nonphilosophy, or nonspeculative thought. It is clear that the twofold task which Hegel in fact endeavors to carry out in the latter part of this text depends for its success upon a prior concept of reason, or speculative thought, a concept which Hegel then proceeds to outline in a series of related paragraphs.

Hegel begins his account of speculative reason in the context of a discussion of the "Need of Philosophy," in the course of which he draws a crucial distinction between understanding and reason. Philosophy, according to Hegel, is not innate in the human spirit but is rather a response to a need created by the rise of culture. That, in turn, generates an opposition between the appearance of the Absolute and the Absolute itself. This diremption, which is generated by the understanding, can be overcome only through reason, in which the elements are seen as related and hence revealed as relative.

Two related implications follow immediately from Hegel's view of the utility of philosophy. It is clear that there is a deep and fundamental opposition on this point between Hegel and Kant. For whereas the author of the critical philosophy suggests that knowledge is the result of the correct employment of the faculty of the understanding, from the Hegelian perspective the appeal to the understanding is merely the prephilosophical presupposition which gives rise to the need for philosophy at all. For it reveals as relative the distinction which the understanding posits as absolute.

Hegel further makes a related point in relation to Reinhold, who, in his concern to think through the critical philosophy, strives to avoid all presuppositions, which Hegel now labels as a task located on the prephilosophical plane. As he notes, "The founding and grounding [das Ergründen und Begründen] gets going before and outside of philosophy" (D 94; II, 25). Now, although the reason which allows Hegel to make this claim about Reinhold's view will not be fully apparent prior to the analysis of it, it is significant to note that in terms of his response to the alleged need for philosophy, Hegel feels justified in characterizing both the critical philosophy and its critical restatement by Reinhold as essentially prephilosophical from the speculative point of view.

Hegel further specifies his view of reason in a discussion of "Reflection as the Instrument of Philosophizing." This paragraph represents a further development, or metastage, in the distinction just drawn between reason and understanding. In order to be consistent with his description of the task of reason as the overcoming of the fixed oppositions generated by the understanding, Hegel must avoid positing a wholly negative relation between these two faculties. He does so by relativizing their distinction so that the task of reason is seen not as a mere cancellation of the determinations generated by the understanding, but rather as an overcoming of them as the merely finite elements are brought together in the synthesis of the finite and the infinite within reason.

Returning to reason, in terms of the distinction previously drawn between it and understanding, Hegel comments briefly at this point on its relation to common sense. The latter is, he observes, a source of isolated truths of pragmatic value for the conduct of life. If inspected from the angle of the understanding, the truths of common sense appear distorted because of their isolation, but they are recognized as true because of an implicit reference to the Absolute. Yet common sense, on the contrary, is unable to grasp the perspective of reason, which it presupposes. For as faith, its relation of limitation to the Absolute, in which only opposition is present to consciousness, precisely excludes the awareness of the identity which is the content of speculative reason.

Hegel's examination of common sense pretends to demonstrate that it necessarily presupposes, but is unable to comprehend, reason. So far he has defined and located reason in respect to its technical and nontechnical alternatives. His point has been that both the Kantian concept of understanding and the popular view of common sense, each of which is essentially limited, point beyond themselves towards the speculative identity which can be revealed only through reason. Now, in terms of his view of reason, Hegel considers briefly three issues arising out of the critical philosophy: foundationalism, transcendental intuition, and the postulate of reason.

The discussion of foundationalism addresses the effort to restate the content of the critical philosophy in more than apparently systematic form. Hegel's discussion of the "Principle of a Philosophy in the Form of an Absolute Basic Proposition [Grundsatz]" is exceedingly dense but of great moment. It helpfully can be viewed as an attempt to elucidate a point that Schelling raises in a work which appeared immediately prior to the *Differenzschrift*. In the *System of Transcendental Idealism* [*System des transzendentalen Idealismus*], published in 1800, Schelling remarks in passing that although since Reinhold "there has been much talk of a first principle from which philosophy must start," in fact "it is easy to see that transcendental philosophy cannot proceed from any theorem, if only because it sets out from the subjective. . . ."[36]

Hegel develops this point in a manner which is highly reminiscent of Kant's discussion in the "Nova Dilucidatio." His argument against the possibility of an ultimate principle follows Fichte's own objection even in its choice of terminology. It can be required, he remarks, that the Absolute which thought seeks to know be already present as its foundation [Grundsatz], as its presupposition. Yet the endeavor to provide an unlimited foundation necessarily must fail. For merely to posit such a principle is to limit it, and hence to require a further principle. Hegel's point, then, which is the basis of his criticism of Reinhold's foundationalism in the latter part of the essay, can be expressed as the claim that any attempt to state the ultimate principle upon which all knowledge depends necessarily must lead to an infinite regress. But although Hegel holds that his predecessors have all been uncritical in their appeal to the formal approach, as exemplified in the strategy of basing all knowledge on one of the two possible forms of identity, he does not at this time put forward his own positive alternative.

In the account of "Transcendental Intuition," Hegel again parts company with Kant. In the critical philosophy, Kant insists on empirical intuition as the real and indeed necessary source of the contents of knowledge. But in order to exclude direct knowledge of oneself suggested in certain forms of rationalism, especially by Descartes, he denies the existence, indeed even the conceivability, of an intellectual intuition, in which such knowledge could be given (see, for instance, B 307 and B 310).

Kant's attempt to rule intellectual intuition out of bounds is contested immediately by both Fichte and Schelling. Although Fichte agrees with Kant that there can be no intuition of a suprasensuous object, he suggests that we do indeed have immediate consciousness of our own activity; and he further suggests that it is difficult to deny intellectual intuition, since it and its sensory form presuppose each other.[37] Schelling follows Fichte's claim of immediate intuitive awareness of our activity, or productive capacity. But he further develops this claim in two ways: in his assertion that aesthetic intuition is merely the objective form of intellectual intuition,[38] which is the basis of his own philosophy of art; and in the further assertion that, as he puts it, "intellectual intuition is the organ of all transcendental thinking."[39] For thought objectifies itself through freedom, and "to intuit that the producing of the object and the intuiting itself are absolutely one . . . is intellectual intuition."[40]

In the *Differenzschrift*, Hegel follows the general post-Kantian insistence on intellectual intuition, renamed here "transcendental intuition," as well as the claim that it is a necessary condition of speculative thought, in a manner reminiscent of Fichte and especially of Schelling. The inability of the critical philosophy to proceed beyond the analytic perspective exhibited in the faculty of the understanding is due, he suggests, to the denial of transcendental intuition, in which alone the speculative identity sought as the completion of knowledge can be exhibited objectively. In fact, as Hegel now insists, utilizing the term *postulate* in the Kantian sense of an absolutely necessary condition (see B 661) against the Kantian view, transcendental intuition is precisely a necessary condition which must be satisfied in order for there to be objective knowledge in the fully speculative sense of the word.

In the final paragraph of the section, entitled "Relation of Philosophizing to a Philosophical System," Hegel provides a coherent, but extremely compressed, statement of the standard which he will employ to judge other systems of philosophy. It follows, it is clear from his concept of speculative thought, that there is a need to suppress fixed separations of any form in a higher unity, or synthesis, which is in fact an objective totality. Hegel then makes two points in this regard:

> In this self-production of Reason the Absolute shapes itself into an objective totality, which is a whole in itself held fast and complete, having no ground outside itself, but founded [begründet] by itself in its beginning, middle and end. [D 113; II, 46]

The initial point concerns the self-contained and hence self-justifying status of the objective totality which issues from speculative reason. Hegel's language, especially concerning the reference to the self-production of the Absolute, seems voluntarily to imitate Schelling. But the view expressed points beyond him to Fichte and further points to the problem of the systematic reconstruction of the critical philosophy. The result of genuinely speculative thought is, Hegel clearly states, a self-contained system which is hence entirely independent of any principle external to it for its justification. By implication, then, genuinely speculative thought can be said to yield the completely adequate system placed on the intellectual agenda by the publication of the *Critique of Pure Reason*. Second, Hegel once again speaks to the problem of the kind of identity provided by genuinely speculative reason, which he describes as both absolute and relative. In fact, every synthesis of reason, as he writes, "as identity of the conscious and the non-conscious is for itself in the Absolute and infinite. But at the same time, the synthesis is finite and limited, insofar as it is posited within the objective totality and has other syntheses outside itself" (D 113; II, 46).

In terms of the need for speculative reason to be both absolute and relative within an objective unity, Hegel then anticipates the kind of criticism which he will develop of other views. His analysis here, although brief, is of the highest interest as much for the specific points he shortly will raise against his contemporaries, as concerns at least one such criticism which is explicitly formulated only later, and as a yardstick accepted by him in terms of which to measure the extent to which his own position can realize its self-assigned tasks. Genuine speculation can, as Hegel says, go astray in two ways: because it fails to manifest itself fully in its system; or, if the view of system does not coincide with the system proposed, if the system tends to cancel opposition but fails to attain complete identity.

After his differentiation of two ways in which speculative thought can go astray, Hegel qualifies his discussion in two interesting observations. Transcendental philosophy can, he remarks, become dogmatism, from which it otherwise is distinguished, if, as it passes into system, it fails to preserve the relative identity. This comment, which is made in passing here, is surely a clear anticipation of his criticism of Schelling's concept of the Absolute, which becomes explicit only later, in the famous simile in the *Phenomenology*.

It is in this respect interesting to note, in regard to Hegel's critique of Fichte from the perspective provided by Schelling's thought, that Hegel's own later criticism of the latter's view is in effect a restatement of Fichte's earlier objection to Schelling's desire to improve on Fichte's transcendental philosophy. In his review of Schelling's system of identity, entitled "On the Exposition of Schelling's Systems of Identity" ("Zur Darstellung von Schelling's Identitätssysteme"), Fichte states, in reference to the latter's concept of the Absolute, that it is even worse not to see that the unitary, absolute reason, which is supposedly all-inclusive, cannot be the indifference of objectivity and subjectivity without also being their difference.[41] Second, if a causal relation between appearance and the Absolute is introduced, both appearance and transcendental intuition become subordinate to it. This point, which in part manifests a reliance on Schelling's view of intellectual intuition, is the basis of the general objection Hegel raises against Fichte—that in the latter's system the identity of subject and object is merely subjective.

That ends Hegel's normative discussion of philosophy. Before we turn to his consideration of his philosophical contemporaries, it will be useful to comment on the relation of the normative discussion to his view of epistemological circularity, which will be developed from a Fichtean perspective in the critical treatment of Reinhold's foundationalism. Hegel's concern to supplement understanding by reason makes clear his intent to surpass the finite in the direction of infinite knowledge. But his rejection of the Reinholdian attempt at foundationalism suggests that reason is to be demonstrated in a nonfoundationalist mode whose outlines as yet are unspecified. If philosophy is in fact to become system, it can be only through a self-grounding, which would in fact attain Reinhold's aim in a manner which avoids the quasi-rationalist recourse to an absolute first principle.

The general lines of Hegel's understanding of antifoundationalist epistemology are translated into a specific epistemological doctrine of circularity in the course of his reading of contemporary philosophy in the remainder of the *Differenzschrift*. This reading of contemporary thought, which is based on the normative conception of philosophy already elaborated, is divided into three unequal parts: a relatively lengthy account, in the context of this essay, of Fichte's thought as system, that is, with respect to the letter of the view as distinguished from the genuinely speculative spirit Hegel attributes to it; two shorter sections, of roughly equal length, which taken together are slightly longer than the account of Fichte's thought; and an untitled section on Reinhold's position, where Hegel criticizes a contemporary form of foundationalism and proposes his own circular, antifoundationalist view of knowledge.

The account of Fichte's position is critical, and is based on prior acceptance of Schelling's view, itself adopted here uncritically. The implicit justification of this approach is that despite their manifest differences, Hegel regards both Fichte and Schelling as representatives of the same system, which he also accepts, the fundamental principle of which is intellectual intuition. The comparative discussion of the positions of Fichte and Schelling is devoted mainly to an inquiry into the significance of the differences between them for a completed philosophical system. Finally, the discussion of Reinhold's position, which closes the circle by returning to the occasional pretext for the essay, is nominally directed towards exposing the latter's incapacity to comprehend the thought of his great philosophical contemporaries. But it is, in fact, perhaps most significant in regard to Hegel's comments on the supposed attempt to reduce philosophy to logic.

Hegel's criticism of Fichte's position is not wholly immanent. It is determined by several external factors, including his own normative view of philosophy, which serves here as a general yardstick against which to measure Fichte's thought; and Schelling's prior criticism of his colleague, which Hegel here follows in detail. After a period in which, according to Fichte, Schelling incorrectly maintained the identity of Fichte's position and his own, Schelling began to distinguish between the two views.

The roots of Schelling's interest in the philosophy of nature [Naturphilosophie], which is the basis of the distinction, can be glimpsed as early as 1797 in his initial account of this domain in *Ideas towards a Philosophy of Nature (Ideen zu einer Philosophie der Natur)*. But the shift in emphasis becomes explicit only in the *System of Transcendental Idealism,* in which Schelling attempts to widen the general Fichtean approach through insistence on the need to supplement the subjective standpoint of transcendental philosophy with the objective perspective provided by the philosophy of nature. Neither science is prior to the other, and both are necessary for a fully developed position; both are further united in a perspective which is neither subjective nor objective, and hence not finite but infinite, which Schelling later called the indifference point [Indifferenzpunkt].

Schelling further developed this perspective in open criticism of Fichte in his *An Exposition of My System of Philosophy (Darstellung meines Systems der Philosophie,* 1801). Although published in the same year as the *Differenzschrift,* Hegel refers to this text at several places in his essay, both implicitly and, on at least one occasion, explicitly.[42] In agreement with Fichte as to the subject-object correspondence as the necessary condition of knowledge, he then draws a further distinction between a "subjective" correspondence on the level of mind, based on reflection, and an "objective" correspondence on the level nature, based on production. Fichte's position, from this perspective, can be understood as subjective idealism, a point on which Hegel insists even as he extends this criticism to Kant.

Hegel's objection can be understood as an extension of Schelling's, although he goes further than his younger colleague. Whereas Schelling argues that Fichte's position was inadequate as formulated, Hegel

makes the further claim that the subjective perspective employed by
Fichte necessarily must fail as a result of its intrinsic limitation. At this
time he does not yet extend his criticism to englobe the founder of the
critical philosophy, which he does as early as the next year in *Faith and
Knowledge*. His basic point is that Fichte's position, like Kant's, suffers
from the intrinsic limitation that, since its goal is the exploration of
human consciousness, it never can go beyond subjectivity to the objectivity in which awareness and knowledge must be grounded.

The relation of Hegel's criticism of Fichte to Schelling's view is
apparent in the general complaint that Fichte's position is a subjective
form of idealism, since it never surpasses the subjective identity of
subject and object which is the ego, as well as in specific points
concerning the philosophy of nature and the indifference point.
Fichte's position, according to Hegel, follows from a theory of intellectual intuition, in terms of which the attempt is made to deduce
empirical consciousness from transcendental consciousness. But although the self-identity of the ego is the principle of speculation,
Fichte is not able to demonstrate the identity sought. Indeed, the
distinction between the subjective ego (= ego) and the objective ego
(= ego + nonego), or, otherwise stated, the difference between Idea
and intuition, reverberates throughout Fichte's position: in the *Foundation of the Entire Science of Knowledge,* where nature can be deduced
neither theoretically nor practically; in the opposition between nature
and reason in the philosophy of right *(Rechtslehre);* and in the difference between freedom and determinism in the treatise on ethics
(Sittenlehre).

In an enterprise such as Hegel's, the problem of interpretation, in
particular the fidelity of his interpretation of texts he criticizes, must
be borne in mind. Clearly the force of his objections in part must
depend upon his reading of the texts. This problem is of special
moment as concerns Hegel's thought. While there is no question that
his penetrating approach to other figures in the philosophical tradition is unusually incisive, it sometimes seems to depend upon an
inadmissible manner of construing the positions in question.

A case in point is the criticism of Fichte's position as subjective
idealism. Indeed, it is precisely because Hegel's influential interpretations of his philosophical contemporaries have seemed increasingly
tendentious that there recently has been growing interest in revising
his readings of the views of Fichte and Schelling. If we concentrate
merely on Hegel's criticism of Fichte and bracket all concern with its
accuracy, the objection still requires some elucidation.

Despite the closely Schellingian manner in which the points are made, and the utilization of Schelling's view as a standard of comparison, as noted, Hegel already has begun to separate his own position, not only from Fichte's but implicitly from Schelling's, as well. From the vantage point afforded by his own concept of reason, Hegel's criticism can be reformulated as the assertion that the perspective of the finite ego is inadequate to reach the infinite, as witness Fichte's inability to demonstrate the unity of subjectivity and objectivity through the derivation of the latter from the former. But since, in view of the failure of the proposed derivation, the identity of thought and being cannot be established from a position located solely within thought, it is necessary to supplement the merely epistemological perspective represented here by a further ontological perspective, in terms of which the problem of their relation becomes a central concern.

Despite Hegel's emphasis on the manner in which succeeding positions build upon their predecessors, it is interesting to note that, historically speaking, his criticism of Fichte represents a reversal of his own view of historical progress through the appeal to an earlier portion of the philosophical tradition. In his rejection in principle of Fichte's approach, Hegel simultaneously rejects by implication the line of epistemological strategy initiated by Kant, which is continued in Fichte's position, in favor of a qualified return to a quasi-rationalist approach.

This point can be illustrated in terms of Hegel's treatment here of Schelling. Hegel purports to consider Schelling's position in comparison to that of Fichte, although in an important sense that task already has been accomplished in the preceding critique of Fichte's position from a Schellingian perspective. Perhaps for this reason, the supposedly comparative discussion is scarcely comparative at all, but is devoted mainly to study of the quasi-rationalist problem of the relation of thought and being.

Hegel here presents Schelling's position in terms of the same principle accepted by Fichte. It follows that although there are indeed two distinct positions, the distinction is merely relative. For there is only one system of philosophy, to which both philosophers subscribe. Hegel makes this point evident in the employment of the word *system* in the singular in the title of the essay. The system, if there is one, is of course the system of idealism, the genuinely speculative form of which originates not in Kant but in Fichte, and in respect to which Schelling's view is more a correction than a fundamental new departure. And there is the additional implication to be drawn that since the two positions are, in Hegel's opinion, only two different versions of the same system, neither is sui generis, and, more important, it can fairly be claimed that one of them has gone further than the other upon the same road.

Hegel's discussion of Schelling begins with some epistemological reflections which clearly prefigure the later break between them over the allegedly abstract character of the latter's concept of the Absolute. Hegel states, in quasi-Schellingian language which seems finally closer to his own position than that he is interpreting, that the Absolute must present itself by turn in the subjective subject/object of consciousness, in the objective subject/object of nature, and in the synthesis of both. So far he is close at least to the spirit, if not to the letter, of Schelling's view.

But there is an important distinction which he now draws. "Both of them, therefore," Hegel comments relative to the opposition of subjectivity and objectivity, "must be posited in the Absolute, or the Absolute must be posited in both forms while yet both of them retain separate standing" (D 157; II, 97). In other words, reason must preserve as merely relative the distinctions of understanding, rather than causing them simply to disappear, although it is Schelling's incapacity to preserve distinction within his featureless Absolute which later precipitated the break between them.

The discussion of Schelling's thought underlines the dualism inherent in his concern to go beyond Fichte's view within the framework prescribed by its basic principle. As noted, according to Schelling, neither transcendental philosophy nor philosophy of nature can supersede the other, since they are located on different planes, attained only by abstraction from the basic thesis of the opposing point of view. Thus, transcendental philosophy begins from subjectivity, and the philosophy of nature starts from objectivity. Nor can the contradiction between them be more than apparent, since each is a self-contained perspective, independent of the other, developed from a separate angle of vision. But from the perspective of the Absolute, both transcendental idealism and philosophy of nature are seen to be one-sided and relative to that which they are concerned to know. It is, hence, permissible to state that each is a stage in the progressive self-construction or evolution of the absolute.

In view of Hegel's concern to transcend dualism, his reaction to Schelling's strategy to overcome this dichotomy is of particular interest. Although it is obvious that forms of dualism are prominent in the philosophical tradition as early as the ancient Greeks, especially in Plato, Schelling is reacting in the first instance to Fichte's position. Fichte's view, in fact, contains no fewer than three analyses of the kind of dualism Schelling is faced with, that is, that between subjective and objective approaches to knowledge. These approaches appear in Fichte's position under the headings of idealism and dogmatism, or theory and practice.

With respect to his problem, in discussions perhaps not wholly consistent with each other, Fichte maintains that 1) since the quarrel between idealism and dogmatism is about first principles, it can be settled only on a prephilosophical basis; 2) neither idealism nor dogmatism can refute each other, but the latter is inadequate as an explanatory principle; and 3) each approach calls for its completion in the other, as theory naturally turns towards practice, and from the angle of practice one necessarily is led towards theory.

It is beyond the scope of this discussion to attempt to reconcile Fichte's several comments on this problem, which may not finally be self-consistent. Here it is sufficient to note that his basic point, which does seem consistent, seems to be that the perspectives of subjectivity and objectivity are equally fundamental and interrelated. In this respect, Schelling's position seems to presuppose, but surpass, Fichte's view in the assertion that the purported epistemological relation is grounded in the status of each perspective relative to an underlying ontological identity. For as Hegel seems to recognize (see D 166; II, 106), in order to relate thought to being, Schelling returns to a quasi-Spinozistic approach in which each can be regarded as parallel through their joint status as aspects of a third thing.

There can be no doubt that Hegel here endorses Schelling's concern to relate thought and being through reinterpretation of the Fichtean concept of the Absolute as a fruitful innovation with respect to the Fichtean view of knowledge. But it would be a mistake to exaggerate the dependence of Hegel, even at this early stage in his career, on his younger contemporary. As Hegel observes, there is an important distinction to be drawn between simple suspension of the difference in perspective between the two sciences, which he labels as merely negative (see D 170; II, 112), and its supersession in a real synthesis. Consistent with his basic distinction between reason and understanding, Hegel suggests that a real synthesis can be attained only through a viewpoint which, as neither subjective nor objective, includes, yet transcends, either form of finitude. Referring again to the contrast between these two perspectives, Hegel writes: "Ordinary reflection can see nothing in this antinomy but contradiction; Reason alone sees the truth in this absolute contradiction through which both are posited and both nullified, and through which neither exists and at the same time both exist" (D 174; II, 115).

Clearly Schelling has gone part of the way in the necessary direction. He at least takes the negative step of suspending the antipathy between the two sciences, although in all fairness it would seem that Fichte also did so. But Schelling here, and arguably later, as well, remains unable to perform the crucial task of uniting these two strands in a real synthesis. Hence, despite his avowed intent, as Hegel later argued in the *History of Philosophy,* although Schelling takes a step in the right direction he fails ultimately to surpass the plane of the philosophy of the understanding already inhabited by Kant and Fichte.

The reading of the positions of Fichte and Schelling as advancing different versions of a single, correct system is highly significant for Hegel's later interpretation of the history of philosophy; it is further significant for his reception of Reinhold's position, which he characterizes, in opposition to the single correct system, despite the latter's concern with system, as unphilosophy. In this regard, Hegel's account of the relation of the views of Fichte and Schelling is helpful, since it indicates his concern with objectivity as opposed to subjectivity in a manner which eschews any hint of dualism. In a sense, the rejection of foundationalism in favor of theory which is circular, and hence self-justifying, or self-grounding, is meant to avoid the dualistic dependence on any principle external to it.

In part because Reinhold's name is now known mainly to historians of philosophy, little attention seems to have been directed to his influence on the constitution of Hegel's initial position and mature thought. At the time Hegel composed his essay, he was as yet unknown; but Reinhold was certainly better known than Schelling, which lends a certain plausibility to Hegel's utilization of the appearance of the former's work as the pretext for his own discussion. It would be unwarranted to devote such attention to one who was completely unknown.

Within the context of his essay, Hegel, in a manner of speaking, closes the circle by turning to Reinhold's view after prior consideration of those of Fichte and Schelling, which here function in that respect as a kind of prolegomena. But beyond the immediate pretext, other factors which conceivably may have impelled Hegel to consider Reinhold here include the latter's rejection of intellectual intuition, which Hegel regards as the basic premise of speculative philosophy in all its forms, as well as the supposed conflation of the positions of Fichte and Schelling subsequent to his more basic inability to treat them as philosophy. In effect, the supposed conflation constitutes a denial of Hegel's concern to point to, and argue for, the significance of a difference between two versions of the same philosophical system.

If Reinhold is correct, then Hegel is certainly wrong to maintain that Schelling's departure from Fichte's thought represents an essential step forward in the progress of the line of argument which issues from Kant's position. In this sense, the study of Reinhold presents a form of hermeneutical counterpoint by means of which Hegel is able to reinforce his basic thesis about the development of post-Kantian philosophy through refutation of one of the principal opponents of his own reading of the modern tradition. Thus, even if, as noted, Hegel later maintained, in his *History of Philosophy,* as he does here, that Fichte and Schelling are the only genuinely important modern thinkers, there is warrant for his critical handling of Reinhold's thought instead of simply ignoring it.

Hegel's analysis takes the form of a scathing refutation of this form of Reinhold's thought in whole and in part. Yet in view of the largely negative characterization, the amount of space Hegel devotes to this phase of the discussion is interesting. Although the thrust of this essay is to argue for the nature and significance of the difference between the positions of Fichte and Schelling, which allegedly was overlooked by Reinhold, Hegel devotes almost as much space merely to setting out Fichte's position as he does to Schelling and Reinhold combined, and equally as much space to a theory he basically accepts at this point as he gives to a view he strongly rejects.

It is, however, not difficult to infer why Hegel accords so much space to Reinhold's view. For although he dismissed (and, it must be conceded, rightly so) the claims of the latter to be a major thinker, he took seriously indeed at least some of the problems with which Reinhold sought to deal, above all the question of the justification of the claims to know. Indeed, that is the reason why, despite the negative character of the discussion here, Hegel returns to Reinhold in *Faith and Knowledge,* again in the *Encyclopedia,* and once more in an important passage at the beginning of the *Science of Logic.* For even if Reinhold could be dismissed as a serious thinker, the problem of foundationalism which he raised in connection with the systematic reformulation of the critical philosophy remained very much on Hegel's mind.

The extent of Hegel's preoccupation, beyond the substance of Reinhold's position, with this problem raised by it is apparent in the manner in which it is discussed. Hegel's treatment of Reinhold principally concerns both his reading of the positions of Fichte and Schelling and the discussion of his own view. In fact, the discussion is concerned mainly with the latter, although comments on Reinhold's interpretation of various positions are scattered throughout this portion of the discussion.

Hegel here makes three general points about Reinhold's grasp of his philosophical contemporaries. In the first place, he simply does not understand that the views of Fichte and Schelling are anything other than pure transcendental idealism. The implication of this point is that Reinhold, rooted as he is in the critical philosophy, has failed to appreciate, or even to perceive, the development of the philosophical tradition subsequent to the appearance of the *Critique of Pure Reason*. Second, his interpretations are questionable, as witness his account of Schelling merely in terms of the introduction to the *System of Transcendental Idealism*, which he, however, misunderstands. Finally, he fails to perceive what is common to the views of Fichte and Schelling as speculative philosophers, since in his interpretation they appear as mere peculiarities [Eigenthümlichkeiten].

Hegel's comments on Reinhold's interpretation of the history of philosophy are limited here to the latter's discussion of his philosophical contemporaries. A wider account would not have been out of place, since, as noted, in his *Contributions (Beyträge)* Reinhold deals in some detail with the history of modern philosophy. This discussion is particularly interesting as concerns Reinhold's view of the importance of the rationalist model for the reformulation of the critical philosophy.

As Reinhold interprets this period, the relevant distinction between Bacon and Descartes is that the former is interested in knowledge in general, whereas the latter is concerned only with philosophical knowledge. Reinhold thereby seems to miss the relevant point that in a fundamental sense for Descartes only philosophical knowledge is worthy of the name, since all other forms of knowledge are parasitic upon it. But one can understand why Hegel would feel satisfied to confine his account of Reinhold's reading of the history of philosophy merely to the latter's interpretation of the contemporary period. For his discussion of Reinhold as a historian of contemporary thought is only a pretext to reinforce the central lesson of his own essay, that is, that despite the fact that Fichte and Schelling are representatives of a single philosophical system, the differences between their positions are significant.

In order to discuss Hegel's treatment of Reinhold's position, we need to distinguish between Hegel's summary of it and his reply, since this distinction is not always clear in the discussion. We need further to separate Hegel's analysis of the central problem, or the attempted reduction of philosophy to logic in order to ground philosophy, from further discussion of related considerations. And finally, we must differentiate Hegel's rejection of Reinhold's proposed strategy for the solution of the problem from the positive doctrine which Hegel here puts forward to the problem which Reinhold has raised.

Hegel initiates his account of Reinhold's own position, as distinguished from the latter's reading of the history of philosophy, by noting that although the attempted reduction of philosophy to logic is only the latest phase, it is an excellent statement of the tendency to found and to ground philosophy [die Begründungs-und Ergründungstendenz] prior to philosophizing (see D 179; II, 122). The suggestion is clear that, beyond the question of the relation of the latest phase of Reinhold's thought to his overall position, a question which temporarily is left in abeyance, his own particular concern to ground philosophy is representative of a more general strategy.

If Hegel has a general tendency in mind, beyond this phase of Reinhold's thought, it should be possible to identify its leading representatives. The obvious candidates are the critical philosophy and rationalism, two forms of thought which correspond closely to this description and which are further conjoined in Reinhold's earlier endeavor to restate Kant's position systematically. For if we abstract from earlier versions of Reinhold's thought, in which this intent was clearly present, we can note that even now the central problem of philosophy, which is at the center of rationalist thought, is to ground knowledge. As he says in a passage on Descartes, the *Meditations* above all are explicitly concerned with the first philosophical task, and begin immediately with the grounding of knowledge [Ergründung der Erkenntnis].[43] And beyond Reinhold, it is clearly the case that despite their differences, the critical philosophy and rationalism are united in their common concern to specify and to satisfy the conditions of knowledge on an a priori plane. For these reasons, Hegel seems entirely justified in the study of the latest phase of Reinhold's thought as representative of a wider philosophical tendency.

Hegel's summary of this phase of Reinhold's position is both accurate and rapid. There are three presuppositions: 1) the love of truth and certainty; 2) faith in truth as truth; and 3) the presupposition of the primordially true [Urwahre]. The third, which is both the fundamental presupposition and the only one discussed here in any detail, is defined by Reinhold—in a passage which, Hegel suggests, reproduces Jacobi's language, although not his insight[44]—"as the primordial ground of everything . . . outside of its relation to the possible and the actual in which it manifests itself, as the absolutely inconceivable, the absolutely inexplicable and the absolutely un-nameable" (D 184; II, 127). There is further, one can note, a clear echo in this passage of Jacob Böhme's mystical view in the utilization of the term *Urgrund* in reference to an uncognizable first principle.

Hegel's response combines subtle interpretation with a critical intent that effectively exposes the weakness of Reinhold's present view. In this position, the true or Absolute is already constituted. Accordingly, reason does not produce that which it knows, but rather only establishes contact with it. The problem, then, is how that which is already constituted in isolation from the knowing subject is to be known. For Reinhold's view leads in this respect to a clear "antinomy," since it contains the requirement that the Absolute is uncognizable and primitively true, although if that is the case, it cannot be known. As Hegel perceptively notes: "If the presupposition of philosophy were the primordially true that is inconceivable, then the primordially true would be announcing itself in its opposite, that is, falsely, if it were to announce itself in something conceivable" (D 185; II, 128).

In the context of the discussion of Reinhold's attempted reduction of philosophy to logic, Hegel also addresses two related issues: the relation of the endeavor to Bardili's position, and the further relation of this phase of the evolution of Reinhold's thought to his thought as a whole.

As concerns the relation between Bardili and Reinhold, Hegel's judgment is based on a sensitive and ultimately negative evaluation of the line of argument which Reinhold pursues at this time. Hegel's basic criticism, as noted, is that Reinhold's line of argument founders on the reef of dualism. Sensitive, however, to Reinhold's intent, although critical of its result, Hegel comments that Reinhold in his book has not availed himself fully of the resources contained in Bardili's work on logic. Reinhold fails to attain the level of Bardili's discussion, since he does not take into account such features as Bardili's insistence on the postulated suitability of the material content to thought; and he further passes over in silence the sense in which there is finally an inherent resistance of materiality to conceptual assimilation.

The remark that Reinhold fails to avail himself of the resources placed at his disposal by Bardili is doubly interesting. It is abundantly clear that even if Hegel does not carry the discussion of the relation between Reinhold and Bardili further, he is constantly aware of the latter's thought. Indeed, even were Hegel not as deeply informed about the history of philosophy, including its latest phase, as he undoubtedly is, that much could be expected in view of the personal association of Bardili and Hegel at the Tübinger Stift.

Second, there is an inference concerning Reinhold's relation to various contemporary thinkers. Bardili's thought is obviously less original than derivative in nature. But just as in prior phases of the development of his position, when he was subject in rather rapid succession to the influence of Kant, then Fichte, and later Jacobi, so in the present phase, largely inspired by Bardili, Reinhold continues to fall below the level already attained by the position from which he draws intellectual sustenance. Now, that is not in itself unusual. Disciples of all kinds generally, indeed routinely, are lesser figures. But in a way, that is just the point, since Reinhold's claim to be an original thinker is, as Hegel implies, indeed negated by the nature of his relation, to Bardili and, throughout his career, to the sources of his thought.

Hegel does not dwell at length on Reinhold's relation to Bardili. He does accord more attention to the problem raised by the latest phase of Reinhold's thought than to the position as a whole. That takes the form of a comparative analysis of Reinhold's view as now stated in comparison to the *Attempt at a New Theory of the Human Capacity of Representation (Versuch einer neuen Theorie des menschlichen Vorstellungsvermögens,* 1798), the first mature statement of the elementary philosophy, with reference also to Bardili's *Sketch of the First Logic.* The relatively extensive treatment of this question is not unexpected. The problem only recently had been raised by Fichte in two separate contexts: in his review of Bardili's book[45] and in his subsequent semipopular response to the publication of Reinhold's *Contributions.*[46] Further, the problem of the relation of successive moments of Reinhold's position to it is obviously significant, since it bears on his claim to effect a genuine philosophical revolution, presumably in the manner of Kant, in the latest version of his view.

Hegel's approach to this question differs significantly from Fichte's, although the conclusion he reaches is nearly identical. The problem of discipleship is obviously a frequent bone of contention in the history of philosophy. Plato was, of course, unable to deny Kant's statements about his position in the critical philosophy, even if Kant was quick to object to Fichte's similar claim to a superior grasp of the critical philosophy. Fichte, in turn, suggested that his own disciples, including Schelling and Reinhold, did not follow his thought adequately.

Despite the effort to stake out a third standpoint between those of Fichte and Jacobi (in much the same manner as that already had been attempted by Reinhold), according to Fichte Bardili does not understand the transcendental philosophy, and his position is merely another version of Reinhold's elementary philosophy.[47] Reinhold's latest view manifests a loss of all traces of the influences of Kant and Fichte, even if he never has understood the latter's thought; but in his acceptance of Bardili's influence, who is already under Reinhold's influence, Reinhold contrives a disguised return to his earlier position.[48]

Hegel, who is obviously unconcerned to defend Fichte's view in the manner of its author, nonetheless agrees with his opinion of Reinhold's position. After a comparison of a number of points in Reinhold's *Contributions* with Bardili's *Sketch,* Hegel remarks that Reinhold's satisfaction with the present state of his thought, the proposed reduction of philosophy to logic, is like that of someone who is entertained with the contents of his own (wine) cellar (D 190; II, 134). That is, in substance, to concede Fichte's point concerning the real sense in which, despite his belief to the contrary, Reinhold's position has not evolved further in its latest statement, but merely returned to its origins in the elementary philosophy.

As if to underscore his agreement with Fichte, whose discussion of this question was obviously familiar to him, Hegel then further enumerates three additional errors supposedly committed by Reinhold: the felt need to abandon the so-called middle standpoint between the views of Fichte and Jacobi; the recognition that despite an earlier belief to the contrary, the positions of Fichte and Bardili are indeed incompatible; and the failure to perceive the incompatibility of Bardili's *Sketch* with Fichte's thought.

In the context of the overall discussion in the *Differenzschrift,* the implication of Hegel's analysis of Reinhold's relation to Fichte is significant. In his stress on the incompatibility of Reinhold's reduction of philosophy to logic and other views, Hegel does more than merely draw attention to the undeniable weakness of the latter's ability to interpret various positions. In the context of Hegel's conviction that Fichte and Schelling are the only authentic contemporary philosophers, the effect of the denial of the compatibility between Reinhold's thought and Fichte's, beyond a vindication of Fichte's own reaction, is to draw an important distinction between philosophy and unphilosophy. In other words, in view of the manifest incompatibility between Reinhold's views and Fichte's, despite his claim to represent a giant step forward in philosophy, Reinhold must be said to stand outside the philosophical pale on the terrain of nonphilosophy.

Beyond his rejection of Reinhold's position, Hegel further considers the more general problem raised by it. This phase of the discussion is an expansion and application to Reinhold's view of the brief remarks on the absolute axiom [Grundsatz] in the initial portion of the *Differenzschrift.* Hegel now supplements his earlier rejection of the concept of an absolute axiom, inspired by Fichte, through a positive view of circularity. He remarks that the strategy of standing outside philosophy and yet philosophizing, which he finds exemplified in Reinhold's proposed reduction of philosophy to logic, is useful but perilous. For there are no longer any constraints as to the possible standpoint to be assumed by reflection.

From a historical angle of vision, this remark is relevant to a cardinal difference between the positions of Fichte and Kant. It is well known that Kant's concern to specify the conditions of the possibility of knowledge whatsoever through a transcendental inquiry is limited, if not rejected, by Fichte, who, in a famous passage, suggests that one's approach to philosophy is unavoidably a function of who one is. Fichte's insistence on an ineliminable subjective element in even the most objective train of argument is rejected implicitly by Hegel, even as he also rejects the more Kantian approach to securing philosophy once and for all in a strongly rationalist sense.

The reason for the rejection is given in a general argument directed against epistemological foundationalism. The task for philosophy, as Hegel understands it, is, of course, to produce an articulated conceptual unity. But the concern to found philosophy from a vantage point prior to it necessarily is related to the production of a series of unresolved and unresolvable dualities. For it fails to reach its middle point, that is, the Absolute in terms of which the relation between inner and outer, essence and appearance, or in this case the appearance of philosophy and philosophy itself, can be understood.

Now, it is true that the attempt can be made to produce a false middle point in the guise of a popular philosophy, whose claim to truth is, however, undermined through its inherent endeavor to do philosophy prior to entering into it. Hence, for the same reason for which he later will reject the Kantian form of transcendental argument as an in-principle impossible endeavor to swim without going in the water, so Hegel now rejects, in a manner entirely consistent with the later, more mature phase of his view, any attempt at foundationalism.

It is absolutely crucial to note that Hegel does not reject the concern to justify the claim to know absolutely. His positive doctrine, which is meant to substitute for foundationalism that requires philosophizing prior to philosophy, is contained in a passage which must be quoted at length. Immediately after his description of the proposed reduction of philosophy to logic as a clear statement of the founding and grounding tendency, Hegel writes:[49]

> Philosophy as a whole grounds itself and the reality of its cognition, both as to form and as to content, within itself. The founding and

grounding tendency on the other hand, with all the crowded press of its corroborations and analyses, its becauses and insofars, its therefores and ifs, neither gets out of itself nor into philosophy. To the rootless worry that grows ever greater the busier it is, every investigation is premature, every beginning is rashness, and every philosophy is a mere preparatory exercise. Science claims to found itself upon itself by positing each one of its parts absolutely, and thereby constituting identity and knowledge at the beginning and at every single point. As objective totality knowledge founds itself more effectively the more it grows, and its parts are only founded simultaneously with this whole of cognitions. Center and circle are so connected with each other that the first beginning of the circle is already a connection with the center, and the center is not completely a center unless the whole circle, with all its connections, is completed: a whole that is as little in need of a particular handle to attach the founding to as the earth is in need of a particular handle to attach the force to that guides it around the sun and at the same time sustains it in the whole living manifold of shapes. [D 179–180; II, 122]

This passage, which consists of four complex sentences, contains at the same time a characterization of foundationalism as a tendency which Hegel, in virtue of his view of the absolute presupposition, rejects, as well as a statement of his own novel, circular form of justification. If we read this passage in the context of his examination of Reinhold's reduction of philosophy to logic as a form of foundationalism, we see that Hegel's point is that even if philosophy cannot be grounded prior to philosophizing, it nevertheless can achieve the same goal through a justification of itself in itself. From this perspective, every other attempt at the justification of philosophy must be abandoned. For if we attempt to justify philosophy before embarking upon it, then, as Hegel notes elsewhere, the problem of the run up (see D 181; II, 123),[50] that is, the problem of getting over the ditch, becomes the only problem and the whole of philosophy. We cannot, accordingly, reach philosophy itself, since we must remain forever in the vestibule but unable to enter the house.

The initial two sentences in the quoted passage serve to indicate Hegel's belief that philosophy must provide its own justification in itself, in terms of which he rejects foundationalism. In the remainder of this passage, he specifies, first in general and then through a decisive metaphor, the sense in which philosophy can be said to justify itself on a non-a priori basis. The claim of science to be self-justifying rests in its positing [setzen] of an identity between knowledge [Wissen] and each of its parts. Each element of science, in other words, is an element of knowledge, which develops in the form of an objective totality. Individual claims to know, the elements of knowledge, are justified in terms of the relation of identity with parts of science. For the justification of knowledge resides in the justification of science, with which it posits an original identity.

In drawing attention to a postulated identity of science and knowledge, Hegel justifies the claim to know and provides for the growth of knowledge in terms of the justification of science. He immediately turns to the sense in which science can be said to be justified through its own growth. A circle, he notes, has the peculiarity that center and circumference are related from the beginning of the latter, even if the middle point as a whole is finally constituted only by the completion of the circle.

If we transpose this comment about the circle to the problem of how science can justify itself, we see at once that Hegel holds that each part of a science, including its beginning point, implies the fully constituted science in terms of which it is justified, but which is fully justified only when it is fully completed. For science justifies itself through the relation of the actually existing part to the at-first only implicit whole; and conversely, when the science is fully constituted, the result justifies the parts in terms of the whole and, as constituted by them, itself as well. Hegel's positive doctrine, then, is that science justifies itself not prior to engaging in it, but progressively through its development and finally through its completion.

The significance of Hegel's recourse to a geometrical image requires some comment. Certainly, as noted, the image of the circle was in the air at the time. It also was appealed to by Reinhold in the introduction to his *Contributions,* where he describes the transcendental movement in philosophy as limited to a curve [Kreislinie] around the sole possible middle point [Mittelpunkt] of subjectivity, which is made secure and completed by Fichte's and Schelling's development of the critical philosophy.[51]

This passage is helpful in that it suggests, beyond the general awareness of circularity, that Hegel may have been thinking of Reinhold's utilization of the circle as a metaphor. This suggestion is further supported by Hegel's recourse at the end of this passage to the famous simile of the Copernican Revolution. But the deeper significance of the recourse to the image of the circle lies not in the allusion but in the revolution in philosophic strategy which Hegel here introduces.

In reference to Reinhold's demand that philosophy found itself in order to justify its claims to knowledge, and Fichte's denial that philosophy can found itself in virtue of its intrinsic circularity, Hegel brilliantly proposes a third strategy. In effect, he reverses the reversal established by Fichte. For he accepts the Fichtean claim for the circular character of philosophy at the same time as he proposes to provide a full justification of it. He thus preserves the traditional demand of philosophy to yield ultimate knowledge on the basis of a circular form of argumentation. The enormous audacity of this argument is surpassed only by the extraordinary skill of Hegel's analysis, which permits him to preserve the traditional concept of philosophy by in effect defusing one of the most powerful arguments to have been directed against that very possibility.

Since the problem for which Hegel's view of circularity counts as a solution is at least proximally of Kantian origin, a word should be said about the relation of this doctrine and the critical philosophy. In view of the tendency in the discussion about Hegel to oppose his position to Kant's, it is important to emphasize that the doctrine in question is thoroughly Kantian. Reference already has been made to Maimon's claim, against Reinhold, that in the critical philosophy a principle can be established only through its use in explaining experience. Now, this point is, to be sure, a paraphrase of Kant's own view. In the *Critique of Pure Reason* (see B 765 and B 357), Kant remarks that through concepts of the understanding, pure reason successfully establishes secure principles in indirect fashion through their reference to possible experience in terms of which they are apodictically certain. In other words, the proof of the principles is given pragmatically by that which they explain.

Hegel's doctrine of circular justification properly can be regarded as an extension of precisely this Kantian point. Just as Kant suggests that isolated principles are established in terms of their capacity to explain experience, Hegel now extends this argument to cover the science, or system of such principles, including its development. It follows that the argument Hegel advances to justify philosophy as science in terms of itself in order to resolve the problem generated by the critical philosophy is not directed against the latter; it is, on the contrary, a creative, indeed brilliant, extension of Kant's own view.

There can be little doubt that Hegel was aware of the significance of the argument he was making. A strong indication is given by his use of an astronomical simile to suggest that no other justification for science can be given and none is necessary. Beyond an implicit reference to his own discussion of the orbits of the planets as circular in his recent *Habilitationsschrift*, Hegel certainly had in mind a famous reference to astronomy in recent philosophy. There can be little doubt that Hegel was subtly, but unmistakably, suggesting, through an allusion to the Copernican world view, that in his own reply to foundationalism he had brought to a close the problem of system posed by the critical philosophy, itself dependent upon the famous Copernican Revolution, in another and final philosophical revolution.

The aim of this chapter has been to demonstrate that the view of circularity which Hegel proposes in the *Differenzschrift* can be regarded as his attempted resolution for the problem of justification raised in the discussion of the critical philosophy. It has been suggested that although Hegel rejects Reinhold's position, he takes seriously the problem raised by the attempted reduction of philosophy to logic. Despite his rejection of foundationalism as a source of unresolved dualism, Hegel, following Fichte, proposes a doctrine of circularity intended to provide a justification of traditional claims to know in an absolute sense. He in effect turns Fichte's doctrine of epistemological circularity against Fichte's position at the same time as he defends a point closely related to Kant's own thought.

Now, it might be objected that the account of epistemological circularity is rather brief, especially in view of the long running start needed to appreciate it in the context of Hegel's discussion. But, then, the explicit indications of this doctrine, which is initially formulated in this text and developed only in subsequent writings, are also unhelpfully sparse. Indeed, that is undoubtedly one of the reasons why this side of the position mainly has been overlooked, despite its fundamental importance for Hegel's view of knowledge. After this initial account of Hegel's view of epistemological circularity in the context of his initial philosophical text, we need to look further at the fate of this doctrine in his later writings, particularly in his mature thought.

IV

CIRCULAR EPISTEMOLOGY

Limiting our discussion to a central theme in Hegel's mature position simplifies our task by relieving us of the responsibility for a general presentation of his thought as a whole, an enormous undertaking never satisfactorily accomplished by Hegel or by any of his students since.[1] The magnitude of such an enterprise is apparent when it is realized that in a sense Hegel devoted almost half his philosophical career to the composition of the various editions of the *Encyclopedia,* that is, to an exposition of his view in outline form. But merely to be aware of how difficult it is to present either the entire theory or an aspect of it does not relieve us of the problem of how to begin, how best to analyze an aspect of the mature position. Nor is this embarrassment specific to Hegel's thought. For there are as yet no standards, after some two and a half thousand years of discussion, which are accepted universally or even widely for the study of a philosophy, either in whole or in part.

From the specifically Hegelian perspective, an adequate analysis must include a presentation of the result, as well as the process leading to it. In that sense, to the extent that an adequate defense for the discussion which follows can be given, it can be marshaled only after the fact. Here it will be sufficient to mention two points peculiar to the present inquiry: its restriction merely to an aspect of Hegel's position, and the problem of how that aspect is best approached.

The problem of the relation of the part and the whole was, of course, central to Hegel's thought on many levels. He was critical of philosophic criticism in general, on the grounds that it demonstrates nothing so much as the incapacity of the critics for philosophy. But he was specifically critical of studies which voluntarily restrict themselves to one or another aspect of a position. He held that the worst fate of philosophy was experienced at the hands of those who were preoccupied with mere judgment of a part of it (see VIII, 17). But although it is correct, as Hegel often emphasizes, that the part is to be understood in terms of the whole, so also is the whole to be grasped, indeed necessarily so, in terms of its component parts. Even if the part has significance only within the context of the entire theory, the part nevertheless must be studied also in terms of itself, lest its particular characteristics be obscured through attention directed merely to the overall theory. One needs, therefore, to scrutinize the parts of the theory closely without losing sight of the larger theoretical framework.

The more delicate point is how best to study the concept of epistemological circularity in Hegel's mature thought. It is surely correct that a theory should be addressed in terms of its own criteria, on pain of being unfair. Although on Hegelian grounds it seems that a unique solution to the problem of how to begin cannot be specified, it does not follow that a plausible procedure cannot be suggested. If we concede that other ways of studying Hegel's thought are possible, it nonetheless appears normal, or at least useful, to raise the problem of epistemological circularity in Hegel's mature thought in a manner closely similar to that in which it is discussed by Hegel.

The problem of how to proceed is closely related to that of which text to select. In his own historical studies, Hegel was mainly unconcerned to justify his choice of texts, which was on occasion more than arbitrary. He frequently dealt with a part of a text or with one out of a number of possible candidates without any significant attempt, or indeed any expression of concern for the need, to explain his procedure. Despite the undoubted insightfulness of Hegel's grasp of other positions, the result of the discussion was often based not on the whole but merely on a part thereof.

A cardinal instance is his consideration of the views of Fichte and Schelling. There is, it should be noted, no more than minor attention to Fichte's position after the initial version of the *Science of Knowledge,* despite the extensive development it later underwent. Nor is there any concern with the many changes in Schelling's thought after the appearance of the *System of Transcendental Idealism,* despite the highly protean nature of his position. In these and other instances, Hegel manifestly failed to observe the criterion which he desired to have applied to his own thought. But if we attempt to be fairer to Hegel than he himself was on so many occasions to others whose thought he construed, or even for procedural reasons misconstrued, we still need to determine how best to approach his writings.

Any study of a position, even a major theme in that position, ultimately must take into account all the relevant textual material. The problem which arises when there is an apparent abundance of such material is whether a single source should be accorded privileged status. This problem is, as noted, especially relevant for Hegel's thought, in view of the different ways it is approached in different languages and literatures. But even if we at least should be aware of trends in Hegel scholarship, that awareness is not a sufficient reason to opt for a particular text.

The choice of one or another text should come not from the current mode but rather from the intrinsic nature of the Hegelian corpus. From the perspective of an adequate exposition of the view in general, or even as concerns the mature doctrine of circularity, the abundance of textual material is more apparent than real. It is significant that in a historical moment when so many philosophers publish with utter disregard for the judgment of time, Hegel published only four major works: the *Phenomenology of Spirit,* the *Science of Logic,* the *Encyclopedia of the Philosophical Sciences,* and the *Philosophy of Right.*

We have Hegel's own testimony as a reason to decline to consider either the *Phenomenology* or the *Philosophy of Right* as an adequate statement of the wider position. It is well known that he regarded the *Phenomenology* as an unusual early work. And the *Philosophy of Right* is described by Hegel, in a passage omitted in the translation (X, par. 487, Zusatz, p. 306), as a systematic account in expanded form of the remarks on objective spirit in the *Encyclopedia.* That leaves us with only two possible candidates between which to choose.

The choice between the *Encyclopedia* and the *Science of Logic* frequently has been decided in favor of the latter on any one of a number of vague grounds, including its intrinsic difficulty, its depth, or simply the belief that ultimately the value of Hegel's thought must stand or fall with this work.[2] But it also has been observed that a generation is insufficient to master the most difficult work of German philosophy, that the *Logic* represents the absolute outer reaches of thought itself, and that, finally, no one understands this book fully.[3] It follows that a decision to concentrate solely, or even mainly, on that text perhaps would enable us to follow its tortuous train of dialectical thought at the same time as it effectively precluded an adequate grasp of the wider position. For it would impose the successful completion of a formidably difficult, perhaps impossible, task as its precondition.

The arguments considered thus far are too vague to be regarded as convincing. A more cogent argument for the preference of the *Logic,* drawn from the chronological relation between it and the *Encyclopedia,* can be answered through mention of the content of the two works. The *Encyclopedia,* which was begun during the period from 1808–1816, when Hegel was rector of the Ägidien-Gymnasium in

Nürnberg, appeared in three successive editions in 1817, 1827, and 1830. It hence is later than the *Logic,* which was published in three installments in 1812, 1813, and 1816. Now, since Hegel was at work on a revision of the *Logic* at the time of his death, that would be a reason to accord precedence to that work. Indeed, the revision of the first volume was published in a second edition, dated November 7, 1831, a scant week before Hegel died.

Yet it is clear that the subject matter is such that the *Logic* cannot supersede the *Encyclopedia,* except as concerns the treatment of special topics, such as those not covered in the so-called *Encyclopedia Logic.* Although these and other topics in any event are covered in great, often bewildering detail in the *Science of Logic,* it is, as Hegel notes, in the main merely the further development of the "previous Logic and Metaphysics" (E 16; VIII, par. 9, Anm., 53; see also par. 24). It is, then, at best a part, indeed an important part, of the system, but still only that as reflected by the role it plays within the *Encyclopedia,* whose stated purpose is to provide a series of theses descriptive of the entire range of Hegel's thought. Indeed, were it necessary to choose between the two texts, the balance necessarily would tip in favor of the *Encyclopedia.* In virtue of its extended exposition of the main lines of the entire position and its appearance in three successive editions revised by Hegel over nearly the entire mature portion of his philosophical career, it enjoys a pride of place in his corpus unrivaled by any of his other writings.

But although I shall consider the *Encyclopedia* as the central text in the Hegelian corpus, it will serve more as a point of reference than as a full statement either of the complete position or of the concept of circularity. Considered as a statement of the entire theory, despite Hegel's extensive and repeated reformulation, the *Encyclopedia* remains intrinsically insufficient. In part, this insufficiency is due to the nature of the work and the historical accident of its composition. As Hegel remarks as early as the initial sentence of the forward to the first edition, the book appeared earlier than normally would have been the case, in response to the need to supply a guide to students enrolled in his classes.[4]

The result, as Hegel twice stresses, was a severely compressed discussion,[5] meant to be supplemented in his courses by oral commentary—in short, not the system itself but a sketch [Grundriss] or series of theses.[6] And the discussion itself is exceedingly uneven; it contains side-by-side illuminating asides to basic points, as well as lengthy digressions and allusions to figures, such as Tholuck, who since have disappeared into the obscurity of the history of philosophy, sustained in memory only by their mention in Hegel's work. It follows that, although in principle, on Hegel's own testimony, the aim of the *Encyclopedia* is to provide the mature Hegelian system, that system is contained only fragmentarily and misleadingly in this work.

The paradoxical status of the *Encyclopedia* means that although it must, for the reasons given, serve as the basic source of Hegel's mature position, it is necessary to use the text, as Hegel also did, as an initial indication of the view to be presented. In the present discussion, the account of the *Encyclopedia* will be supplemented through forays into other Hegelian writings, either to understand better the genesis of the view, as in the account of the *Differenzschrift,* or to round out the former text. In particular, it will be useful to consider a passage in the *Science of Logic* which both confirms and extends the view of circularity presented in the *Encyclopedia*. From the point of view of continuity, this text is valuable, since it is almost the last thing Hegel wrote. In sum, although the *Encyclopedia* will serve as the main source of the mature view, use of the relevant portion of the *Logic,* as well, attenuates the problem of which text is to be accorded preference.

Another difficulty concerns the exposition of the mature doctrine of circularity. Although there is no reasonable alternative to the *Encyclopedia* as the basic source of the mature view, it should be noted that here as elsewhere the concept of circularity never is thematized. Hegel's failure to provide a systematic statement of this concept does not indicate its unimportance for his position. In fact, the claim that circularity lies at the heart of Hegel's thought partially explains his failure to discuss it in detail, even in a treatise such as the *Encyclopedia,* whose purpose is to describe the general outline of the wider position. For to the extent that the entire position rests precisely on this concept as its conceptual underpinning, there is no convenient standpoint from which it can be considered at length. Any such vantage point would necessarily find its locus only on a remove prior to the theory. But even if the concept of circularity is mentioned no more than in passing, it is neither absent from other writings nor absent from this text. In fact, it is present in different ways on a number of levels, including the title of the work, its relation with other works within the corpus, the interrelation of its parts, in the various paragraphs, and above all in the introduction of the book.

The doctrine of circularity is suggested directly by the name which Hegel gave to the exposition of his mature system, that is, the *Encyclopedia of the Philosophical Sciences*. The term *Enzyklopädie,* like its English cognate, is derived from the French term *encyclopédie,* which the French *encyclopédistes,* especially Diderot and d'Alambert, employed in the eighteenth century to describe their attempt to provide a compendium of human knowledge. The French term has two basic meanings, both of which are present in the related German word: "the entirety of knowledge," and "a secondary work covering all domains of knowledge." These meanings are the result of a later differentiation of one meaning suggested by the etymology common to all three modern cognates: *enkyklios paideia,* or more precisely *enkyklios* (*en* = "in" + *kyklos* = "circle"), "in a circle, general," + *paideia,* "education," from *paideuein* = "to educate, bring up a child," from *pais, paidos,* "child," that is, "education running in a circle."

From the etymology, it is obvious that the term *Enzyklopädie* has two root meanings: the cycle or circle of all knowledge, and the process of education running in a circle. The former meaning obviously is preserved and expanded in the later appearance of the term *encyclopedia* and its cognates. But the latter sense of the term, as an inherent circularity, does not seem to have been preserved in ordinary usage, in which the awareness of the relation of the term *cycle* with its meaning of circularity seems to have been obscured.

It hardly seems possible that Hegel was not aware of either of the meanings of the term *encyclopédie* which, with the word, were taken up in the German language, or of the Greek etymology. In his writings, Hegel apparently uses the term *Enzyklopädie* in at least four senses. First, the book of that name is the entirety of the knowledge of the philosophical sciences in outline [im Grundrisse]. Second, it is the presentation of that knowledge in the form of a secondary work. It is further an exposition of Hegel's own system of philosophy, in which this knowledge is presented in the form of a system exhibiting necessity throughout. Finally, it is a theory which, as philosophy, is, as Hegel insists, necessarily circular. It is in this last sense that Hegel preserves in his own use of the term *Enzyklopädie* the primary meaning suggested in its Greek etymology, that is, the sense in which the cycle of knowledge is itself in fact and necessarily a circular process.

The emphasis on the cycle of knowledge as a process which is inherently circular, in the etymological sense, is already implicit in Hegel's initial approach to the statement of his system of philosophy in the so-called *Nürnberger Schriften.* The entire text is not, as we know, an authentic Hegelian work. It is, rather, a compilation by Karl Rosenkranz of manuscripts he discovered.[7] Nonetheless, even if every word is not of authentic Hegelian origin, which is incontestably the case, the general distinction drawn here between two forms of encyclopedia, which underlies Hegel's work of that name, is important for a glimpse of the role of circularity in Hegel's presentation of his system.

The central idea of the Hegelian form of an encyclopedia is given in the first paragraph of the *Nürnberger Schriften:* "An encyclopedia has to consider the entire circumscribed circle [Umkreis] of the sciences with respect to its object and its basic concept" (IV, 9). Hegel here insists on the need to elaborate the description of the cycle of sciences according to an object and concept undetermined by empirical considerations. The usual form of encyclopedia considers the sciences simply empirically (see par. 5), whereas in the philosophical kind the principle guiding its development is the necessary connection of concepts (see par. 6).

The distinction drawn in these two paragraphs is emphasized again in the next paragraph (par. 8), where Hegel stresses that although the sciences differ as to their empirical or rational form, they share the same content. We see, then, that to the extent that this text is genuine, which at least for this portion of it seems entirely likely, Hegel insists on the fact that his own encyclopedia is not a *somme,* not a mere compilation of what is known, but rather unfolds according to the intrinsic logic of the concepts. It hence differs from the French form of encyclopedia, which is a mere compilation, as well as from the writings of certain dogmatic German thinkers, such as Wolff, in the reliance on the immanent necessity of the concept. But since the concept itself is circular for Hegel, so also is the *Encyclopedia* in which it unfolds.

This kind of circularity is, it must be admitted, more implicit than explicit, depending as it does for recognition on previous knowledge of basic aspects of Hegel's position. The concept of circularity immediately is given explicit standing, even before we enter into the main body of the work, in Hegel's preliminary discussion of philosophy in the introduction to the *Encyclopedia.* This short, but exceedingly dense, text is composed of eighteen numbered paragraphs, many provided with additional written commentary by Hegel.[8]

By some "dialectical" quirk, it is precisely those paragraphs which deal most closely with epistemological concerns, and hence which are most relevant here, which are presented in their original stark simplicity, bereft of further comment. How difficult it is to grasp Hegel's meaning in these several paragraphs, as well as the tortuous progression from paragraph to paragraph within the introduction, is mirrored by Hegel's statement at the close of this short text. Hegel there stresses the general difficulty of providing an introduction, and perhaps as well his own frustration in that regard, when he writes: "As the whole science, and only the whole, can exhibit what the idea or system of reason is, it is impossible to give in a preliminary way a general impression of a philosophy" (E 28; VIII, par. 18, 63).

For present purposes it will be sufficient to comment not on the entire introduction but rather on those aspects most related to the doctrine of circularity. Now, despite the Hegelian claim that the proper way to begin is to begin, the introduction cannot begin just anywhere, in view of its particular role with respect to the exposition of the mature position. More precisely, we can infer the need for a double relation which must exist as concerns the three elements of the main text, the introduction to that text, and the first paragraph of that introduction. Just as the introduction constitutes the beginning of the exposition which is to follow and should announce its principal themes, in the same way the role of the first paragraph is to give to the introduction its basic direction by indicating the main themes to be studied there. Accordingly, there is reason to believe, even before inspecting the text, that the first paragraph should be exceptionally important for comprehension of its general lines, which justifies its study in some detail.

The crucial first paragraph is less than a page in length, twenty-seven lines in the original German. This numbered paragraph, which is divided into two indented, unnumbered paragraphs, concerns three themes. There is first a comparison between philosophy and the other sciences. This comparison is followed by another between philosophy and religion. Finally, mainly in the second unnumbered paragraph, there is a brief discussion of philosophy as such.

More generally, we are concerned here with a comparative discussion between philosophy and the two other forms of knowledge, that is, the sciences and religion, in an analysis which leads finally to the Hegelian concept of philosophy. The connecting thread, which links the three phases of the discussion in this numbered paragraph, and which at the same time enables Hegel to distinguish philosophy from other forms of knowledge, is an aspect of the problem of knowledge. For in this strategically significant point in the discussion, at the very beginning of the book in which his system is described, Hegel immediately raises again the problem of epistemological justification discussed previously by him in numerous places, above all in the account of circularity in the *Differenzschrift*.

The first comparison, which concerns the relation between philosophy and the other sciences, in German occupies a single sentence, formulated with unusual clarity. "Philosophy lacks the advantage enjoyed by the other sciences of being able to *presuppose* [*voraussetzen* zu können] its objects as directly given from representation as well as the cognitive method for the beginning and continuation" (E 3; VIII, par. 1, 41). The significance of this initial sentence for Hegel's position scarcely can be overemphasized. Indeed, in a sense, fully to grasp the meaning of this apparently simple, in fact complex, claim is to grasp in large part the nature of the position advanced here and elsewhere in the corpus.

The sense of the claim Hegel makes here can be brought out against the background of the history of philosophy he has constantly in view. Certainly the result of the statement that philosophy can assume nothing is to range the Hegelian position, as Hegel was fully aware, within the Platonic tradition, broadly conceived. In the philosophical tradition, at least since the *Republic,* there has been the persistent and widely held conviction that philosophy differs from all other forms of science through its insistence on, and indeed ability to provide, full justification of the claim to know because of its anhypothetical status. Such justification concerns the other sciences, to which philosophy is conceptually prior and which are incapable of justifying themselves, as well as philosophy itself.

This point requires additional comment; for it is basic to Hegel's view of philosophy and, accordingly, to any interpretation of it. In order to see what is at stake, it is important to emphasize the continuity in the philosophical tradition between modern and ancient views of knowledge and its attainment. It is well known that the Cartesian view of knowledge as absolute and philosophy as a presuppositionless science dominates later thought. It is perhaps less widely known that this view is not specifically modern. For the concept of knowledge as necessarily perfect is already apparent much earlier, for instance in Parmenides.

It should further be noted that the association of perfect knowledge with presuppositionlessness is well established in Greek thought. This point can be demonstrated both linguistically and conceptually. The specific vocabulary was already extant in ancient Greek. Hegel's term for presupposition [Voraussetzung], from the verb *voraussetzen* (*voraus* = "in front of, in advance, beforehand" + *setzen* = "to place, to put"), widely current in German thought, means "to take as given." It can be construed literally as "to place before" what follows. *Voraussetzung* is the strict German equivalent of the Greek *hupothesis,* from the verb *hupotithemi* (*hupo* = "under, beneath" = *tithemi* = "to put, to place").

The Hegelian claim that philosophy must be presuppositionless science is formulated clearly by Plato, especially in the *Republic,* that work which more than any other determined the course of the later discussion of the problem of knowledge.[9] In the famous discussion of the divided line (*Republic*, Bk. VI), Plato distinguishes between the spheres of the sensible and the intelligible before writing:[10]

> In such a way that in one section the soul, using as images what before were models, is compelled to investigate from hypotheses [eks hypotheseon], proceeding from these not to a first principle [ouk ep'archen], but to a conclusion [epi teleuten]. The other section, which leads to a first principle that is not hypothetical [to ep'archen anupotheton], proceeding from a hypothesis [eks hypotheseos] without using the images of the other section, by means of the Forms themselves and proceeding through these. [510.8]

The crucial distinction is drawn here between hypothetical and anhypothetical approaches to knowledge. The latter is the higher, indeed the highest, and only adequate form. This distinction is underlined again by Plato in a slightly later passage, in the discussion of dialectic (in Bk. VII). Here Plato says that dialectic differs generically from other forms of study in its concern with things as they really are (see 533 B). He then writes:[11] "Now dialectic is the only subject which travels this road, doing away with hypotheses [tas hupotheseis anairousa; from *anaireo*, Lat. *tollere* = "to sublate"] and proceeding to the first principle where it will find certainly [ep'auten ten archen hina bebaiosetai; *bebaio* = "to confirm, establish"]" (533 C).

Beyond its obvious influence on the later history of philosophy, the Platonic doctrine of philosophy as presuppositionless science is specifically relevant to the present discussion.[12] Hegel's qualified return to a Platonic view of philosophy is doubly interesting. On the one hand, if philosophy is necessarily presuppositionless, which Hegel interprets with Fichte against Reinhold as meaning "without a foundation," then it must be circular. For it is only in this way that the result can justify its beginning point. On the other hand, as circular the initial presupposition can be "confirmed" so that the inevitable initial dependence of the theory upon its beginning point can be sublated in a quasi-Platonic sense.

This result points, as early as the first sentence of the *Encyclopedia*, to an important elaboration of the doctrine of epistemological circularity in the mature position. In the first formulation in the *Differenzschrift*, this doctrine was advanced as an alternative to the quasi-rationalist form of justification invoked by Reinhold, but not further justified. In the context of a qualified return to a Platonic concept of philosophy as necessarily without presuppositions, Hegel then provides a form of justification for the doctrine of circularity. For the wider significance of this doctrine is not that it represents an alternative to Reinhold, but that it now appears as a consequence of the concept of philosophy itself as a necessarily presuppositionless science.

After this single sentence on the character of philosophy as such, Hegel proceeds to a comparison between philosophy and religion, a theme already evoked in several other texts, notably in the final chapter of the *Phenomenology*. In the context of the intial paragraph, this further comparison constitutes the second stage of the attempt to situate philosophy in respect to other forms of knowledge, in terms of a general doctrine for the justification of claims to know. In order to elucidate this phase of the analysis, it will be convenient to divide it into two parts, concerning the comparison as such and the lesson which Hegel draws from it.

The parallel between philosophy and religion is that both treat the real infinite, which is God, from the vantage point of the finite world. There is, hence, a parallel concerning the immediate finite object and the true, ultimate infinite. In effect, for Hegel philosophy and religion concern the same object, the same reality, and are therefore inseparable in this sense. There cannot, however, be a conflict between them, except in case of error. For in view of the fact that both means of knowledge aim at the same object, they must agree. On the contrary, Hegel stresses elsewhere, as we know, the enormous difference between philosophy, which justifies itself through reason and is therefore conceptual, and religion, which is based on faith and is nonconceptual. For Hegel, then, religion is a primitive form of philosophy, and philosophy is a more highly perfected form of religion.

We still do not know how philosophy effects the transition between the study of the finite and the true infinity. Hegel now tells us in drawing the lesson of the parallel sketched in order better to understand philosophy. The central idea is simple enough. It can be stated as the claim that we need to presuppose an awareness of, and interest in, the contents of consciousness, which then is transformed into concepts. Hegel's meaning can be summarized in a series of three propositions, the last of which tells us how the transition is to be made.

In the first place, Hegel properly insists on the need to distinguish between an epistemological presupposition, which relates principally to the fashion in which knowledge is attained, and a pre-epistemological presupposition, which concerns the presence of an object to be known. It seems that Hegel does not contradict himself, since he still has not allowed an epistemological presupposition. Second, he calls our attention, as Fichte already has done, to the difference between the attitudes of daily life and of philosophy. The former, which is strictly a prephilosophical attitude, is the necessary condition for the birth of philosophy. On the former level, there are not as yet concepts but only thoughts, since philosophy has yet to begin. The work of philosophy, then, can be described as the transformation of the preconceptual content into properly philosophical content, or concepts.

We have arrived by this train of thought at the Hegelian definition of philosophy. According to Hegel, philosophy is the activity of the thinking mind. More precisely, it is the activity which transforms the immediate given of consciousness, the images which come to us from the study of the finite world, in order to arrive at the true infinity. We understand why Hegel criticizes those philosophers who believe that it is possible to arrive at truth directly by a sort of intellectual intuition (e.g., Jacobi and Schleiermacher). According to Hegel, the search for truth necessarily must pass through the state of the apprenticeship with the finite. And we understand also the difference between philosophy and religion, since the latter lacks a conceptual dimension.

The comparison between philosophy and religion leads up to the third stage of the discussion, the description of philosophy as such. In this phase, Hegel insists on three themes: that which is to be demonstrated, the general justification of philosophy as a discipline, and the basic methodological problem that follows from his concept of philosophy. Turning first to the thinking mode of the study of the object, he insists clearly on the need to prove its content, that is, both its being and its mode of being. In regard, then, to the critical philosophy, for which it is a scandal that philosophy is unable to demonstrate even the existence of the external world, Hegel insists that philosophy can and must carry out the task which Kant undertook in his attempted "Refutation of Idealism." Second, Hegel responds to the question as to why philosophy is necessary by a formal exclusion of any other possibility of arriving at knowledge in the full sense. With respect to the preceding portion of the discussion, the new element here is the assimilation of mere assurances of all kinds to presuppositions which philosophy cannot admit.

This concept of philosophy imposes a heavy methodological burden, as Hegel is aware. In the last sentence of this paragraph, he completes the circle by returning to the problem posed in the initial sentence in the distinction between philosophy and the other sciences. "The difficulty of making a beginning arises at the same time since a beginning as immediate makes a presupposition [Voraussetzung] or rather is itself one" (E 4; VIII, par. 1, 41). The meaning of this statement is easily understood if we remember that in order to pretend to knowledge of the truly unlimited, nothing can be presupposed.

Any theory necessarily begins somewhere or other, wherever that may be. But we must avoid having the truth of theory depend on its undemonstrated initial principle. How is that possible? The response which Hegel gives here, already foreshadowed in the discussion of Reinhold in the *Differenzschrift*, is a brilliant attempt to go beyond the simple requirement that philosophy be presuppositionless in now suggesting how that is practically possible. Since philosophy cannot justify itself through its deduction from its initial principle, its beginning, which itself is not justified, it must be the case that the result of the theory justifies its beginning. In other words, the beginning of a theory cannot already contain in merely implicit form the proof which follows from it. On the contrary, it is the result which justifies the entire reasoning process, including its onset. In a word, philosophy, which must justify itself in part and in whole, can carry out this process only through a return to itself in the form of a circle.

I have dwelt at some length on the initial paragraph of the *Encyclopedia* for two reasons: as the beginning of the description of the system as a whole, and because in this strategic moment in the discussion Hegel reaffirms his doctrine of epistemological circularity. It remains now to indicate more briefly the way in which the initial statement of the concept of epistemological circularity is developed further in the introduction to this text through selective commentary on those aspects most related to the doctrine of circularity.

In the same way as the remainder of the initial paragraph serves to bring out the concept of philosophy as necessarily circular, expressed in its initial sentence, so the remainder of the introduction further elaborates the theses expressed in the first paragraph. Hegel turns first to the form of philosophy and, immediately, to the description of philosophic activity in relation to its object. The activity of philosophy is described as "this *thinking study* of things. . . ." (E 4; VIII, par. 2, 41) Although it often has been said that the difference between human beings and animals lies in the former's capacity for thought, not every instance of it is properly philosophic. To highlight this point, Hegel then introduces a distinction between feeling, intuition, and representation [Vorstellung], forms of thought [Denken] which exhibit consciousness of an object. These forms of thought are now contrasted with Reflection [Nachdenken], which, as self-consciousness, has thought itself as its object in the relation of thought upon thought. In this respect, philosophic activity is said to consist in the transformation given to thought by subsequent reflection upon it, that is, in the replacement of mere representation by thought, categories by concepts.

As important as these remarks are, they do not break new ground, but are rather an expansion on the already implicit distinction between the immediately given representation and the mediation of philosophic thought, which recurs below. Where Hegel does break new ground, but in a less happy manner, is in his brief remarks on the relation of the representation to the concept and concerning the intelligibility of philosophy, both topics outside the immediate scope of this essay. It will be sufficient to note that representation is a kind of metaphor which points to the concept it cannot grasp, but which it necessarily includes within itself. This point again emphasizes the manner in which philosophy differs from, but builds upon, more mundane forms of experience and thought.

After this further qualification of his concept of philosophic activity, Hegel returns at once to the comparison between it and ordinary modes of thought and religion. As concerns the former, philosophy must demonstrate its reason for being. As concerns the latter, it must prove its own need and justify any difference in the two perspectives. Both of these statements are merely further affirmations of philosophy's acknowledged requirement to make no presuppositions.

Hegel further refines the distinction between philosophic and non-philosophic modes of thought in a reference to the "old saw" that the truth can be attained through reflection only. He remarks that a failure to respect the implicit distinction is apparent both in the view of some that no prior preparation is needed to do philosophy, here in a reference above all to Jacobi and perhaps Schleiermacher; and in the recent popularity of a theory of immediate knowledge, "the theory of immediate or intuitive knowledge" (E 9; VIII, par. 5, 46). Each of these approaches can be ruled out of bounds as the result of a failure to observe the distinction between philosophy and other forms of thought already drawn.

After these remarks on form, Hegel then turns (par. 6) to content in a series of comments relating to actuality, experience, and appearance which are as illuminating as they are brief. These rapid observations, which are important to connect the *Encyclopedia* with other parts of his corpus, are by no means a simple expansion of his earlier remarks. Philosophy, we are told, must understand that its content, which is restricted to what comes into the world in the inner and outer contents of consciousness, is actuality itself [Wirklichkeit]. In this way, Hegel insists (properly so) on the continuity between the position outlined here and that of the *Phenomenology,* since actuality is circumscribed by the contents of consciousness which we call experience [Erfahrung].

Hegel further restates the doctrine of the *Phenomenology* when he distinguishes between the concept of actuality and mere appearance [Erscheinung]. This doctrine is addressed here in the *Zusatz* to the remarks in the introduction to the *Philosophy of Right*. He further takes a stance against those who see a rupture between philosophy and experience. Referring again to the distinction in form between philosophy and other kinds of thought, he stresses the need for philosophy to agree with actuality and experience. Indeed, this agreement is not only a least external measure of the truth claims of philosophy; and one further can say that the entire aim of science is in fact to bring about through the knowledge of this agreement "a reconciliation of the self-conscious reason with the *objectified* reason [mit der *seienden* Vernunft], with actuality" (E 10; VIII, par. 6, 47), in other words, to provide in actuality the total identification of thought and being which is the central theme of the *Phenomenology* and, according to Hegel, all philosophy.

In terms of its place within the introduction, this phase of the discussion has a double function: to reaffirm the need of philosophy to be entirely self-sufficient and hence fully self-justifying, against those who would submit it to a higher arbiter; and to stress the constitutive role of experience for philosophy in terms of the distinction between actuality and mere appearance. Taken together, these points are, despite their intrinsic interest, further qualifications of the Hegelian view of philosophy as reflection, mentioned as early as the second paragraph. Hegel again qualifies this view in a series of limitative comments on the relation between philosophy and experience just invoked.

He begins with a historical remark, which anticipates his later criticism of British empiricism. Reflection, we are told, already existed, albeit in abstract form, in Greek thought. When it reemerged in the wake of the Protestant Reformation, thought then revealed a new interest in the phenomenal world, in terms of which philosophy has come to be understood as an endeavor to determine the stable element in the flux of experience. In a passage which has important political overtones, whose consequences can be seen in the Hegelian view of the relation of the individual and the state, Hegel writes of "the principle of *Experience*," which is the demand that through either external sense or internal thought or consciousness the subject be directly present so that "we must find such content in unity and combined with the *certainty of itself*" (E 12; VIII, par. 7, 49). The clear parallel here between epistemological and political doctrines takes on added significance in the light of Marx's critique of the *Philosophy of Right*. Hegel's interest in the immediate context lies merely on the contemporary epistemological plane.

Hegel notes that sciences which observe this principle are frequently called philosophy, especially in England. This understanding of the term is, as Hegel quickly adds (par. 8), overly restrictive, since however successful the pursuit of knowledge within this sphere might be, it excludes consideration of such topics as freedom, spirit [Geist], and God. In this way, Hegel in principle rejects any attempt to restrict philosophy to experience, which he will criticize elsewhere in his discussion of the philosophic tradition. This rejection of an overly simple, sensationalistic criterion is further evident in his interesting remarks on the relation between spirit and experience.

But as Hegel notes in the next paragraph (par. 9), from the perspective of his normative view of philosophy empirical science is doubly deficient as concerns the criterion of necessity: on the one hand, there is an unresolved duality between the universal and the particular; and on the other hand, there is everywhere the depiction of the beginnings of this approach in terms of immediacy, givenness, and presuppositions. Now, again asserting the preeminence of philosophy without further explanation, Hegel writes: "Hence reflection, whenever it sets itself to remedy these defects, is *speculative thinking*, the thinking proper to philosophy" (E 15; VIII, par. 9, 52), which moves properly in concepts only. Although in the *Zusatz* Hegel makes an interesting remark on speculative logic as a further development of previous logic and metaphysics as supplemented through categories, the bare, unsupported claim of the priority of philosophy with respect to other sciences, which follows directly from the definition of reflection, does not advance the argument.

The consequence of Hegel's refusal to equate the realms of philosophy and experience is that the problem of justification is posed anew. For if philosophy is wider than experience, the claims of the former cannot be supported merely through an appeal to the latter, even if philosophy cannot remain indifferent to it. Hegel's answer to this problem, which he clearly recognizes, is in effect a plea for its postponement to a later date. "This thinking of philosophical modes of knowledge [Erkenntnisweise] itself requires to be justified [gerechtfertigt zu werden] as well with respect to its necessity as its capacity to know the absolute objects [die absoluten Gegenstände zu erkennen]" (E 16; VIII, par. 10, 80–81).

But any satisfactory, that is, philosophic, answer is forthcoming within philosophy itself only on pain of failure to meet philosophic standards. This reply is, to be sure, in itself a response, although only of a preliminary kind. For instead of resolving the problem at hand, it has three other consequences. In the first place, it again affirms the Hegelian doctrine that the justification of a theory lies in its results. Second, it affirms the correlative doctrine, dependent on that just evoked, that a provisional characterization of philosophy is not possible without embarking upon it. Taken together, these two points can be restated as the claim that no practice, including philosophy, can be justified in a provisional manner prior to engaging in it, since the practice is itself its only possible justification. There is an unmistakable echo here of the Aristotelian doctrine that there are some practices for which knowledge can be acquired only by engaging in them. Third, Hegel applies this point as a standard for the evaluation of recent discussion tending to justify claims to know by Kant and Reinhold.

Hegel's remarks on Kant are well known. The subtle criticism of Kant's endeavor to provide a justification of the conditions of the possibility of knowledge whatsoever is summed up in the widely cited statement, as noted, attributed to a scholastic, in which the critical philosophy is compared to a scholastic's decision *"before venturing into the water* to learn *to swim"* (E 17; VIII, par. Zusatz, 54).

One should not minimize the significance of this attack, which shakes the foundations of the critical approach to philosophy. For it represents an implicit rejection of the basic Kantian distinction between the a priori and the a posteriori without which the critical approach cannot be pursued. But although Hegel is surely correct that the discussion of knowledge is itself part of the knowing process, it does not follow, as Dewey incorrectly later concluded, that the problem of knowledge therefore disappears. Rather, this problem is merely transported within that process, as a moment of it, as Hegel himself notes elsewhere in his comments on skepticism.

As Hegel recognizes, his summary rejection of the Kantian solution to the problem of epistemological justification does not dispose of it. In a further comment, he then turns briefly to Reinhold. Hegel's treatment here of Reinhold is much more rapid than in the *Differenzschrift,* but similar in intent. Reinhold understood the difficulty just identified with respect to the critical philosophy. In his own thought, he proposed that one should proceed cautiously, as Hegel says, "to begin in a prliminary manner [vorläufig] with a *hypothetical* and *problematical* philosophizing and to continue in this, one knows not how, until it finally results, that one arrives by such a route to the primordially true" (E 17; VIII, par. 10 Zusatz, 54).

The obvious similarities between this new, briefer treatment of Reinhold's view and the earlier, more extensive discussion include concentration on the phase influenced by Bardili, acknowledgment of the genuine importance of the problem even as the proposed solution is rejected, and the suggestion that the process of knowledge is self-justifying. And although at this point Hegel does not feel the need to justify this latter doctrine in terms of detailed discussion, the basic doctrine is clearly continuous with that expressed in the *Differenzschrift*.

The passage on Reinhold is part of the larger account of the relation between reason and its philosophical comprehension. The result of Hegel's remarks concerning the asymmetry between philosophy and experience can be evaluated from two perspectives. Certainly the comments on the history of philosophy, beyond their interest in clarifying the outlines of Hegel's view, serve here to open the way for further criticism of others from this perspective, such as in this work in the discussion of the "Attitudes of Thought to Objectivity" and elsewhere. But from the systematic perspective it does not appear that this passage brings Hegel closer to the goal of demonstrating that philosophy can fulfill its assigned task of self-justification. In this respect, the single positive result lies in the suggestion that the necessary justification is not forthcoming on an initial plane.

Fortified by what can be regarded only as a justification of why a justification cannot now be provided, Hegel temporarily abandons this problem to address the need for philosophy. The innermost self, Hegel tells us, is thought, which develops in and through the resolution of contradictions. "In this business it happens," Hegel observes concerning thought, "that thought entangles itself in contradictions, that is, loses itself in the rigid non-identity of thoughts, so that instead of reaching itself, rather it remains embarrassed in its opposite [in seinem Gegenteil befangen bleibt]" (E 18; VIII, par. 11, 55).

The point, clearly of Fichtean inspiration, that philosophy is essentially a response to experience then is developed further in a series of paragraphs (pars. 12–14). Hegel returns first to the problem of the relation of philosophy to science, already raised in the first paragraph. Going beyond Aristotle's claim that philosophy begins in wonder, he asserts that the stimulus for philosophy is to be found in a specific problem, whether in ordinary experience or in the realm of the various empirical sciences, as a result of which philosophy assumes against itself a negative attitude. Philosophy hence takes up the role of bringing about a peaceful resolution of the many conflicts which arise in experience of the day, a point Hegel also makes elsewhere in the famous definition of philosophy as its own time comprehended in thought.

The purpose of the application of philosophic reflection to the contents of experience is that by raising understanding to the level of reason, necessary connections between them are thereby revealed. Applying this general concept to the realm of philosophy, Hegel redevelops an important point about the nature of philosophy and of its relation to the prior tradition. It is possible to demonstrate necessity only within empirical experience. Similarly, although the history of philosophy seems to be composed of a myriad of positions related merely by chance, and containing irreconcilable principles, it is in fact the record of the stagewise manifestation of the single spirit.

After his remarks on the relation of any position, including his own, to the preceding tradition, Hegel returns to the nature of philosophy. The immediately preceding comments (pars. 11–13) serve to locate the development of philosophy in relation to experience as given in time and space. Hegel then abstracts from the historical element just discussed in order to consider the development of thought merely within the element of thought.

In a series of observations on the nature of philosophy, Hegel makes two points related to themes previously discussed. To begin with, he notes that concrete thought, which he also previously has called the concept, can be called Idea or Absolute, as well. This point is left in suspense, since what a concrete thought might be is not made clear either here or in preceding sections of the introduction. But an immediate result is to reinforce the relation of this work to the *Phenomenology* through the latter's discussion of the Absolute, as well as to reemphasize the sense in which philosophy, like religion, is preoccupied with truth as such. Hegel's second, perhaps more imposing, point consists in the assertion that as science philosophy is essentially a system of the whole that develops through the unfolding of concrete thought. "The science [of concrete thought—T.R.] is essentially system," Hegel writes, "because the true as *concrete* can only as such be in itself developing and in unity comprising and holding, that is, it is a *totality,* and only through differentiation and limitation of its differences can the necessity and the freedom be" (E 24; VIII, par. 14, 59).

This point already has been raised obliquely, both here and in the *Differenzschrift,* for instance in the account of the relation of part and whole. A full discussion of the concept of the whole, or totality, which here emerges into clear view, would take us too far afield. Here it can be noted that the implications of this concept for knowledge seem rarely to have been perceived, and then mainly by Marxists.[13] But it should be emphasized that although Hegel states this principle clearly only at this late date in the introduction, it follows closely from the earlier discussion, particularly from the constant emphasis on necessity as the hallmark of philosophy. This principle is further important, in the introduction, to the account of circularity, to which Hegel then turns.

The remarks in this paragraph (par. 14) close the parenthesis which Hegel opened immediately after the declaration that the only justification of philosophy can be given within philosophy itself (par. 10), which is in turn a further qualification of the claim that philosophy can presuppose nothing. In fact, that remark was misleading, since, despite the implied difference between philosophy and nonphilosophy, the introduction is elaborated throughout on an appropriate philosophic plane. The result is to render it difficult, and perhaps not possible, to separate the introduction from the system to follow, which it introduces and of which it forms an integral part.

It is, thus, not entirely clear whether Hegel is correct in his assertion that the justification of philosophy must be postponed to a later date, since the justification of the postponement is, as noted, a philosophical argument. In this sense, Hegel would seem to be engaged here in philosophizing prior to philosophy. Were that the case, it would further count against the objection to the critical philosophy raised earlier (in par. 10). But although Hegel does not return here or elsewhere in the introduction to the problem of justification as such, after the close of the parenthesis mentioned, he does focus his attention once again on epistemology (see pars. 15–17) in a manner which indirectly illuminates this problem.

Hegel then provides a metaphorical further description of philosophy in quasi-geometrical terms in a passage which extends the earlier comparison between theory and circularity in the *Differenzschrift*. Each part of philosophy, Hegel states, is a whole, or self-contained, circle. Hegel's meaning seems to be that each part of philosophy is itself a self-contained unity, articulated within a specific context.

This claim can be justified in various ways, such as by the preceding remarks on the concept of the whole, as well as those concerning the relation of philosophy to experience in general, in particular to the empirical sciences. Each of the latter, for instance, could be said by analogy to possess a particular, or specific, content and to constitute itself as a self-enclosed whole which evolves according to its own rules. But if, as Hegel suggests in quasi-Platonic fashion, the empirical sciences are not self-justifying, at the same time as each is a closed unity it also appeals implicitly to a higher plane for which it serves as content.

If we now transpose this point to the relation of empirical science and philosophy, following Hegel we can say that although self-enclosed, an empirical science founds a higher form of generality, or, as Hegel says, that each circle breaks through the limits of its special domain, or again, still following the circle metaphor, gives rise to a wider sphere. But if we return for a moment to the relation of philosophy and the empirical sciences, the result is a wider totality which includes both as elements of a whole structured, or articulated, through a relation of necessity. In an important passage, Hegel then writes: "The whole produces itself as a circle of circles, of which each is a necessary moment, so that the system constitutes the entire idea of its particular elements, which even so appears in each" (E 24–25; VIII, par. 15, 60).

The description of philosophy here as the circle of circles represents a notable advance over the comparison between philosophy and circularity in the *Differenzschrift*. The emphasis in that text on progressive self-justification is now widened in several respects. One such respect concerns the emphasis on the relation between the various sciences and philosophy in a manner which reinforces the mature view of philosophy as necessarily presuppositionless. Hegel's view of philosophy as the circle of circles is now seen to agree with Plato's in another sense. For the two concepts share the stress on the fact that the individual sciences are not self-justifying, and hence depend on philosophy, which, as the science of sciences, justifies both itself and all other claims to know.

The description of philosophy as the circle of circles goes beyond the *Differenzschrift* in another respect. Hegel earlier left open the problem of how the claim for theory to provide knowledge could be justified through the relation of part to whole. It already has been noted that this topic is alluded to in paragraph 6, in the claim that theory must agree with reality and experience. From this perspective, the idea that philosophy is the circle of circles is doubly suggestive.

On the one hand, Hegel here brings out the relation of philosophy to the other sciences, as noted. On the other hand, he stresses that philosophy cannot depend on its starting point for its claim to provide knowledge. It follows that the final touchstone of evaluation must be the ability of self-enclosed theory to explain reality and experience.

He thus goes beyond his earlier view of the justification of the elements of the theory in terms of the entire theory by providing what is obviously a pragmatic standard for the theory as a whole.

Taken together, these two points suggest that in virtue of its circular character, philosophy must be evaluated as a single conceptual unity independent of the relation of a theory to its starting point. But since any theory, including Hegel's, must begin somewhere, it remains to be seen how the element of contingency, which hence is inevitable, can be defused. Hegel, who was aware of this problem, did not respond to it at this time but turned first to a brief comment on the *Encyclopedia* to follow (see par. 16), before returning to epistemological matters (in par. 17) and a final word on the *Encyclopedia* (in par. 18).

In his comments on the *Encyclopedia*, Hegel is above all concerned to limit the legitimate expectations of his readers. Once more returning to the relation between philosophy and the particular sciences it can be held to include, which has just been given definite form in the description of philosophy as the circle of circles, he writes: "As *Encyclopedia* the science will not be expounded in detailed development of its particularity, but is limited to the beginnings and fundamental concepts of the particular sciences" (E 25; VIII, par. 16, 60).

In view of the previous discussion, this statement is clear. Also clear is the comment on it in the *Zusatz* to the paragraph, where Hegel once again recalls the role of necessity within philosophy as a distinguishing trait, and accordingly excludes various sorts of fortuitous relations from the *Encyclopedia* in which the system is sketched. Of particular interest here is a series of remarks on positivity [Positivität], a concept already evoked elsewhere, particularly in the *Phenomenology*, as concerns sciences which are not fully self-justifying. The force of this passage is to underline again the quasi-Platonic view of philosophy Hegel proposes here.

Hegel then continues his discussion of the problem of knowledge in an important passage which summarizes and further clarifies the relation he has established in the introduction between the problem of the beginning and the circular character of philosophy. In a manner similar to the earlier allusion to the difference between philosophy and religion (in par. 1), Hegel begins with an observation concerning the asymmetry between philosophy and the other sciences. It may seem as if philosophy, like the other sciences, can start only with a subjective presupposition, such as taking thought as the object of thought. But in fact the beginning is a free act of thought through which philosophy produces and gives to itself its own object.

The claim that philosophy is unrestrained and hence free follows from the earlier insistence on its conceptual priority with respect to all other sciences. But it is unclear in which sense thought, which endeavors to know being absolutely, as is the case for philosophy, is unhindered by the social being in which it arises. (Hegel also raises this point elsewhere against earlier forms of philosophy, for instance in the *Phenomenology* and in the *History of Philosophy*.) Nor is it apparent at this point how philosophy is able to avoid the merely subjective presupposition of the other sciences.

Hegel, who is sensitive to this point, responds by once again drawing attention to the circular character of philosophy described above. The answer is that since the immediate presupposition with which philosophy starts returns at the end, as its result, in mediated form, philosophy can be said to form a circle which is bereft of a beginning in the ordinary sense. As the immediate presupposition is mediated through the process to which it gives rise, the theory is freed of dependence on its initial point, and accordingly the initial point is freed of its merely subjective status. In other words, the beginning point remains subjective in its relation to the subject, but not as concerns its relation to the position to which it belongs. In a passage which sums up this line of reasoning, Hegel writes:

> Further the very point of view, which appears as *immediate* becomes within science its *result,* and truly its final result, in which science has its beginning in the manner of other sciences, so that the beginning has only a relation to a subject, which as such wants to decide to philosophize, but not to science as such. [E 28–29; VIII, par. 17, 63]

This point is, as Hegel recognizes, of utmost importance if philosophy is to preserve its unique claim to self-justification. Perhaps for this reason, Hegel then seems to abandon the intellectual reserve he has displayed since postponing the problem of justification (see par. 10) in order to insist on the sense in which the relation of the beginning point and circularity suffices to protect the edifice of knowledge. Now extending the earlier description of philosophy as reflection in circular form, he adds that the entire philosophical process is directed solely towards grasping the object of contemplation in order to arrive at the concept of the concept, that is, to attain self-consciousness, and hence to achieve its own return and satisfaction.

Hegel's choice of apparently ethical, or perhaps even religious, language at this important point in his analysis is significant, since he is so careful in his choice of terminology. Several times in this paragraph where one might expect the verb *sein,* he employs the verb *müssen* in an impersonal form in order to express obligation. Examples are the requirement that philosophy must be self-reflective, that its starting point must appear as the result of the thought process, and that philosophy must grasp its own concept as science. But although Hegel already has made clear in the prior discussion why his concept of philosophy requires the self-sublation of its beginning, he has not yet shown how this requirement can be met. Hegel's use of the imperative formulation is accordingly significant, since it can be construed as an indication that he is aware of the distinction between the requirement specified by his normative view of philosophy and its fulfillment.

The concluding paragraph of the introduction has a double role: to bring to a close that portion of the work in which it functions as a limit, and to provide a link between the introduction and the work to follow. This selective account of some main themes of the introduction is, as noted, neither complete nor intended to be. But it is sufficiently detailed to enable us to draw some conclusions regarding the mature doctrine of circularity. Although the mature doctrine is in no sense inconsistent with its initial formulation, its restatement expands and alters its significance for the position as a whole.

In comparison with the *Differenzschrift*, at least five significant differences can be detected in the manner in which epistemological circularity is described in the *Encyclopedia*. To begin with, in the mature position the doctrine of epistemological circularity is central, and not merely eccentric to the normative description of philosophy. In the *Differenzschrift*, the account of epistemological circularity occurs in a virtual appendix to the text, in what may be regarded as its most occasional, and least integral, portion. But in the *Encyclopedia,* this doctrine arises in a central portion of the work, as a principal theme in the first paragraph, in fact in the initial sentence.

Second, there is a change in the apparent relation of circularity to the historical context. In the original statement of the doctrine, its relation to Reinhold's response to the critical philosophy is clear. But in the restatement of the position, Hegel effectively conceals the relation between the systematic doctrine and the problem in the history of philosophy towards which it counts as a solution. Although Hegel insists in the *Encyclopedia* and elsewhere on the inseparable relation between a result and the process it brings to a close, the occasional context which led to the concept of circularity is not indicated here.

A third difference already has been implied in the discussion of epistemological circularity in terms of a normative view of philosophy as presupposing nothing. This point is of interest, since in the restatement of philosophy as the traditional, quasi-Platonic concept, Hegel provides a retrospective justification of the earlier rejection of Reinhold's foundationalism in favor of an alternative model. Self-justifying theory is now revealed as more than a mere alternative, in fact as the authentic restatement of the normative view of philosophy which has been central to the entire philosophic tradition.

A fourth difference concerns the elaboration now of epistemological circularity in the description of philosophy as the circle of circles. The interest of this metaphor is that the original relation of the part to the whole has been widened to reflect the relation of the other sciences to philosophy. This more inclusive view of circularity now includes the original relation of the parts of the theory to the theory, as well as that of philosophy to other forms of knowledge.

A fifth difference, which also has been noted, concerns the evaluation of theory in terms of experience. In calling attention to this relation, Hegel clearly goes beyond the original, Platonic concept of philosophy, which disdains the realm of the mutable. For the problem of justification is now seen to possess a third dimension, beyond that of the relation of the part to the whole, or of other forms of science to philosophy. Philosophy's claim to provide knowledge must further be tested on a third level of circularity, the circular relation between theory and experience. It is this latter relation between thought and being which is the most significant change in the view of circularity. By addressing this relation, Hegel provides a fundamental new dimension for his view of circular justification at the same time as he specifies the standard by which all views of epistemology, including his own, must be evaluated, that is, in the circular relation between thought and the experience of being.

That brings to a close the discussion of the introduction from the perspective of circularity. Although it might be thought that more could be learned by according an equal amount of attention to other texts, such is not the case. Among the mature texts, the references to circularity in the introduction to the *Encyclopedia* constitute the most extensive consideration of the doctrine as an integral part of the argument, as distinguished from illustrative appeals to it. For this reason, it seemed useful to provide a careful, if incomplete, account of this doctrine in the context of the basic outline of the mature position.

It remains now to round out our understanding of circularity in Hegel's mature thought. As already noted, discussion of circularity in the introduction to the *Encyclopedia* is systematic, and not historical. To complete this systematic approach to Hegel's mature doctrine, it will be useful to consider rapidly other systematic allusions to circularity in the body of the *Encyclopedia* and a single, important passage in the *Science of Logic*. An account of the relation of Hegel's mature doctrine of circularity to his mature reading of the history of philosophy will be postponed to the following chapter.

In the text of the *Encyclopedia,* the doctrine of circularity, although not always in epistemological dress, can be detected in at least the following numbered paragraphs: 119, 154, 181, 189, 235, 266, 270, 329, 337, 346, 387, and 574–79. Our task now will be to examine these references to circularity in order to determine whether they cast any new light on it.

The *Encyclopedia* is divided into three main sections. In the first section, entitled the "Science of Logic" (also known as the "Encyclopedia Logic" or "Lesser Logic" to distinguish it from the so-called "Greater Logic," or simply "Logic"), there is a clear reference to circularity in the account of mediation. In the course of a remark on the opposition between identity and nonidentity, Hegel notes that a circle is not yet a concept, and then writes: "In the concept of a circle, center and circumference are equally essential; both marks belong to it and yet center and circumference are opposite and contradictory to each other" (E 221; VIII, par. 119, 245). This passage is an obvious restatement of the metaphor used in the *Differenzschrift* in the discussion of Reinhold. The substitution of the word *Zirkel* here for *Kreis* and the failure to mention the inherent circularity of theory can both be explained by the fact that Hegel is here thinking of geometry and not of philosophy.

A perhaps more relevant allusion occurs in the discussion of essence, in the account of reality, where Hegel insists that the development of externality is "a *circle* of the limitations [Bestimmungen] of possibility. . . ." (E 266; VIII, par. 147, 288). The view that an existent being forms a totality is restated twice in close succession: in the next paragraph (par. 148), where Hegel writes of "the complete circle of conditions" (E 272; VIII, par. 148, 292); and in the succeeding paragraph (par. 149), where he mentions necessity as mediated through the "circle of the surroundings" (E 273; VIII, par. 149, 294). The result is to add another level of circularity to the view of knowledge, which now includes inherently circular objects, studied by self-enclosed, or circular, sciences, and known in the full sense by philosophy as the circle of circles.

A different aspect of circularity is in evidence in paragraph 154, where, in the transition to the concept of reciprocity, Hegel notes that from this perspective endless progress is sublated "in that the rectilinear movement out from causes to effects, and from effects to causes is *bent around* and *back into* itself [in sich *um-* und zurückgebogen ist]" (E 279; VIII, par. 154, 300). Theory, then, by implication, shares with causal reciprocity a similar interrelation—not, however, of causes and effects, but of conceptual moments.

The description of the object as circular is supplemented by a series of passages in which thought is similarly qualified. In the discussion of the syllogism, Hegel ends his initial description of this form of reasoning with the statement "The actual is one, but also the diverging of the conceptual moments, and the conclusion of the circulation [Kreislauf] of the mediation of its moments, through which it posits itself as one" (E 163; VIII, par. 181, 332). Thought and being resemble each other in their intrinsic circularity. From the vantage point of the history of philosophy, Hegel is restating the original pre-Socratic doctrine, which is the basis of his own rejection of "linear" forms of epistemology.

Other passages record an insistence on the circularity of thought. In paragraph 189, in a discussion of the full development of mediation, Hegel reports that that can occur in only one manner, "that is, as a *circle* of opposing, presupposing mediations. . . ." (E 323; VIII, par. 189, 340). That is a further specification of the claim that the syllogism is inherently circular. Finally, in the discussion of the Idea, which immediately precedes the account of the Absolute Idea, Hegel provides a preliminary definition of the latter concept as the result of the overcoming of distinction through further unfolding of the concept: "This life which has returned to itself out of the difference and finitude of knowing and becomes identical with it through the activity of the concept is the *speculative or absolute Idea*" (E 373; VIII, par. 235, 387–88).

The references to circularity in the *Philosophy of Nature,* the middle section of the *Encyclopedia,* although relevant to Hegel's account of nature, do not always concern epistemology. More than once circularity is invoked merely as an illustration. In the account of the finite form of Mechanics, referring to Newton's *Principia,* Hegel follows Newton in illustrating centripetal motion through the example of a stone in a sling which "moves from the hand in circles" (PN 52; IX, par. 266, 70). Hegel again refers to Newton, in particular the Newtonian law of gravitation, when he writes that a body in a gravitational field describes "*not a circle* or *in place of it a conic section,* but is *only* the *ellipse*" (PN 66; IX, par. 270, 86). This passage, like the preceding reference to circularity, has no obvious relation to the epistemological form of that concept. It is, however, interesting as a correction to

Hegel's youthful discussion of circular orbits in his *Habilitationsschrift*, as noted.

Other allusions to circularity do have more general epistemological significance. In the latter portion of the *Philosophy of Nature*, Hegel returns to the theme of being as circular, which he illustrates on various levels. In a remark on the physics of total individuality, concerning chemical processes, Hegel invokes the image of concentric circles in his description of chemical processes as composing "a circle of *particular processes,* each of which is the presupposition for the others. . . ." (PN 241; IX, par. 329, 298). The metaphor further contains a difficult analogy between processes and theory which is itself presuppositionless.

A similar remark occurs in the discussion of organic physics, where Hegel describes the real totality of the body as the unending process in which "the individual defines itself as particular or finite and this at the same time negates and comes back into itself, in the end of the process reconstituting the beginning. . . ." (PN 373; IX, par. 337, 337). This account of the realization of the idea in existence is further restated in the discussion of geology, where Hegel discusses the growth of plants as the process of the external manifestation in roots and leaves "in which each simultaneously relates itself to the exterior, and preserves its inner circulation [Kreislauf]" (PN 322; IX, par. 346, 394).

In the final portion of the *Encyclopedia*, the *Philosophy of Spirit*, the concept of circularity is evoked in two places: near the beginning in the account of subjective spirit, and in an important passage, spread over several paragraphs, on the nature of Hegel's system. In a remark on the self-differentiation of spirit into different stages, Hegel distinguishes between spirit and culture [Bildung], or education [Erziehung], when he comments about the former: "This circle relates itself *only* to the *individual* subjects as such, that the general spirit in them is brought into existence" (PM 26; X, par. 387, 39). Beyond the obvious reference to circularity, the importance of this remark is that Hegel here differentiates the progress of individual spirit from that of spirit as such, thus elucidating in passing his famous allusion to the "we" [wir] in the *Phenomenology*.

Of the various references to circularity in the main body of the text, by far the most significant occurs in the final paragraphs of the work, in a connected argument. Echoing now his view that that syllogism is circular, Hegel indicates that his own system is composed of three syllogisms. Each of the conclusions, which is in each of the three cases a different major division of the work, is derived from premises composed of the other two divisions of his thought. In the first syllogism, the conclusion has "the *logical* as its beginning point and *nature* as its middle. . . ." (PM 314; X, par. 575, 393). The following syllogism from the perspective of spirit, "which the mediator of the process is, *presupposes* nature and binds it together with the *logical*" (PM 314; X, par. 576, 394). Finally, in the third stage we have the idea of philosophy, "which has the self-*knowing reason,* the absolute-universal as its middle. . . ." (PM 314; X, par. 577, 394). In effect, at the close of the summary description of his mature system of philosophy, Hegel attempts to close the circle opened by his metatheoretical discription of philosophy as presuppositionless science, and therefore circular, by showing that his own system in fact meets this standard.

That ends the review of the main passages concerning circularity in the body of the *Encyclopedia.* On consideration, we can see that, taken together, these passages are all consistent with, and often supplement in important ways, the doctrine of circularity set forth in the introduction to the book. The most important result of our brief review of such passages is the disclosure of a significant expansion of the present epistemological thesis. The double thesis presented in the introduction, which is that philosophy is both circular and the circle of circles, is supplemented here by the further point that the object is itself circular. The result is twofold. On the one hand, we can perceive a triple circularity, encompassing the object, the nonphilosophical sciences, and philosophy. On the other hand, we perceive the return by Hegel to the pre-Socratic doctrine, further exemplified in Plato's thought, according to which both thought and its object are circular. But the doctrine remains specifically modern in the further circle between thought and experience.

The discussion of the mature doctrine of circularity has been limited so far to the *Encyclopedia.* Although reasons have been advanced as to why it is the preferred source of the mature position as a whole, it would be a mistake to overlook the *Science of Logic.* Although the *Encyclopedia* was revised twice, the first volume of the *Logic* was, as noted, the last work revised by Hegel. Hence, it is of interest to examine this text. But rather than study the entire work, it will be sufficient to concentrate on a single passage in the chapter, "With What Must the Science Begin?" It is Hegel's latest and final statement of the vexed problem initially considered in response to Reinhold in the *Differenzschrift,* and later restated in the introduction to the *Encyclopedia* (in par. 10).

This chapter has no direct equivalent in the *Encyclopedia Logic.*

Accordingly, it should be regarded not as an expansion of other theses but as a further addition to the mature view. It occurs in a strategically important place in the work as a whole, immediately after the introduction and immediately prior to the general division and discussion of being. The point of the chapter is to analyze the question of the beginning of science in order to provide a transition for the discussion of being, through a demonstration that science can begin at this point only.

Now, although it is common practice to approach the various works in Hegel's corpus, including this one, as if they were self-contained, there are at least two presuppositions in this phase of the discussion which clearly refer beyond this book: to the passage in the *Phenomenology* from immediate consciousness to pure knowledge [*zu reinem Wissen*], as a result of which the discussion of pure knowledge in the *Logic* can occur; and to the prior, normative definition of philosophy as presuppositionless science in the *Encyclopedia*.

The latter presupposition, which, unlike the former, is not acknowledged here, is the more important of the two. For it is only because philosophy cannot employ presuppositions that the problem of the beginning point for pure knowledge arises in this context. Hegel's analysis of this problem is complex. After a statement of it, he offers what purport to be two separate arguments for being as the initial point for a discussion of pure knowledge, followed by critical evaluation of other possibilities. After stating that the problem of finding a beginning for philosophy has recently been noted, Hegel writes: "The beginning of philosophy must be either *mediated* or *immediate*, and it is easy to show that it can be neither the one nor the other; thus either way of beginning is refuted" (SL 67; V, 65).

By stating the problem in this manner, Hegel appears to accept the distinction between mediacy and immediacy as exclusive alternatives, and further appears to accept the view that neither of the two alternatives is viable. Were that the case, the problem of how to find the beginning of philosophy, more precisely how the beginning of science must be made, would become an insoluble difficulty. But Hegel's manner here of stating the problem is misleading. Although he does not challenge the distinction between mediacy and immediacy as an exhaustive account of the possible approaches to determine the beginning point, his suggestion is that the concept of immediacy, which he shows to be identical to pure being, provides the necessary solution.

Hegel's overall claim for immediacy, as distinguished from mediacy as the necessary starting point of science, is based on two arguments, which he apparently regards as separate. The first argument is that in order to be acceptable, the beginning point must be objective and first in the choice of thought; logical, since it concerns pure knowledge; and absolute, since it presupposes nothing. From this enumeration of the three characteristics which the beginning point must possess, Hegel concludes that it must be immediacy as such, or pure being. The unexamined assumption in this chain of reasoning, for which Hegel argues elsewhere, is, of course, that there is an identity, which he does not demonstrate, between thought and being, that is, between the initial concept in the analysis and pure being. In the second argument, which is presented here more rapidly, Hegel merely says that if we abstract from consideration of all determinations of being in order to make a pure beginning, nothing is before us but being, and we see what it is.

Hegel also considers, as noted, two alternatives to his suggestion. One proposal he examines is Reinhold's suggestion, which he already has analyzed elsewhere, that philosophy must begin with a hypothetical and problematic truth. It follows that to philosophize is the process for the seeking, as distinguished from the finding, of what is sought. Although the account of this phase of Reinhold's position is summary in comparison with the earlier account in the *Differenzschrift*, yet fuller than that in the *Encyclopedia*, Hegel here provides nearly the same analysis of Reinhold's thought as he has provided elsewhere.

Hegel concedes that Reinhold's suggestion presents a real interest for the speculative nature of the philosophical beginning point, which is merely another designation of that perspective. He then remarks that the consequence of Reinhold's approach is "that progress [Vorwärtsschreiten] in philosophy is rather a retrogression and a grounding, or establishing by means of which we first obtain the result that what we began with is not something merely arbitrarily assumed but is in fact the *true*, and also the primary *true*" (SL 70-71; V, 70).

In other words, the significance of Reinhold's suggestion is to provide a response to the difficulty which arises, since the absolute is a result which presupposes an initial truth. For the initial truth is established as such by the double movement in which forward progress is a return to the beginning, and a grounding of the theory, whose beginning hence is revealed as true. Hegel expresses the point at issue when he writes in part: "It must be admitted . . . that the advance is a return into the *ground*, to what is *primary* and *true*, on which it depends and, in fact, from which it originates, that with which the beginning is made" (SL 71; V, 70).

This statement, indeed the entire rapid review of Reinhold's later thought, adds another dimension to Hegel's argument. In order to argue for being as the necessary beginning point, Hegel here makes two claims: that the process of the development of science is inherently circular, and that the intrinsic circularity suffices to establish the truth of the starting point. Both of these points are restatements of views Hegel has held consistently since the initial treatment of Reinhold's thought.

What is perhaps most surprising is that even though this passage was revised after the last edition of the *Encyclopedia,* as concerns circularity it falls below the level of that work. For no mention is made here of the important point that philosophical science must justify itself through an appeal to experience. The result is a tension in the account presented here of science. "The essential requirement for science," Hegel writes, "is not so much that the beginning be pure immediacy, but rather that the whole be within itself a circular process [Kreislauf] in which the first is also the last and the last is also the first" (SL 71; V, 70). But this point is incomplete, since a theory could well be of this type and yet fail the test of experience, in terms of which the claim to provide knowledge must be justified.

In a manner consistent with his tendency to appropriate all that is of value in the preceding tradition, Hegel's treatment of Reinhold's suggestion here is not an outright rejection but rather a qualified acceptance of it. He is less charitable in his reception of the other alternative he considers, the suggestion to begin with the self [Ich]. Hegel's treatment of this suggestion, although consistent with his thought since the *Differenzschrift*, is not directly related to his doctrine of circularity and hence need not detain us long.

Although he does not enter into detail, Hegel probably has in mind Fichte, primarily, as well as Kant and certainly Descartes, as representatives of the ego philosophy, or views of science which begin from the subject and accordingly privilege subjectivity above objectivity. Hegel willingly concedes that from the perspective of the self, one arrives at the standpoint of pure knowing. But he objects that that is only in terms of a subjective postulate, since the necessity inherent in the movement from immediate consciousness to pure knowledge has not been shown. The pure self is, then, merely the pure knowing which results from the absolute act of self-elevation of the individual consciousness, but nothing more than that. It follows that the advantage which supposedly results from this perspective disappears. What we have here, then, is a cryptic restatement of Hegel's frequently repeated earlier criticism of Kant and Fichte, and by implication

Descartes, as philosophers who, through the transcendental analysis of the ego, remain imprisoned within it, unable to progress beyond subjectivity to objectivity.

This chapter has been concerned with providing a sketch of the doctrine of circularity in Hegel's mature thought. Its results can be summarized in terms of the difference in the treatment of this doctrine in the *Encyclopedia* and the *Logic*. The latter phase of the discussion reveals a basic continuity with the initial version of the doctrine, whereas in the *Encyclopedia* it is, as noted, expanded considerably. In this respect, three main ways can be noted in which the mature view of epistemological circularity expands on earlier discussion. There is, to begin with, a realization by Hegel that in a fundamental sense the claim of philosophy to provide knowledge must rest on its intrinsic circularity. Second, there is an extension of the doctrine to include not only philosophy but also nonphilosophical science and the objects of knowledge. Third, Hegel now clearly associates the justification of the claim for inherently circular, because presuppositionless, science to provide knowledge to its capacity to meet the test imposed by experience.

V

CIRCULAR EPISTEMOLOGY AND THE HISTORY OF PHILOSOPHY

The task of this chapter and the next one will be to complete our grasp of Hegel's mature doctrine of circularity through an account of its relation to his reading of the history of philosophy. We will review first, very briefly, the relation of Hegel's mature doctrine of circularity to history in general.

A consideration of history and the history of philosophy introduces the dimension of time. According to Hegel, the change of the historical object over time is paralleled by the development of theory. In the course of its development, a theory can be said to sublate its starting point by realizing what at first was only implicit and potential. The historical object, and history itself, constitute a process through which the potentials originally implicit are progressively realized.

Hegel maintains this view concerning both history and the history of philosophy. His corpus contains two main texts on the philosophy of history in general [Weltgeschichte]: the final paragraphs (pars. 341-60) of the *Philosophy of Right,* his last major work; and the series of notes covering the courses he gave a total of five times in the period from 1822/1823 to the fall of 1830/1831, at two-year intervals. These notes, which were not written explicitly for publication, since have appeared in several different versions, most recently under the title *Lectures on the History of Philosophy (Vorlesungen über die Geschichte der Philosophie).*[1]

The brief comments in the *Philosophy of Right* indicate Hegel's belief that history must be regarded as intrinsically rational in order to be known. In paragraph 341, he insists that there is a rational element inherent in the process of historical change. "The element of the existence of general spirit," he writes, ". . . is in *world history* spiritual

111

reality in its whole compass of internality and externality" (PR 216; VII, par. 341, 503). He carries this claim further in the next paragraph, where he asserts that world history presents the theater of the "interpretation and actualization of the universal mind" (PR 216; VII, par. 342, 504), the sphere in which reason can be known in externality because it is immanently present.

In the following paragraph, Hegel again insists on the presence of a rationality which is progressively manifested in, and known through the study of, world history. "This grasping," he writes concerning spirit's insight into history, "is its being and principle, and the *fulfillment* of the grasping is at the same time its externalisation and its transition to a higher stage" (PR 216; VII, par. 343, 504).

Although the general point is clear, it is not obvious how Hegel can assert that reason is indeed immanent in history. His answer seems to be that although in one sense that is a necessary presupposition, as the condition of historical knowledge, the truth of this assumption is revealed through historical phenomena. The result of this line of reasoning is a clearly circular relation between the assumption that reason is intrinsic to historical phenomena and the demonstration that such is the case.

This point is made perhaps most clearly in the *Lectures on the Philosophy of History (Vorlesungen über die Philosophie der Geschichte)*. It is well known that Hegel here differentiates three main concepts of history: the original view, the reflective view, and the philosophical view. The philosophical view is defined by Hegel as the thoughtful contemplation of history. The significance of this normative concept lies in the point that reason, which is revealed in the interpretation of the historical phenomena, is intrinsic to these phenomena. "The only thought, which philosophy brings with it," Hegel writes, "is the simple thought of *reason,* that reason rules the world, that it therefore also traverses world history" (PH 52; XII, 20).

This presupposition is evidently necessary as a condition for the interpretation of the historical phenomena in rational fashion, which can yield knowledge only if they are rational and hence knowable. But the interpretation of historical phenomena has as its result the demonstration of their intrinsic rationality, which further yields the proof of the initial assumption. Hegel writes:

> It is only an inference from the history of the world, that its development has been a rational process; that the history in question has constituted the rationally necessary course of the world spirit, of spirit, whose nature truly always one and the same is, which however makes its nature explicit in the existence of the world [PH 54; VII, 22]

In other words, the analysis is clearly circular, since reason can be revealed in the phenomena of history only on the assumption that it is already there.

Hegel also insists on the unified character of the rational course of history, as a manifestation of the relation of history to the life of a people. In a passage from the *Philosophy of Right* (par. 343), he stresses the importance of self-consciousness. In the *Lectures on the Philosophy of History*, the self-awareness of a people—its reflection on its own views of right and morality, in brief on the material which is the content of philosophy—is described as "the innermost unity in which spirit can be with itself" (PH 130; XII, 100).

In the same way as history is intrinsically circular, so Hegel insists on the sense in which the history of philosophy forms a single tradition, a single system; this system, developing in and through time, builds upon and makes manifest the principles present in, and ever more explicitly realized in, the historical process of philosophical change. In an important passage, Hegel writes: "The *history of philosophy* shows in the different appearing philosophies in part only one philosophy in different stages of development, in part that the particular *principles*, which underlie a system, are only *branches* of one and the same whole" (E 22–23; VIII, par. 13, 58).

The view expressed here is, of course, substantially identical to that presupposed in the *Differenzschrift* as the basis of the study of the positions of Fichte and Schelling as manifestations of a single system in its post-Kantian phase. It may seem late, however, to be interested in Hegel's own reading of the history of philosophy. Even such sympathetic commentators as the editors of the recent Hegel edition believe it is no longer possible to read Hegel to learn about the history of philosophy, but only about his own views of it.[2]

This attitude is neither entirely unjustified nor wholly correct. Certainly subsequent progress in the study of the philosophic tradition has rendered many details of Hegel's discussion obsolete. And, as noted, his influential misunderstandings of his contemporaries have been widely reproduced in the later philosophic literature, where they have contributed in a significant manner to the misunderstanding of such thinkers as Fichte and Schelling, and to an imperfect evaluation of Hegel's own relation to his historical moment. But even if Hegel's grasp of the history of philosophy requires correction as to detail or the interpretation of individual positions, it remains the most impressive framework for the interpretation of the history of philosophy in the widest sense since Aristotle. Even were Hegel's grasp of the history of philosophy unrelated to his doctrine of circularity, it would be worth more than the cursory treatment it usually has received.

In the context of the present inquiry, there is a specific reason which justifies our concern with Hegel's mature reception of the history of philosophy. For Hegel is explicit in his claims, as noted, that later philosophy must be understood as continuous with, and the result of, prior historical moments, from which it emerges and whose principles it has to carry to a higher level.

As a first step in the process of analyzing Hegel's mature reception of the history of philosophy, it is necessary to choose an appropriate source from among several possibilities. Hegel's writings on the history of philosophy fall into four main categories: 1) occasional comments in the context of more systematic writings, such as the well-known remark on Spinoza's concept of determinate negation in the *Science of Logic;* 2) thematic investigations of a restricted topic, such as in the *Differenzschrift, Faith and Knowledge,* and the important article on skepticism from the *Jenaer Schriften;* 3) the monumental *History of Philosophy,* whose present shape is due mainly to Michelet's controversial reconstruction of Hegel's lectures from a series of notebooks, and whose status as an authoritative statement of Hegel's view hence must be questioned;[3] and 4) the discussion of the "Attitudes of Thought to Objectivity" in the *Encyclopedia.*

Each of these sources of Hegel's reading of the history of philosophy has its merits, and none should be omitted in a full-scale study of his reception of preceding thought. Nonetheless, since we are concerned here less with the fine structure than with his mature, general view as it relates to epistemological circularity, it will be useful to emphasize the latter source, supplementing it where necessary by a cautious appeal to the less certain *History of Philosophy.* Caution is necessary in this regard, since Hegel never prepared the *History of Philosophy* for publication, although it was clearly an interesting and important source of his views. Placing primary reliance on the "Attitudes of Thought to Objectivity" has the further advantage that, for the reasons given in the preceding chapter, the main source for Hegel's mature reception of the history of philosophy will be the authorized presentation of his position as a whole.

As we turn now to the "Attitudes of Thought to Objectivity," we can note immediately that interpretation of any kind presupposes a conceptual framework, as Hegel often emphasizes. As part of the analysis of his reading of the history of philosophy, it is appropriate to locate its conceptual framework within the *Encyclopedia.* The point concerning the interpenetration of systematic and historical elements within the Hegelian position is illustrated here by the location of an explicit discussion of the history of philosophy within the first part of that work, in the so-called "Encyclopedia Logic."

The initial portion of the "Encyclopedia Logic," entitled "Preliminary Concept [Vorbegriff]," bears to it a relation like that of the introduction to the work as a whole. The "Preliminary Concept" is composed of two interrelated moments: a brief discussion of objective, or philosophic, thought, developed in systematic fashion; followed by a systematic reading of the philosophic tradition in terms of that discussion, as stages in the manifestation of objective thought on the historical plane.

In his discussion of objective thought, Hegel underlines the relation of his view of logic and metaphysics, recently discredited in the critical philosophy. It follows that his normative view of logic, and hence the reading of the history of philosophy which depends upon it, can be viewed as a renewal of the earlier metaphysical tradition, especially in the Aristotelian form rejected by Kant. Accordingly, in the analysis of Hegel's conceptual framework for, and reading of, the history of philosophy, it will be useful to emphasize the relation between the Hegelian endeavor to renew the metaphysical tradition and the function of the concept of epistemological circularity for objective thought.

To put this point somewhat differently, Hegel's view of epistemological circularity is doubly determined: from a systematic perspective, as noted in the account of the introduction to the *Encyclopedia*, through the effort to complete the argument necessary to justify the claim to know; and from the historical perspective by the inner logic of the unfolding of the concept of objective thought. Indeed, precisely this kind of interrelation between historical and systematic aspects of the position could be expected, since, at the limit, as Hegel remarks, system and history are merely two aspects of the same process through which objective thought achieves knowledge.

The normative discussion of thought in the "Preliminary Concept," which precedes the related reading of the history of philosophy, provides further clarification of the concept of reflection. Particularly important is Hegel's rejection of traditional logic as the science of the form of thought, devoid of content—a point further developed in the "Doctrine of the Concept [Begriffslogik]—as a possible candidate for the science of the self-development of the content of thought. Utilizing traditional terminology, with novel intent, Hegel defines logic as "the science of the *pure idea*" (E 19; VIII, par. 19, 67). He rejects the view that logical concepts are valid in themselves in favor of the already noted underlying concept of totality, of which they designate mere aspects.

Rather than analytic, Hegelian logic is synthetic in nature, since it does not undertake to understand an object which is already present.

It rather undertakes to bring forth the self-developing totality of laws and determinations which it gives to itself and knows, which Hegel describes as "the self-developing totality of its proper determinations and laws, which it gives to itself, does not already *have* and in itself finds" (E 30; VIII, par. 19, 54). The implication is clear that rather than a formal study of the laws of thought, in abstraction from all content, Hegelian logic is, on the contrary, ontologic—that is, an analysis of the internal logic of the self-development, within thought, of its own object, a general science of the knowledge of objects brought forth within thought.

After this rapid differentiation of his own view of logic from the traditional form, Hegel turns to the thought which is its content. His discussion here is reminiscent of the *Phenomenology.* The content of thought is the universal [Allgemeine], and thought itself is described as the self-active universal [das tätige Allgemeine]. With respect to an object, thought is a reflection upon it, whose universality, the product of the activity of thought, has the status of the essential, the internal as opposed to the external or merely contingent, and as true.

Recalling a specific argument made in the introduction to the *Phenomenology,* Hegel further suggests that through the medium of reflective thought, that which is merely perceived is transformed so that its true nature comes to consciousness. This point, which also is repeated in different form in the "Doctrine of the Concept," is further significant as a demonstration—against those who would separate the *Phenomenology* from Hegel's later, more logical writings—of the continuity between the logic of objective thought and of consciousness. Conversely, since the nature of the object is apparent to consciousness only through the activity through which it is produced, it can be regarded as the product of my spirit, that is, as produced by me on the level of thought through freedom.

After this account of the nature of objective thought, Hegel makes two remarks of great interest for his theory of logic, as well as for his reading of the history of philosophy. Drawing the conclusion suggested by the concern of logic, as he views it, not with form but with content, Hegel acknowledges the inseparability between logic and metaphysics. "*Logic,* then, coincides with *metaphysics,* the science of *things* grasped in thoughts, which therefore serve to express the *essences* of *things*" (E 45; VIII, par. 24, 81). Logic is, hence, the metaphysics of the contents of consciousness, a point also relevant to the unfortunate concern of many Hegelian students to separate logic and phenomenology in Hegel's mature thought.

Hegel further stresses that since knowledge is by its nature unlimited, it necessarily oversteps the limit of finite forms, established in the critical philosophy, concerned only with the understanding, in order to take as its object the absolute object. In this way, Hegel again underlines the claim of logic to renew with the metaphysical tradition, which the critical philosophy had attempted to banish from the ranks of the legitimate pretenders to scientific status.

The significance of Hegel's endeavor to renew the metaphysical tradition as the science of objective thought can be seen against the background of the historical tradition he knew so well. This book is certainly not the place to embark on a full-scale discussion of metaphysics, a complicated topic with a lengthy history. But it is common knowledge that metaphysics originates as early as Parmenides' poem and that the term initially was applied by later Hellenists to designate Aristotle's treatise on theology, or first philosophy. In his objection to metaphysics, beyond Leibniz and Wolff, Kant also is taking aim at Aristotle's view of metaphysics as the science of being as such. Since it is the Aristotelian concept of first philosophy to which Kant objects and to which Hegel makes a qualified return, it will be useful to contrast Aristotle's and Kant's positions in this regard.

With regard to metaphysics, the contrast between Kant and Aristotle could hardly be clearer, even if Kant's own concept of it is by no means clear. Aristotle is explicit in his view of theology as one of the three basic theoretical sciences (Meta. Epsilon 1, 1026a 18–20). As the science of first principles (Topics 100b; Post. Ana. 100b 12–17; NE VI, iii, 1–4), theology is concerned with knowledge of being, specifically that which is that it is and that which is not that it is not. Knowledge of being as such, which is not an object of experience, of that which is in Aristotle's view most knowable, is the aim of theology. It is well known that for Kant, on the contrary, the limits of knowledge are drawn more narrowly to begin with experience only.

At least three senses of the term *metaphysics* can be discerned in Kant's writings:[4] 1) in the widest sense, the systematic unity of pure philosophy (B 869, B 875); 2) the system of pure philosophy as opposed to critical philosophy (B 869); and 3) more narrowly, the division into speculative and practical uses of pure reason in respect to the metaphysics of nature and of morals. The former, which is rejected by Kant as surpassing the bounds of possible experience, is described by him as follows: "The former contains all the principles of pure reason that are derived from mere concepts . . . from the theoretical knowledge of all things. . . ." (B 869). But there is a tension in his view in this respect, since, in the passage where he characterizes the well-known Copernican Revolution, he writes in part: ". .

whether we may not have more success in the tasks of metaphysics, if
we suppose that objects must conform to our knowledge" (B xvi). The
implication would seem to follow that the completion of the task of
metaphysics, which is manifestly Kant's intention, belongs to another,
positive form of metaphysics.

The contrast between Aristotle and Kant concerning metaphysics is
by no means a historical curiosity; it is, rather, a fundamental disagreement which divides two basically different concepts of the
nature of philosophy. The disagreement between metaphysical and
antimetaphysical perspectives, sometimes miscategorized as a conflict
between positivism and the antipositivism inherent in a metaphysical
point of view, echoes throughout the entire philosophic tradition. A
recent example is provided in contemporary phenomenology, whose
post-Husserlian phase in part can be viewed, despite Heidegger's
claims, as a revolt against the antimetaphysical strictures of Husserl's
thought.

In briefest terms, if we appeal to the most restrictive of the forms of
metaphysics distinguished in Kant's position, that is, as a science of
first principles closely modeled on Aristotle's concept, we can note an
area of agreement circumscribing a basic difference of opinion. Both
Kant and Aristotle believe, as did Plato, that philosophy necessarily
must yield knowledge in the full sense of the term, as distinguished
from mere opinion. The disagreement, which cannot be explained
merely as a difference of perspective, concerns whether, as the science
of first principles, philosophy provides knowledge of reality as such,
as Aristotle believes, or whether, on the contrary, reality cannot be
known, since knowledge is limited to mere appearance, as Kant holds.

This disagreement provides a standard against which to understand Hegel's project. Hegel's project can be regarded as the endeavor, characteristic of his thought, to mediate both perspectives
within the compass of his own. But it must be doubted whether a
genuine unity in fact can be achieved on the basis of different, indeed
fundamentally opposed, points of view. Despite Hegel's reluctance to
take sides and his concern to take up into his own thought all that is of
value in the preceding tradition, his own inclination here points to an
earlier moment. Although he is sympathetic to the concern within the
critical philosophy, in the wake of Locke, to relate knowledge to
experience, there is perhaps no stronger point of opposition between
Kant and Hegel than in the problem of whether knowledge is limited
to experience, evident in Hegel's reading of the critical philosophy as
a form of empirical skepticism. For in his claim that through experience we in fact achieve knowledge, not merely of appearance but of

reality which appears. Hegel clearly transgresses the epistemological limits drawn by Kant in order to renew the Aristotelian metaphysical claim to know reality.

The Hegelian endeavor to renew the metaphysical claim to know reality can be said to exercise a double function in his thought. From the systematic perspective, the renewal of this concept functions as a constitutive idea which Hegel seeks to incorporate into his own thought. Conversely, from the historical perspective, the concept of philosophy as metaphysics functions as a regulative idea in terms of whose realization all preceding positions in the history of philosphy are to be measured.

This metaphysical standard is largely in evidence in Hegel's reading of the history of philosophy. Hegel here distinguishes a series of stages, or conceptual models, which he in part relates to specific positions, most extensively to the critical philosophy. Hegel interrogates these conceptual models in order to bring out the intrinsic limits in the capacity of each of them to grasp the relation of thought and being.

The relation should be noted between this typology of various epistemological approaches and Hegel's doctrine of epistemological circularity. In simplest terms, the latter systematic doctrine, which Hegel briefly indicates in the introduction to and in other places in the *Encyclopedia,* as well as elsewhere, must depend for its justification upon the exclusion of other alternative strategies available in the history of philosophy. In the *Differenzschrift,* as noted, Hegel indicates his interest in objective knowledge in part through the rejection of Reinhold's foundationalist form of epistemological strategy. In the mature reconsideration of the same problem in the "Attitudes of Thought to Objectivity," Hegel provides a broader treatment in order to exclude not only Reinhold's form of unphilosophy but the main philosophical alternatives to his own approach.

It follows that concerning the solution of the analysis of the relation of thought to objectivity, the discussion of the other approaches represented in the history of philosophy is essentially negative. Nevertheless, for a consideration of Hegel's mature doctrine of epistemological circularity, the treatment of other attitudes of thought to objectivity is of great importance as a source of insight into Hegel's reasons for the rejection of other strategies for knowledge in previous philosophy.

The impact of the critical philosophy on later thought, including the constitution of Hegel's own view and his reading of the relation of the views of Fichte and Schelling, has been noted. Significantly, Hegel's mature account of different forms of epistemological strategy represented in the history of the philosophical tradition is organized around Kant's position. It is relevant to note that of the fifty-eight numbered paragraphs devoted here to all forms of the relation of thought to objectivity, fully twenty of them, slightly more than a third, directly concern the critical philosophy.

Here, as in his previous discussions of and lectures on the history of philosophy, Hegel continues to regard Kant as a central figure. But the emphasis has shifted to include increased attention to the centrally limited nature of his insights, especially as concerns the restriction of knowledge to mere appearance, earlier criticized in the distinction between reason and understanding. Nevertheless, Hegel's view of philosophy, despite his increasingly critical attitude towards Kant, remains broadly Kantian, especially in his reading of the history of philosophy as a series of attitudes of thought towards objectivity, which is formulated in terms of pre-Kantian, Kantian, and post-Kantian approaches.

Since Hegel here regards the history of philosophy as providing a series of alternative epistemological approaches to objective thought, it is important to be clear about how he understands the latter concept. In the paragraph immediately preceding the initial phase of the three attitudes distinguished here, Hegel writes: "The term *'Objective Thoughts'* indicates the *truth* which is the absolute *object,* and not merely the *goal,* of philosophy" (E 57–58; VIII, par. 25, 91). This statement, which is formulated in voluntarily Kantian language, employed with anti-Kantian intent, is important. It reaffirms at a crucial point in the discussion Hegel's oft-expressed normative belief, present as early as the *Differenzschrift,* that philosophy does not only strive for but in fact attains the absolute object. To make the same point in even more Kantian language, Hegel here explicitly indicates that it is not regulative but in fact constitutive of the philosophic task to reach knowledge, not of appearance but of reality as such.

Hegel's summary statement of his view of the relation of thought to objectivity has two immediate consequences for his reading of the philosophic tradition. In opposition to Kant, to begin with, it is clear that Hegel regards philosophy as making the kind of claim to knowledge of reality, or the unlimited, which is excluded as an illegitimate employment of reason in the critical philosophy. Here we have a clear expression of a fundamental opposition between the views of Hegel and Kant. But on a more general plane, Hegel clearly indicates that the central problem of philosophy is the proper grasp of the relation of thought to objectivity, or the relation of subject and object. For this reason, the various philosophic models he examines in his review of the tradition appear as a series of ever more adequate views of the relation of thought to objectivity; and, conversely, the aim of his own position must, therefore, be to provide that analysis of the relation of thought to objectivity which carries forward and completes the work already undertaken by the preceding tradition.

In his discussion, Hegel distinguishes three broad attitudes of thought towards objectivity. He begins with the "First Attitude of Thought to Objectivity," subtitled "Metaphysics," which coincides roughly with that portion of the history of philosophy which Kant called prior metaphysics [vormalige Metaphysik]. Hegel here considers that form of thought which, although unprejudiced, uncritically asserts, but does not know, that through reflection objects of consciousness are known as they are. The defining characteristic of this approach, shared by all beginning forms of science, is the reliance on what may be called a theory of immediate, naive perception. "In this believing," Hegel writes in magisterial language, "the thinking goes directly to the object, reproduces the content of sensation and intuition from it as the content of thought, and is thus as from truth contented" (E 60; VIII, par. 26, 93).

Who are the representatives of this view? Hegel does not mention any names, so we can only infer whom he has in mind. Although this form of naive realism is still present (no less so then than now), it is most widespread, as he notes, in the older, pre-Kantian metaphysics. From his appeal to the division of this attitude towards objectivity, following Kantian practice, into the realms of ontology, rational psychology, or pneumatology, cosmology, and natural, or rational, theology, Hegel seems to have in mind what Kant called the Leibnizian-Wolffian philosophy, that is, those thinkers who merely held, but were unable to demonstrate, that thought corresponds to the object. But the defining characteristic here applies equally well to other thinkers, including perhaps Plato, Aristotle, and above all Descartes. To put the same point in another way, in his discussion of previous metaphysics, Hegel seems to be adopting a perspective similar to Kant's in the Copernican Revolution. For like the author of the critical philosophy, he classes together all pre-Kantian theories of knowledge in which the relation of thought to objectivity is not active, in which the subject does not in some sense produce what is known but in passive fashion merely observes its object, already constituted and fully independent.

The very generality of Hegel's insight, which permits him to isolate an element common to many particular instances, renders it difficult to test its quality through comparison with any single view. Hegel, to be sure, does not insist on the parallel between thought and time, which, if interpreted rigorously, is certainly too broad. If he does have in mind here the Kantian view of active subjectivity as a standard, then we can note that a similar view is largely anticipated in Plato's doctrine of perception in the *Theaetetus*.

This similarity is not surprising in view of Kant's well-known claim to know Plato better than he knew himself. For it is difficult to imagine how one could be closely familiar with, but uninfluenced by, a great thinker. And we can note also a perhaps even closer anticipation of the Kantian view that thought can comprehend what it produces only according to a plan of its own (see B xiii) in Vico's concept of *verum et factum convertuntur*,[5] a position which Hegel seems not to have known. But if, as also seems likely, Hegel is less concerned with the chronological order than with the description of a particular, but unreflective, attitude of thought towards objectivity, it would seem that in the passive relation of the subject to the object, fully constituted and independent of it, he has identified a significant type of epistemology, widespread throughout the entire philosophic tradition.

Hegel then advances a series of criticisms—each of which already has appeared in earlier writings, although not necessarily in the same form—against the claim of thought to go directly to objectivity. Pre-Kantian metaphysics is, according to Hegel, in a sense more advanced than the critical philosophy, for it presupposes that being can be known through thought. But it is nonetheless naive, for instance in its supposition that abstract predicates are adequate for an exhaustive description of the object as present to consciousness.

Hegel's rejection of abstract description, if correct, counts against any quasi-propositional approach to knowledge, such as those following from Aristotelian logic, in which the epistemological process is understood as one in which qualities are predicated of a subject. Second, this attitude presupposes uncritically that the object itself is given as already fully constituted, although the finished state within thought, the object for us, is reached only through an intellectual process. Finally, Hegel remarks, the view becomes dogmatic through its presupposition, supposedly as a result of the reliance on finite determinations, "that of two *opposed assertions* . . . the one must be *true* and the other *false*" (E 66; VIII, par. 32, 98). In this and other passages,[6] Hegel is expressing his misgivings concerning what since Aristotle has become known as the law of the excluded middle.[7]

Hegel's criticism of the naive attitude of earlier metaphysics is asserted but not developed. As a result, his discussion takes the form of more the counterposition of one attitude to another, on the basis of a rival theory, than an immanent critique. In part, the abstract

character of Hegel's criticism is imposed by his concern here with a
general attitude, as distinguished from its specific instances. Had he
wished to illustrate his discussion, he would have been forced to
abandon the lofty plane of his analysis in order to demonstrate his
insight in concrete terms. As he does not, his account here is subject to
the charge of abstractness which he brings against the form of metaphysics he considers here. But despite its abstract character, his criticism surpasses that leveled by Kant against the same doctrine in
virtue of his insistence on the developmental character of thought
through time. For the latter can only condemn without reserve the
Leibnizian-Wolffian philosophy, and by extension all prior forms of
metaphysics, from the unexpectedly pragmatic perspective of their
essential inutility (see B 61, B 865), but Hegel's wider perspective
enables him to recognize in this attitude the initial stage which makes
possible further progress in the endeavor of thought to know objectivity.

To sum up this phase of the discussion, Hegel's point is that although initially thought claims to go directly to objectivity, this abstract, naive claim cannot be demonstrated. Hegel then turns to the
second attitude, subdivided by him into empiricism and the critical
philosophy. These are aspects of what he regards as a higher, but still
inadequate, conceptual moment called forth by the inadequacy of the
earlier metaphysics. The common characteristic, shared by both sub-
forms of this attitude, is that the realm in which thought can legitimately pretend to relate to objectivity no longer is unrestricted but is
defined as coextensive with the realm of experience.

Hegel's brief treatment here of empiricism is important, both in
itself and for the light it sheds on his understanding of the critical
philosophy. Empiricism, which Hegel regards as a reaction against
previous thought, is defined as the form of theory "which instead of
seeking the true in thinking, goes to fetch it out of *experience*, the outer
and inner present [Gegenwart]" (E 76; VIII, par. 37, 107). But although the goal of empiricism, as of all forms of philosophy, is
manifestly knowledge of objectivity, Hegel nonetheless regards it as a
form of subjectivism.

In his appeal to the Fichtean form of Kant's distinction between
theory and practice, Hegel notes that empiricism makes a positive
contribution in its insistence that, unlike the ought [Sollen], the true
must appear in reality and for perception. But this approach to
objectivity is doubly limited. For it fails, through its voluntary restriction of the scope of knowledge merely to the finite, to account for the
existence and possible knowledge of the nonsensory, as a result of

which thought remains on an abstract plane. Following Kant, Hegel here plainly is thinking of his frequent insistence, in this and other texts, that universality and necessity are the hallmarks of knowledge in the full sense. And although it is correct to distinguish between content and form, to which universality and necessity belong, since knowledge is drawn only from the perceptual sphere the claim for universality and necessity is unjustified within this attitude.

Once again, perhaps because of his concern with an attitude in general as distinguished from instances of it, Hegel does not illustrate his discussion by reference to particular thinkers, apart from an incidental mention of Hume in connection with skeptical thought. Indeed, the scope of his reference to empiricism in this text as a whole is surprisingly limited. Hume's view further recurs in Hegel's attempt to demonstrate the sense in which Kant's position remains within the empiricist fold. But it is interesting to note that although their positions are described by Hegel in his *History of Philosophy,* with special emphasis accorded to Locke, neither Locke nor Berkeley is mentioned at all in the *Encyclopedia.* Yet, despite the rapidity of Hegel's discussion, it provides a penetrating insight into the empiricist approach to objectivity on several planes.

Hegel is correct, following Kant and others, in drawing attention to skepticism as a consequence of the empiricist standpoint, as reflected, for instance, in the position of Hume. His originality lies in his extension of the claim to include Kant. This point, which he already had discussed at length in the important article on skepticism from the Jena period, is of importance for his understanding of the critical philosophy as having drawn the limits of knowledge too narrowly so as to exclude its genuine form. We merely can note in passing that the related criticism, concerning the incompatibility of perception and necessity, which recurs in the discussion of Kant and is clearly drawn from Hume, successfully anticipates a widespread objection later brought against logical atomism.

The general defect of empiricism is that it is overly restrictive as to its admissible sources of knowledge and, like prior metaphysics, fails to justify its claims to know. Still within the compass of the "Second Attitude of Thought to Objectivity," Hegel then turns to the critical philosophy. His account here is, it should be noted, unlike both prior and succeeding accounts of the "Attitudes of Thought to Objectivity." Rather than a general overview of a type of philosophy, Kant's view is studied explicitly through a careful description and criticism in a manner basically similar to earlier treatments of it, especially in the *Differenzschrift* and in *Faith and Knowledge.*

The reasons for the relatively detailed treatment Hegel here accords to the critical philosophy can only be inferred. He may have
considered Kant's view too important to be subsumed under a more
general heading. Or he may have believed that as an original perspective, the critical philosophy was sui generis and could not fairly be
regarded as the species of a higher genus. Both reasons seem likely
and are compatible with each other. Indeed, the possibility that both
reasons influence Hegel's position here can be inferred from the
discussion in the *Differenzschrift* in which Kant's position is regarded as
a central, but centrally deficient, formulation of philosophy as such
from the perspective of the letter of his theory. But whether for these
or other reasons, as a result of the direct attention which it alone
receives among the conceptual attitudes considered here by Hegel,
Kant's thought occupies a central position fully equivalent to its central importance for the positive constitution of Hegel's own view.

Hegel begins his consideration of the critical philosophy with two
general paragraphs, which set the stage for his interpretation of
specific aspects. His immediate concern is to describe the overall
structure of Kant's position, and to grasp its relation to empiricism.
Hegel here makes two related points, both of which depend on a
quasi-ontological interpretation of the thing-in-itself. An interpretation of this kind is suggested by Kant in his well-known remark (see B
xxvi-xxvii), perhaps incompatible with his depiction of the doctrine
elsewhere (see, e.g., B 566), that it is absurd for there to be an
appearance without anything which appears.

On the one hand, Hegel notes that the critical philosophy shares
with empiricism the restriction of the epistemological sphere to experience, which it, however, regards as a source not of truth but of
knowledge of appearance. This claim, which fairly reproduces Kant's
view that experience concerns appearances, not things-in-themselves
as such (see B 1, B 33), leads to the inference that since reality cannot
be known, the critical philosophy does not transcend the form of
skepticism already present in empiricism, especially in Hume's
thought.[8]

On the other hand, Hegel calls attention to the subjective character
of Kant's view. As a consequence of the inquiry into the concepts of
the understanding, Kant reworks the dichotomy between subjectivity
and objectivity in such a manner that both subject and object fall
within subjectivity, and only the thing-in-itself is excluded. But since
knowledge is a relation of thought to objectivity, in the critical philosophy it retains a subjective element. In a word, even before he has had
a chance to grapple with the details of the position, Hegel's initial

statement of Kant's thought in relation to empiricism leads him to the conclusion that the critical philosophy shares with other forms of empiricism an intrinsic skepticism, which, in virtue of the concern with an analysis of the capacity to know, is compounded with subjectivism. Since Hegel above all is concerned with knowledge of objectivity that Kant's position doubly excludes on subjectivistic and skeptical grounds, the severe tone of his discussion of the critical philosophy is expected. Indeed, it hardly could be otherwise.

After these introductory remarks, Hegel turns his attention to exposition and criticism of the Kantian position, wholly oriented to the three *Critiques*. Here the objections raised on an abstract plane are restated in the closer context of successive developmental phases of the critical philosophy. Although the exposition concerns all three main Kantian works, major attention is properly given, in view of its preponderant influence on Kant's later thought, to the *Critique of Pure Reason*. Kant's examination here of the capacity for theoretical knowledge is characterized as subjective idealism. As noted, this term was borrowed from Schelling as early as the *Differenzschrift* to describe the views of Fichte and Kant, which lack a philosophy of nature, as philosophies of the understanding.

If we bracket the allusion to Fichte's position, which need not concern us here, the implied criticism of Kant's view is not adequate as it stands. Although it is correct that Kant, in a famous passage, indeed indicated that it is a scandal that philosophy is unable to prove even the existence of the external world, the point of his own "Refutation of Idealism" was to carry out this task. One can conclude only that for Kant philosophy must remain within the subjective sphere if it is presumed that the proposed refutation fails. But Hegel does not even take up this theme here. And it would not be correct to accuse Kant of subjectivity in virtue of his restriction of knowledge to appearances, since such knowledge is, he holds, wholly objective.

According to Hegel, the second, more significant side of the critical philosophy's examination of the faculty of knowledge concerns its relation to the sphere beyond experience, which Kant notoriously held to be inaccessible to human reason. In this respect, Hegel considers Kant's own treatment of the themes of the older metaphysics. With regard to the problem of knowledge of the soul, Hegel suggests that Kant's discussion of the paralogisms rests on a restatement of Hume's point, concerning, as noted, the incompatibility of necessity and perception. Hegel also takes the opportunity here to raise again his charge of subjectivism.

His evaluation of Kant's discussion of the antinomies that arise from the endeavor to know the world is more positive. Although Kant's attitude towards knowledge remains subjective, since the contradiction is located by him in appearance and not in reality, his awareness that contradiction arises through the application of the categories of the understanding to the objects of reason is hailed by Hegel as one of the most important modern insights. The unfortunate shallowness of Kant's solution, unequal to his grasp of the problem, lies in his failure to grasp the immanence of contradiction within reality, as well as the restriction of it to four forms only. Once more, rather than a thoroughly immanent critique, Hegel clearly is invoking his own position as the prior standard of comparison.

Hegel then turns to Kant's treatment of the proofs of God's existence, which he divides into that from being to thought and the converse. He again remarks that the treatment of the cosmological proof in the critical philosophy is a restatement of the point from Hume already noted; and he accepts Kant's well-known analysis of the ontological proof, even if in the "Subjective Spirit" doubt is expressed as to the conception of God implied therein (see par. 552). Hegel's criticism is directed less to the analysis of the proofs than to the reduction of reason here and elsewhere in the Kantian view, as concerns knowledge of the nonexperiential, to a mere abstraction. As a result, the critical philosophy merely reproduces in its analysis the absolute unity of self-consciousness with which it begins, in the negative critique of knowledge that is missing an other than negative doctrine of reality.

Although suggestive and often profound, Hegel's account of Kant's critique of reason is insufficient to decide the issues which separate their two positions.[9] In large part, that is because Hegel's analysis lacks a concern to demonstrate the appropriateness of its objections to the critical philosophy. That is certainly not to deny the discussion its legitimate merits. The strength of Hegel's discussion lies above all in the characterization of the critical philosophy as subjective idealism with a skeptical bent.

According to Kant, in his analytic restatement of his epistemological theory (see *Prolegomena*, par. 58; see also B 884), his aim was to steer a middle course between dogmatism and skepticism through an objective analysis of the conditions of knowledge as such. From that perspective, Hegel's discussion of the critical philosophy, including his account of the arbitrary assumption of the categories, can be interpreted as an indication of the inability of Kant's position to fulfill its own goals. But the force of the alleged failure of Kant, beyond his examination of reason, to provide a positive doctrine for knowledge of reality is attenuated if (as he believes, but Hegel denies) such knowledge is in principle to be excluded.

Hegel's treatment of the remainder of Kant's position is more rapid and fails to break new ground. He remarks correctly that Kant's grasp of practical reason is based on an abstract identity of the understanding, and hence remains formal. Here it will be sufficient to note that this point since has been widely accepted by students of Kant; in fact, it was closely anticipated by Fichte, prior to the publication of the *Phenomenology*, where it is elaborated at length.

Hegel's immediate aim is less to reveal the intrinsic limit of Kant's ethical view than to demonstrate its parallel to the concept of theoretical knowledge, based on the transcendental unity of apperception. Although on the plane of perception Kant once again confines the discussion to mere appearance, Hegel regards the concept of internal teleology as the sole speculative side of the critical philosophy. Once more construing the critical philosophy in a manner more congenial to his own thought, he expresses regret at Kant's failure to develop further the concept of immanent teleology, which Hegel regards as superior to the merely mechanical approach to nature. Although this remark makes sense from the perspective of Hegel's position, the criticism is at best external to the critical philosophy. For a concept of teleology as in fact constitutive of nature is counter to the spirit and letter of Kant's thought.

Similarly, Hegel correctly observes that in terms of the character of the argument, for Kant the good as such reduces to the good for us, and hence remains ineliminably subjective. But it scarcely would have been possible for Kant to argue otherwise within the limits he set himself in his epistemological analysis, and which he continues to respect in his later thought.

Hegel's discussion of Kant's views of practical reason and judgment hardly can be held to be thorough, or even adequate, treatments of these portions of the critical philosophy, although that may not have been Hegel's intent. But the discussion here is sufficient to achieve another purpose. For it reveals that, since these sides of the critical philosophy presuppose the earlier critique of reason, the objections raised against Kant's view of theoretical reason also can be brought against the subsequent aspects of his position. Yet despite its intrinsic interest, the immanent criticism of various aspects of the critical philosophy is not easy to relate to the larger topic, against whose background it occurs, that is, the "Attitudes of Thought to Objectivity." In this respect, greater significance must be attached to Hegel's rapid but profound summary of the significance of the critical philosophy for knowledge.

In the course of his summary, Hegel makes two interesting points. In the first place, he attacks the fundamental distinction between reality and appearance which is the conceptual basis of the Kantian position. According to Hegel, the critical philosophy, like all forms of dualism, exhibits an utter inability to unite within itself what it acknowledges as in fact unified. In particular, it is inadmissible to suggest that knowledge is restricted merely to appearances (which we, however, know absolutely), on the grounds that that is the absolute limit of knowledge. For awareness of a limit necessarily presupposes that we already have transcended it. To put the point in another way, in Hegelian language, knowledge of the finite presupposes as its condition knowledge of the infinite.

This point, which is of the utmost importance for Kant's position, is difficult to meet on strictly Kantian grounds. Kant himself sometimes holds a similar view, as witness his distinction in the *Prolegomena* between a limit and a bound.[10] As a result, Kant is put in the difficult situation, often noted by commentators in respect to his concept of the thing-in-itself, of knowing what is unknowable, or in this case that which is nonexperienceable, as a condition of experience. In this way, Hegel demonstrates to his own satisfaction that, despite Kant's epistemological injunction to limit knowledge to appearance, a distinction between appearance and reality cannot be made out; for we in fact do know the latter.

In the present context, it is not necessary to follow the systematic implications of this argument further, other than to remark that if correct, it would appear to undermine all forms of dualism by tending to reveal an underlying monism. In the context of the examination of "Attitudes of Thought to Objectivity," this argument demonstrates that, on grounds conceded by Kant within the critical philosophy, knowledge of reality is indeed possible. The corollary of this point is that, despite Kant's intention, the critical philosophy itself provides a basic reason, at the same time as it unsuccessfully strives to limit knowledge to appearance, to surpass this limit.

Second, Hegel returns to the problem of the relation of the critical philosophy to empiricism in a manner which supports the preceding point. Despite its interest in sensory perception, Kant's position differs from simple empiricism by its insistence on a level of spiritual reality, a suprasensible world. Now, empiricism is, of course, monistically inclined in its refusal to admit anything other than experience. But the critical philosophy is a dualism: it combines, on the one hand, the contents of perception and reflective understanding, and, on the other, the self-critical faculty of reason, which, although similar to that of prior metaphysics criticized by Kant, is emptied of all content and, accordingly, any claim to authority.

Kant was certainly not unaware of this problem. If we interpret the different critiques of various capacities to know as aspects of human being, then, as he indicated in a later work, his entire critical enterprise can be grasped as an endeavor to respond to the question "What is man?"[11] Nevertheless, it must be conceded that his repeated efforts, in terms of the faculty of judgment, to relate his views of theoretical and practical reason are unavailing. Hegel does not attend to the consequences of the unresolved dualism in Kant's concept of subjectivity, so important for the genesis of Fichte's thought. He merely states that the concept of a fully self-contained, wholly free reason belongs to the prejudice of the present day as Kant's legacy. Yet, it should be noted that as Hegel interprets the critical philosophy, the concept of independent reason is necessarily self-stultifying. For even as it transcends the empirical sphere, it remains empty and hence forfeits its claim to know.

The limitation of reason within the critical philosophy, as Hegel interprets it, to make room for faith allows only for finite knowledge drawn from experience; but it consigns reason itself, as deprived of any possible content, to a purely negative role. In the last section, the "Third Attitude of Thought to Objectivity," Hegel considers the contrary position, the denial of knowledge of the finite which through faith claims knowledge of the infinite. Once again, as is his custom here except with respect to Kant, Hegel does not attach his general analysis to specific positions, preferring instead the unrestricted freedom of pure assertion. In order to appreciate Hegel's treatment of what he calls immediate knowledge [das unmittelbare Wissen], it will be helpful to relate this kind of attitude to specific positions.

The type of attitude which Hegel here examines is exemplified perhaps most closely among post-Kantian thinkers by Jacobi and Schleiermacher. It is possible that Hegel also has Schelling in mind, for Schelling's early insistence that knowledge is possible only through the assumption of a featureless absolute—a view spelled out in detail in the *System of Transcendental Idealism,* which Hegel took as the basic statement of his friend's thought—can be interpreted as a denial of the epistemological value of the finite in favor of the transfinite absolute.[12] Finally, Hegel clearly also has Descartes again in mind, as can be seen from the direct mention of the Cartesian position. Indeed, it is well known that Descartes's intent is to attain knowledge independent of faith. In that sense, his stress on immediate knowing, on direct cognition of the given, as distinguished from sensory perception, is the major precursor of later forms of intuitionism.

If we pause for a moment, it is perhaps surprising to note that nearly as much space is devoted to Jacobi and Schleiermacher as to the author of the critical philosophy. That is surprising in view of Hegel's well-known belief that Fichte and Schelling are the only contemporary thinkers worthy of notice. Yet, although it must be conceded that neither Jacobi nor Schleiermacher is a thinker of the first rank, for the former, and by extension for the latter, we can infer why, as in the case of Reinhold, Hegel would find it important to deal, even in oblique fashion, with their views. In fact, it may be supposed that the reason which attracts Hegel to these three thinkers of relatively minor stature in the history of philosophy is the same in all cases. At the time Hegel was writing, their positions were significant as leading representatives of a widespread, but basically mistaken, philosophic perspective, whose error, accordingly, required demonstration.

Since the names of Jacobi and Schleiermacher are scarcely household words, it will be useful to recall the views which Hegel here opposes. As an early opponent of the critical philosophy, Jacobi rejected the view that knowledge could and indeed must be drawn from experience. He held that it was in principle impossible to develop the unlimited from the limited.[13] But from his view, which Hegel did not share, that all justification is provisional and based ultimately on faith, he drew conclusions which Hegel sought to avoid. For he also held that knowledge in the full sense occurs in the form of direct revelation [Offenbarung] in consciousness which is not itself in need of justification.

According to Jacobi, the concept of direct certainty not only requires no grounds but simply excludes them, since it is in and of itself a representation in agreement with the represented thing. A similar view of unmediated, direct knowledge, despite differences in their respective positions, was held by Schleiermacher.[14] In his well-known book *On Religion: Talks to the Educated among Their Contemptors,* he speaks of direct intuition of the universe;[15] and he further defines religion as neither thought nor activity, but intuition and feeling.[16]

Hegel's treatment here of the general attitude of immediate knowledge represented by Jacobi and Schleiermacher, and perhaps Schelling and Descartes, as well, is preceded by discussion of Jacobi's position in *Faith and Knowledge*. This essay ostensibly is directed to the relation named in the title, which continues to recur in different forms throughout Hegel's writings. Hegel here approaches Kant and Jacobi as representatives of opposing views inadequately synthesized in Fichte's thought.

Jacobi shares with Kant the emphasis on absolute finitude, formal knowledge, and belief, but differs from the critical philosophy in that he accords objective status to finitude and subjectivity (FN 97; II, 333). Hegel notes that Jacobi's attempt to reconcile individual and universe through love, which he himself had defended earlier, is the highest point that can be reached within Protestantism without abandoning subjectivity, as in Schleiermacher's work on religion (see FN 150; II, 391). But he rejects the view that knowledge can be grounded in subjectivity. Further important, since the attitude of direct knowledge forms the final stage in Hegel's consideration of attitudes to objectivity, is the summary at the close of the essay. There Hegel suggests that with Kant, Jacobi, and Fichte the old metaphysics has run through the full cycle of possibilities (see FN 189; II, 430). As a direct consequence, it is possible only now to advance the correct system of thought.

Hegel's discussion of immediate knowledge in the *Encyclopedia* is patterned on his treatment of Jacobi's thought in *Faith and Knowledge*. There it is opposed to the critical philosophy, in which the final, unsurpassable vestige of subjectivity remains in the abstract unity of the understanding, as distinguished from concrete universality. This opposing standpoint treats thought as the activity of the particular which renders it unable to grasp truth. "The opposed standpoint," Hegel writes, "is that thinking as activity grasps only the *particular,* and for this reason is to be described as incapable of grasping truth" (E 121; VIII, par. 61, 148). Mediate knowledge, in this view, is confined to the finite contents of experience, but reason, which is defined as direct knowledge, or faith, gives us knowledge in the infinite, the eternal, God.

Following this brief exposition, Hegel's discussion immediately takes the form of a direct attack on the concept of immediate knowledge as such, that is, knowledge that has been asserted but not demonstrated. Although Hegel's main targets are Jacobi and Schleiermacher, the assault on immediate knowledge is launched in terms of an examination of the Cartesian view. Descartes himself, Hegel points out, regarded the cogito not as the result of a deduction but as a proposition from which others could be deduced (see par. 64). This interpretation, which Hegel uncharacteristically supports by quotation, is of great interest. For it would appear to undermine recent criticism of the Cartesian epistemology in terms of the so-called Cartesian circle.

But if Hegel's interpretation is correct, Descartes's theory of knowledge is not threatened by circularity because of the prior relation between thought, being, and appearance. Nor are mathematical truths immediately evident; or rather they provide direct knowledge only as mediated by a chain of proofs (see par. 66), so that the "immediate" is indeed mediated. And the frequent claim for direct knowledge of God, the right, and morality as essential must rest on education, as Plato has shown (see par. 67). In short, the implication follows that there are, in fact, no items of immediate knowledge which can be advanced in support of the Cartesian position or later versions of it, since immediate knowledge, strictly speaking, does not exist.

As the rejection of immediate knowledge, anticipated by Kant, has been largely followed in later thought, nothing more needs to be said on this point. Of greater interest is Hegel's attack on the one-sidedness of a view in which consciousness, not its content, is the criterion of truth. It is this attitude which, according to Hegel, leads to the enfranchisement of every superstition, as well as knowledge that God is, not what God is, in virtue of the rejection of mediation. But it should be noted that from the kind of perspective in which a clear distinction cannot be drawn between the object in itself and for us, which Hegel often seems to presuppose, it admittedly becomes difficult to make out his objection.

Hegel further raises the problem of the internal consistency of the view of immediate knowledge as such. The principal interest of this perspective, he suggests (see par. 64, 69), is to make the transition from our subjective idea to being, for instance, from our concept of God to God as an existent being. But whereas Kant, in his well-known treatment of the ontological proof, drew a distinction between predicates and existence, Hegel is content here to make a weaker point. He notes that immediate knowledge depends on an interrelation between thought and being, which contradicts the claim of immediacy. It follows that even if, as Hegel here leaves open, through thought we can arrive at knowledge of the absolute subject, such knowledge is mediate, not immediate, since it depends on the interrelation of the concept and its object.

This point is quite general, and bears an interesting similarity to Hegel's earlier criticism of Kant's position. In the discussion of the critical philosophy, Hegel suggests, as noted, that the endeavor to prove the limits of knowledge necessarily requires one to overstep the limits drawn. Similarly, in the account of immediate knowledge, Hegel maintains that its immediate character presupposes the mediate relation of thought and being. The evident similarity lies in Hegel's contention that any attempt to restrict knowledge, by eliminating either the finite or the infinite elements, fails, since it presupposes within it what in principle is excluded. The inference follows that a satisfactory relation of thought and being will comprise both finite and infinite dimensions, as well as their interrelation.

The overall judgment passed on the "Third Attitude of Thought to Objectivity" is unusually bleak in view of Hegel's predisposition to find everywhere a positive conceptual legacy in even the most insignificant development of the philosophical tradition. The principle of immediate knowledge resides, Hegel points out (see par. 74), in the endeavor to cast off the finite knowledge of the metaphysical identity of the understanding—in a word, to distance itself from the stance assumed by the critical philosophy. But it has been shown to be factually false to assert that there is immediate, or unmediated, knowledge, since no such instance can be advanced.

Hegel now asserts, although he does not here demonstrate his claim, that it is factually false to hold that knowledge cannot rid itself of its mediate status. He thus refutes, at least to his own satisfaction, the principal claim of immediate knowledge. But since, through the rejection of finite knowledge within this view, we are left only with the abstract relation of thought to itself, or the abstract identity, as the criterion of truth, Hegel observes that, despite its intention, the theory of immediate knowledge does not differ significantly from, and in fact coincides with, the critical philosophy. "*Abstract thinking* (the form of the reflecting metaphysics) and *abstract intuiting* (the form of direct knowledge)," he writes, "are one and the same" (E 137; VIII, par. 74, 164). To put the point somewhat differently, the attempt to correct the error of the critical philosophy through a theory of immediate knowledge results in a position not significantly different from, and in fact relevantly similar to, that which it rejects.

The bleakness of Hegel's evaluation of the post-Kantian attitude of thought to objectivity, considered as such, is justified by its alleged inability to furnish knowledge of the kind proposed, its internal inconsistency, and its failure to demarcate itself from the critical philosophy. More generally, Hegel suggests that the deeper error lies in the interest simply to negate the results of prior thought in an attitude which, since it is incompatible with his own way of reading the prior tradition, is certainly responsible for his failure to provide a more positive evaluation of it.

Hegel in fact challenges the claimed discontinuity of immediate knowledge in respect to the prior tradition. For in this form of immediate knowledge, the tradition makes a qualified return to its beginnings in the "First Attitude of Thought to Objectivity," so-called unprejudiced metaphysics, as exemplified in modern times in the Cartesian position. Hegel suggests (see par. 76) that these views share a common stress on the inseparability of thought and being, the indivisibility of the concept and existence of God, and the attitude towards sensory consciousness.

Despite the evident similarity between the attitude of immediate knowledge and that of unprejudiced metaphysics, it is the differences which are more significant. Descartes begins from unproven and unprovable assumptions through a method which has been found widely useful in modern science. But when the representatives of immediate knowledge argue that a finite method can lead only to finite knowledge, they thereby take up a position similar to Anselm's; and they similarly refuse the Cartesian and all other methods in favor of a merely arbitrary approach. The inference is clear that from the comparative perspective, the latest "Attitude of Thought to Objectivity" falls below that to which it makes a qualified return. But although the Cartesian view (and traditional metaphysics in general) is in this sense superior to later philosophic developments, Hegel again points out that it is not acceptable as such. For it begins from assumptions, whereas it belongs to philosophy as such that it can presuppose nothing (see par. 78).

The purpose of this discussion of Hegel's analysis of the "Attitudes of Thought to Objectivity" has been to understand his mature view of the problem which the concept of epistemological circularity is intended to resolve. If, as I have suggested, the *Encyclopedia* is the official source of the mature position, any discussion of Hegel's later reading of the history of philosophy must begin at that point. In the analysis of the "Attitudes of Thought to Objectivity," Hegel studies three prominent strategies in the modern philosophical tradition concerning the problem of knowledge. In the course of his inquiry, each of the three strategies is rejected for reasons already given in the initial formulation of his normative view of philosophy in the *Differenzschrift*, which, however, lacks a systematic account of alternative strategies. Thus, prior metaphysics is held to go to the object in an uncritical manner, and empiricism is said to result in dualism. Further, the concept of immediate knowledge is merely asserted but not demonstrated. Nor can it be demonstrated, or even exist, since knowledge can only be mediate.

If we reflect now on Hegel's accounts of the "Attitudes of Thought to Objectivity," its limitations are apparent. The paradox has been noted that although the *Encyclopedia* is the official version of the mature position and as such the primary source for it, in an important sense that position is not wholly contained in this text. An analogous point must be made about the problem of knowledge, which Hegel approaches through the relation of thought to objectivity. His concept of epistemological circularity clearly is intended as an analysis of this relation which succeeds where other strategies fail. But his account of this problem in the "Attitudes of Thought to Objectivity," where any discussion of his mature view of it must begin, is severely flawed by its formulation in terms of the critical philosophy. Although it is correct, as the *Differenzschrift* clearly shows, that Hegel's own thought is intended to bring to a close the revolution in philosophy begun by Kant, but in a wholly critical manner, the discussion of the epistemological problem in the *Encyclopedia* is severely foreshortened.

To state this point differently, in centering his discussion of the epistemological problem around Kant's position, we have at best a discussion of its treatment in modern philosophy, but not within the wider philosophical tradition. In this sense, although in the *Encyclopedia* Hegel indeed develops further the philosophical terrain surveyed earlier in the *Differenzschrift,* above all through broadening it to include Descartes and the empiricists, he remains within roughly the same compass. For he still surveys only the modern moment, but not the entire history of philosophy.

A reflection on Hegel's discussion of the "Attitudes of Thought to Objectivity" reveals a peculiar deficiency: the absence of any analysis, direct or indirect, of Greek thought. This absence is even more remarkable in view of Hegel's known fondness for, and immersion in, this philosophical moment. Certainly an account of the epistemological problem would be incomplete without a substantive analysis of the Greek phase of the philosophical tradition unless it were held that Greek philosophy as such is not concerned with objectivity. Yet there is no reason to believe that that is, in fact, Hegel's view. But within the framework of his discussion, Greek thought could fall only under the heading of pre-Kantian, dogmatic metaphysics.

Now, in a sense that is indeed its correct place within Hegel's rubric. For with respect to Kant's position, it is both chronologically and conceptually precritical, and hence by definition dogmatic as well. But even if Greek thought is not critical, it is not clearly dogmatic in the sense that Kant employs this term to refer to his predecessors in the modern portion of the philosophic tradition. Nor is there reason to believe that Hegel here attempts to assimilate Greek thought to pre-Kantian, modern metaphysics.

If this point is correct, two inferences immediately can be drawn. It follows, in the first place, that Hegel's account of the "Attitudes of Thought to Objectivity" can fairly be regarded as a systematic restatement of the main attitudes in the modern portion of the philosophical tradition, but not as an analysis of the entire preceding tradition. That is the case even if, as seems likely, the mature exposition of his own positive philosophical view in this work presupposes, in fact is influenced by, his reading of the entire history of philosophy, especially including its Greek portion. To put this point more strongly, consideration of Hegel's discussion of the "Attitudes of Thought to Objectivity" from a general perspective will show that the problem with which he is concerned in the discussion of contemporary philosophy is older, and that it is of Greek origin.

Second, it follows that to understand completely Hegel's mature grasp of the epistemological problem, it is necessary to venture beyond the safety of the official version of the mature position to consider the less reliable, unofficial series of manuscripts published as the *History of Philosophy*. As will be seen in the next chapter, this source does not, as concerns the problem of knowledge, contradict our prior understanding; rather, it provides a more extensive version of that analysis which aids in understanding the epistemological problem the concept of circularity is meant to resolve.

VI

THOUGHT, BEING, AND CIRCULAR EPISTEMOLOGY

> Denn da das Objekt ausser mir und die
> Erkenntnis in mir ist, so kann ich immer
> doch nur beurtheilen: ob meine Erkenntnis
> vom Object übereinstimmen. Einen solchen
> Cirkel im Erklären nennen die Alten
> Diallele.
>
> Kant[1]

In the preceding chapter, a start was made towards understanding the problem for which epistemological circularity is intended as a solution, through examination of Hegel's analysis of the "Attitudes of Thought to Objectivity." In that context, the suggestion was made that Hegel's analysis of different modern epistemological strategies refers to the answer to a problem which has traversed the entire philosophical solution since its inception. Our task here is to extend the discussion of that topic through consideration of the *History of Philosophy* in order to provide a more adequate understanding of Hegel's grasp of epistemology and to evaluate the concept of epistemological circularity.

To avoid misapprehension, it immediately should be noted that the discussion to follow will rest on a triple distinction between the origin of the epistemological problem in ancient philosophy, whose continued study ties together the ancient and modern phases of philosophy in a single tradition; Hegel's specifically modern approach to that problem, only partly in evidence in the analysis of the "Attitudes of Thought to Objectivity," which is supplemented here by detailed discussion of Descartes's thought; and the adequacy of the proposed solution. Accordingly, the discussion will develop in three stages, beginning with a reexamination of the epistemological problem in both the ancient and modern portions of the history of philosophy, followed by analysis of Hegel's detailed consideration of the Cartesian view, and ending in an evaluation of the concept of epistemological circularity as a solution to the epistemological problem as Hegel grasps it. Throughout, the emphasis will be less on offering a new version of Hegel's reading of the problem of knowledge than in supplementing that acquired through the relevant portions of the *Encyclopedia* by further discussion of *History of Philosophy*.

In order to comprehend how Hegel views the problem of knowledge in the historical context, we require both a general statement of that topic and its identification against the historical background. The problem of knowledge is easily described, for instance in terms of the repeated rejection of dualism in the formulation of the normative conception of philosophy in the *Differenzschrift*, and in the criticism in terms of this standard of other positions both in that text and in later writings. An adequate grasp of the relation of thought to objectivity will require, it can be inferred, a demonstration of the unity in terms of which the diversity of thought and being can be established.

It follows that an adequate grasp of the relation will need to resolve that problem which, according to Hegel, is central to the entire philosophical tradition since its inception and to thought itself. "The task of philosophy," Hegel writes, "is defined as making the unity of thought and being, which is its fundamental idea, into an object and grasping it, that is, to grasp the innermost necessity, the concept" (HP III, 409; XX, 314).

According to Hegel, this problem is coeval with philosophy itself. An account of Hegel's grasp of the ancient origins of the problem of knowledge could be provided in several ways, for instance through the detailed study of his reading of the different philosophical positions as variations on a single theme. Here it will not be necessary to do more than merely indicate how that might be done in some general remarks on Hegel's understanding of ancient philosophy.

For Hegel, any claim for the unity of thought and being must be demonstrated. But it is characteristic of Greek philosophy that the required unity was merely asserted, but not proven. The problem of the unity of thought and being arises nearly with philosophy itself. As Hegel reads Parmenides, the latter's main insight is that thinking produces itself as thought, so that thinking and being are identical and there is nothing outside of being. The basic problem of the relation of thought and being is not resolved by Parmenides, but is transmitted as an ongoing concern to later thinkers.

According to Hegel, Plato's analysis of the one and the many in the theory of forms, which is meant to resolve the Parmenidean question, founders on the inability to explain the concept of participation. From Hegel's standpoint, a more adequate analysis is provided by Aristotle's concept of activity [energeia] as the unity of thought and what is thought. "The main moment in the Aristotelian philosophy," Hegel writes, "is that the thinking and the thought is one—that the objective and the thinking (the activity) one and the same is" (HP II, 148–49; XIX, 162–63).

This interesting passage deserves a more extensive analysis than can be given here, especially in view of Hegel's clear insistence on the centrality of activity for Aristotle's positive view. This point, which is only rarely made by commentators, is of great significance for an appreciation of the development of the Greek philosophical tradition, as well as for Aristotle's own position. Here it will be sufficient to stress Hegel's indication of the relation between thought, what is thought, and being, as three forms of the same thing.

In more general terms, the significance of Aristotle's introduction of the concept of activity is that in place of the formal unity, un-demonstrated by Plato, he substitutes a dynamic relation. According to Hegel, the relation of thought to being is not fixed. It is, rather, "activity, motion, repulsion" (HP II, 149; XIX, 148). In consequence, Hegel can hold that even though the Aristotelian position lacks the necessity which, as Hegel concedes, cannot be demanded of the thought of the time, in modern terms his thought can be charac-terized as a monism based on a speculative unity in diversity, of which the highest example is the circular movement of God with which Hegel ends the *Encyclopedia*.

To put this point differently, despite the lack of a concept of neces-sity, which appears only later in the history of philosophy, the Aristo-telian position offers what can fairly be called a monistic view of the unity of thought and being in terms of a concept of activity. This activity expresses itself, on the level of thought and being, in a circular motion: "As the essence, the true, is accordingly to postulate that which in itself moves therefore in a *circle;* and this is not only in thinking reason to see, but also through the deed [ergō], that is, ready to hand, existing *realiter* in the visible nature" (HP II, 145; XIX, 160). In that sense, there is a circularity present in the relations between thought and being, knower and known, thought and objectivity.

Hegel's treatment of the relation between Plato and Aristotle can be summarized by saying that both are concerned with a similar prob-lem, that is, the unity of thought and being. Aristotle advances beyond Plato, in that he provides in his position a concept of activity as a means to think the unity which Plato merely asserts. As Hegel notes, Aristotle's concept of activity differs from movement [kinesis] in that it ". . . is in its distinguishing at the same time identical with itself" (HP II, 148; XIX, 164). But Aristotle is not yet able to demonstrate the necessity of the unity of thought and being which philosophy must provide.

The result of the discussion is to show that the problem of knowledge, or the relation of thought and being, arises early in Greek thought, whose evolution can fairly be regarded as an ongoing endeavor to resolve it. This same problem similarly recurs as a continuing concern in modern philosophy, which links together the positions of the main modern philosphers beginning with Descartes. The specific phase of the discussion initiated by Kant and continued by his successors is the endeavor to grasp the unity in question with innermost necessity:

> The *Kantian* philosophy formulates the task, but has only the abstract absoluteness of reason in self-consciousness as its result . . . on the other hand it has the *Fichtean* philosophy as its continuation, which grasps the essence of self-consciousness as the concrete ego, but does not surpass the subjective form of the absolute from which the-*Schellingean* philosophy begins, which it discards, and proposes the idea of the absolute, the true in and for itself. [HP III, 409–410; XX, 314–15]

The identification of the Greek origins of the problem of knowledge and description of its presence as a continuing concern in the entire philosophical tradition together broaden our appreciation of Hegel's understanding of epistemology in the historical background. We perceive here a breadth and concreteness which were not apparent in the abstract discussion of modern epistemological strategies in the account of the "Attitudes of Thought to Objectivity." But it must be stressed that Hegel's approach to the solution of the problem of epistemology, despite his awareness of its historical roots, remains specifically modern. For his own position is determined by its post-Cartesian status, in particular by his reading of Descartes's position. A fundamental difference between the *Encyclopedia* and the *History of Philosophy* is that the latter text provides the detailed analysis of Descartes's position, which alone makes Hegel's dependence on that view visible.

Despite the importance of the critical philosophy for the constitution of Hegel's thought and for his reading of the modern tradition, for the problem of the relation of thought to being Descartes, not

Kant, is the more important thinker. From this perspective, Kant's significance for modern philosophy is primarily methodological. For he substitutes his own critical approach for the dogmatism and skepticism attributed by him (with reason, according to Hegel) to Descartes and Hume. Hegel's treatment of the Kantian position focuses consistently on the extent to which the critical philosophy is not genuinely critical. The problem of a genuinely critical position is twofold as it applies to Kant: on the one hand, to be "critical" means "to surpass the supposed dogmatism in the Cartesian position in a manner which successfully avoids the skeptical consequences of empiricism"; and on the other, to be "critical" means "to be self-critical."

Hegel's reading of the critical status of the critical philosophy is basically skeptical. Although he concedes its genuinely critical intent, he questions its success in avoiding either skepticism or dogmatism, as well as its claim to be self-critical. It is, then, only in intent, but not in practice, that Kant can be said to advance beyond Descartes. Further, the critical philosophy is determined by the Cartesian position, since both the problem in general with which it is concerned and even its specific approach are broadly Cartesian in inspiration. In a word, Hegel's treatment of Kant, important as it is, is not self-contained but points backward to the Cartesian view.

In order to understand Hegel's reception of Descartes's position, we need to set this position in the context of Hegel's reading of modern philosophy. According to Hegel, modern philosophy shares with ancient thought the perspective of real consciousness, and further includes the medieval insight on the diversity of thought and what is thought. The specific characteristic of modern thought is the thought of thought and objectivity. "The main concern is there not so much to think objects in their truth, as to think the thinking and grasping [Begreifen] of the objects, this unity itself" (HP 160; XX, 63).

The task, then, of understanding Hegel's reception of Descartes implies an understanding of the latter's contribution to this specifically modern approach to the relation of thought and objectivity. It is this specific Cartesian contribution which is doubly presupposed, but never directly discussed, in the analysis of the "Attitudes of Thought to Objectivity" and as the legitimate conceptual context against which the doctrine of circularity conceivably might resolve the problem of the relation of thought and being.

To understand Descartes's contribution, we need to distinguish his intention from the result of his position. Descartes's intention is to provide a position based on self-subsistent, and hence fully independent, reason. But in fact, in his own position Descartes provides a dogmatic, uncritical approach, in essence what Hegel regards as a mere philosophy of the understanding [Verstandesphilosophie]. Although the intent of the Cartesian philosophy can be regarded as to bring about the separation of reason and faith inherent in the concept of independent reason, at best Descartes can be held to have set this uncompleted, but crucial, task as a challenge to future thought.

The sense in which the Cartesian position represents an attempt to liberate reason from faith can be seen against the background of Hegel's reading of the modern period. In his consideration of this phase of thought, Hegel discusses earlier thinkers, such as Bacon and Böhme. But he holds that Descartes's position is doubly distinguished: as the first new position since neo-Platonism; and as the revival of philosophy, hence the true beginning of modern thought. Now, the single theme which above all others is typical of modern philosophy, as Hegel reads it, is its emancipation from religion through the insistence on independent reason. This form of reason, which Hegel refers to variously as "the Protestant principle" or "the principle of thinking," is defined by him as "thinking free for itself, what must count, what must be acknowledged" (HP III, 217; XX, 120). To restate this point in another fashion, it is only when reason has been distinguished from faith that it can think the unity of thought and being.

This interesting description of the principle of modern philosophy calls immediately for two comments on Hegel's view of the relation between Lutheranism and modern thought. Hegel's suggestion is that just as the Protestant Reformation marked the beginning of the modern period of Western religion, so the onset of modern philosophy can be regarded as the result of the reflection of the spirit animating this religious upheaval onto the philosophical plane. The relevant similarity lies in the fact that in Lutheranism, the same separation between the subjective, religious principle and philosophy occurs in virtue of which inner conscious thought becomes the criterion of truth (see HP III, 221; XX, 123) as occurs in the Cartesian position.

In that sense, despite his Catholic faith, Descartes legitimately could be cast in the role of the Luther of modern philosophy (!), which, precisely, is modern because of its quasi-Lutheran, rational emphasis. Indeed, to the extent that modern philosophy represents the continuation of the Protestant Reformation with other means, it properly can be held to originate, as clearly is suggested by at least one of Hegel's disciples, in Luther's revolt against the strictures of the Roman Church.[2] One therefore should not overlook the philosophical significance of Hegel's proud claim, made early in his study of the *History of Philosophy*: "I am a Lutheran and want to remain so" (HP I, 23; XVIII,

94). Beyond an acknowledgment of his religious affiliation, Hegel is also indicating his attachment to the principle of independent reason, as revealed in consciousness, as the standard he makes his own—the same standard further advanced by Kant in the critical philosophy.

Second, Hegel's stress on the relation of modern philosophy and Lutheranism casts a significant light on his understanding of the relation between Kant and Descartes. For the critical side of the Kantian position now can be seen as a further, major moment, although not the last step, in the process of the full emancipation of reason. In other words, beyond evident dissimilarities revealed by Hegel's reading of the tradition, due to the inherent dogmatism of Descartes's position and the skeptical result of the critical philosophy, Descartes and Kant are united by their desire to complete the Lutheran undertaking of the divorce between reason and faith; indeed, that is a necessary condition of the real possibility of philosophy from the modern perspective.

In intent, if not in execution, Descartes's position is wholly imbued with the concept of independent thought. The novelty of his position, in terms of which it marks the beginning of modern philosophy, lies in its attempt to free thought from theology. Descartes, according to Hegel, "is in fact the true beginner of modern philosophy insofar as it makes thinking its principle. Thinking for itself is here distinguished from theology, which it places on the other side; it [i.e., thinking—T.R.] is on a new foundation [Boden]" (HP III, 221; XX, 123). It is important to note that although Hegel characterizes the result as a new ground [Boden], this term is understood here in a non-Cartesian sense. *Boden* is a permissible translation for the Cartesian words *fondement* and *fundamentum*. Descartes insists more than once on the need to provide philosophy with a *fundamentum inconcussum*, a principle which is both certain and able, by means of deduction, to provide for the development of a certain philosophy on this basis.

Hegel, on the contrary, apparently is unconcerned with the foundationalist side of Cartesian epistemology. Both here and in the *Encyclopedia,* he is interested mainly in the cogito, not as a foundation but as an example of the immediate relation between thought and being, as the relation which will give rise in the critical philosophy to the concept of the transcendental unity of apperception which Kant, following Descartes, regards as the highest principle of philosophy.

This new foundation upon which Descartes has placed philosophy is understood by Hegel not in the sense of the foundation of knowledge, which Descartes clearly intends. Rather, Hegel in effect stresses the equally obvious continuity between Descartes and Plato in his interpretation of the concept of the foundation as the decision to abandon all presuppositions in order to rely on thought alone. That is so even if, as is the case, the non-speculative, Cartesian cast of mind employs thought only under the mode of understanding, and not yet as reason: "By setting aside all presupposition, he began from thinking, truly in the form of determined, clear understanding; one cannot call this thinking speculative thinking, speculative reason" (HP III, 221; XX 123–24). To put the same point in more Hegelian terminology, Hegel is clear in distinguishing the new foundation upon which Descartes has placed philosophy—that is, that of thought as such, under the form of the understanding—from the Cartesian concern with foundationalism [Grundlage], expressed in a series of popular, naive writings (see HP III, 223; XX, 126).

In the *Encyclopedia,* especially in the discussion of the "Attitudes of Thought to Objectivity," there is little direct mention of Descartes. In the *History of Philosophy,* this relative oversight is corrected, and the importance of his thought for modern philosophy and Hegel's position is clearly in evidence. Hegel's discussion of Descartes in that text is divided into three points, concerning Descartes's new turn [Wendung] and his views of extension and of spirit. Although the latter two points are interesting for Hegel's grasp of his predecessor, they do not require our attention here. The former point is highly relevant to the present discussion, since it casts significant light on the relation of Hegel's thought to Descartes's view, as he reads it.

In a gloss on Descartes's new turn, Hegel writes: "He began, that every presupposition must be set aside, thought must start from itself; all previous philosophy, especially that which began from the authority of the Church, was set aside" (HP III, 224; XX, 126). This simple statement is important, because it describes the novelty of Descartes's new turn in terms which Hegel makes constitutive of his own concept of philosophy. In the space of a single sentence, he makes two important points: he relates his own mature, quasi-Platonic view of philosophy as necessarily presuppositionless to the conceptual advance made by Descartes, in virtue of which nothing other than thought is to be admitted; and he further rests the possibility of such thought on the possibility of an effective distinction between reason and faith.

In order to understand why Descartes is unable to carry out his self-defined program, we need to follow Hegel's subtle discussion of it under the headings of "thought as such" and the "certain" [das Gewisse], and above all as concerns the transition from "certainty to the limited [zu Bestimmten], or truth." It is significant, in view of his earlier insistence that the true legacy of the critical philosophy lies in Fichte's thought, that Hegel's account of Descartes's position is largely a restatement of it in Fichtean form as a series of related theses.

The first thesis is that a beginning from thought as such is an absolute beginning. But although Descartes insists on the need for thought to presuppose nothing, he nevertheless presupposes, as Hegel notes, that which is not presupposed by thought—that is, that which is thought in thought as given to it in immediate intuition, as well as the interest of freedom; in other words, the freedom of the conceptually unfettered subject. Descartes's second principle is the direct certainty of thought, in which thought is certain of itself alone in independence of any other standard. Here it is interesting to note that for Hegel there is a point of convergence between Fichte and Descartes. "Descartes begins therefore with the standpoint of the self [Ich] as that of simple certainty [des schlecthin Gewissens], as Fichte also begins: I know, it posits itself there in me" (HP III, 228; XX, 130).

In the context of Hegel's reading of modern philosophy, his proposed identification of the positions of Descartes and Fichte is significant, since it seems to reaffirm his earlier conviction of the role of Fichte's position for the modern tradition. Much like Reinhold, Hegel seems to suggest that after the critical philosophy, further progress requires a qualified return to a form of rationalism. The link between the critical philosophy and rationalism cannot arise from Reinhold's attempted reformulation of the critical philosophy. It is, rather, provided in Fichte's position, which is both the true result of the critical philosophy and at the same time essentially Cartesian in key respects, including the adoption of the standpoints of the subject and of subjective certainty. It is no accident that Hegel's reading of Descartes is conducted from a Fichtean perspective, since he merely is maintaining his initial approach to contemporary German thought in the wider context of the modern philosophical tradition.

If we follow the Fichtean character of Hegel's reading of Descartes's thought, the problem which arises is how to mediate the two principles identified so far, that is, how to relate an absolute beginning in thought and subjective certainty in order to achieve knowledge. From a similar perspective, as Hegel reads him, Fichte was able to deduce a series of concrete limitations on the basis of subjective certainty. "Fichte also afterwards again began with the same absolute certainty, with the self, and continued from there, to develop all limitations from this point [Spitze]" (HP III, 230; XX, 132). But it should be noted that if Hegel rejects Fichte's attempted transition from the subject to the objective world, he also rejects the Cartesian solution.

Hegel's objection to Descartes's proposed transition from certainty to truth, or definiteness, concerns the series of problems which have come to be known as the Cartesian circle. The objection based on the so-called Cartesian circle, already formulated by Arnauld and known to Descartes, turns on the claim that in his reasoning Descartes commits a petitio principii. In the context of his thought, it is alleged that he makes good the veracity of clear and distinct ideas in terms of the existence of God, which in turn is demonstrated only in terms of such ideas.[3]

Whether that is in fact a petitio is a matter of continuing controversy which falls outside the scope of this essay. But it should be noted that Hegel's criticism does not depend on the objection that Descartes's argument fails because of the form in which it is expressed. Nor is he in a position to object to circularity as such. Unlike Descartes, who in his response to Arnauld seeks to dissipate even the appearance of a circle in his own reasoning, Hegel makes of it an integral part of his analysis of knowledge. Hegel is, then, entirely consistent in his suggestion that the problem is not the form in which Descartes states his argument, but rather that he employs an assumption which he cannot demonstrate as its basis. Hegel's objection, which is accordingly not formal but substantive, contains the inference that Descartes's view is not in principle incorrect, provided that a satisfactory manner to advance the point at issue can be found.

Hegel's objection turns on the assertion that Descartes's naive transition from certainty to thought rests on an undemonstrated unity of thought and being. His account of this unity is triply significant in the context of his own thought. In the first place, Hegel's insistence on the relation between the epistemology and metaphysics, or ontology, in the Cartesian position is important in regard to his own thought. In his own position and in his interpretation of other views, he is consistent in rejecting all attempts to compartmentalize philosophy into discrete regions. For to limit claims to know merely to the level of consciousness is to restrict knowledge claims to mere certainty, which has no call to truth.

Second, there is an interesting suggestion in the description of the principle of the unity of thought and being as new with Descartes. This statement is puzzling, since a very similar assertion was made as early as the dawn of the Western philosophical tradition, as Hegel himself notes in his discussion of Parmenides (see HP I, 252; XVIII, 289–90). Perhaps Hegel has in mind that Descartes's originality lies in the initial statement of this idea in modern times, although not as such. But from another perspective, the evident novelty in Descartes's formulation of this point lies in its restatement—from the peculiarly modern, subjective angle of vision—from the perspective of thought which has as its task to know being. This task is indeed begun by Descartes's creation of the modern epistemological tradition.

Third, we have Hegel's clear description of this principle as "the most interesting idea of modern times *überhaupt*" (HP III, 233; XX, 136). Thus, for Hegel, at least, the importance of the concept enunciated by Descartes ranges far beyond its immediate philosophical concept. If, as he suggests, Descartes is unable to prove the relation he necessarily assumes to hold as a condition of knowledge, a point Hegel largely follows, it is obvious that the reasons for Descartes's failure are a matter for careful consideration.

To determine whether Descartes fails to realize his intention, the intention must be identified. Hegel regards the Cartesian line of reasoning as a further development of Anselm's original version of the ontological argument. This argument depends on the concept of degrees of perfection to argue for an essentially more limited identity of thought and being. More generally, the ontological argument for the existence of God is a specific instance of the transition from certainty to truth, both of which rest, in this analysis, on an undemonstrated unity between thought and being.

The Cartesian argument is reconstructed by Hegel in five stages, concerning: 1) grades of reality; 2) the relation between the concept of a thing and its existence; 3) the principle *ex nihilo nihil fit;* 4) the relation of a concept and its cause; and 5) the ontological proof. It is interesting to note, concerning the last point, that Hegel remarks on, but does not follow, the line of reasoning which Kant earlier develops against the proof. Although Kant's suggestion is indeed significant, there is nonetheless an identity of predicates, or more broadly essence and existence within the concept, that is, as thought.

Hegel's objection is formulated in terms of the alleged inability here, as in the demonstration of the cogito, to deduce specific content, or indeed any content at all. This line of reasoning is anti-Kantian, and reminiscent of Schelling. The Cartesian claim that we have an idea of a perfect being which cannot be due to us and hence exists is, according to Hegel, merely a presupposition. More precisely, the content of this idea is not demonstrated since, as is the case for the cogito, the unity of thought and being merely is asserted. It is relevant here to recall that Hegel suggests in his analysis of the cogito that the proof offered by Descartes is not a conclusion, since it lacks syllogistic form (see HP III, 229; XX, 131), as Descartes also admits (see *Encyclopedia*, par. 64). Although it is true that there is indeed a unity between thought and being for both the cogito and the proof of the existence of God, in each case this result is arrived at merely on an empirical, and hence nonphilosophical, basis.

Enough has been said about the details of Hegel's reception of Descartes's view to allow us to make some more general comments. A clue as to how to proceed is suggested by Hegel's own procedure. In his study of the history of philosophy, Hegel is careful to distinguish the problems with which particular thinkers are concerned from the solutions proposed by them. This procedure is not difficult to justify; even if the position in question constitutes a genuine step forward, it is rarely, if ever, the case that the problems under study unambiguously can be held to be fully resolved. More generally, the nature of the case study of the history of philosophy reveals that there are fewer problems (which constantly recur under novel and less novel formulations) than there are proposed solutions for them.

If we apply a Hegelian approach to the history of philosophy to Hegel's own account of Descartes's position, we easily can detect a fundamental tension between the proposed solution and the problem for which it is advanced. As Hegel reads the Cartesian philosophy, there is a manifest tension between the reliance on independent thought, on the one hand, and the claimed unity of thought and being, on the other. For in the decision to render thought independent and hence self-subsistent, the central theme of his position, Descartes renounces the dependence on any and all presuppositions. Certainly that is the intent, if not the necessary effect, of his reliance on the cogito as an Archimedean point to defeat skepticism and end the quarrel of the schools.

Descartes's thought is not presuppositionless, since it relies on a unity between thought and being, which is presupposed but not demonstrated, as Hegel points out, at two crucial points in the chain of reasoning: in the ontological proof necessary in order to effect the required transition from certainty to truth, and in the cogito itself. Accordingly, Descartes's position is shown to rest on a presupposition. In other words, the assurance of the Cartesian position, whose proudest claim lies in the pretended freedom of thought from presuppositions, is shown on the contrary, to repose on a presupposition which is not eccentric to it, but is lodged at its very heart.

Hegel's demonstration of a tension in the Cartesian view between the method and the problem to which it is addressed affects both his reception of the immediate position and the succeeding portion of modern philosophy which it begins and which remains conditioned by it. Descartes's philosophy is, as Hegel indicates, no more than the "course [Gang] of clear understanding" (HP III, 240; XX, 144). In virtue of the tension intrinsic to the development of his argument, his use of thought does not as yet attain the wholly critical and self-critical standard of reason, for which it, however, constitutes the indispensable initial stage.

Even if Descartes's position must be regarded as unsatisfactory, in view of the demonstrated inability to meet the standards intrinsic to it, which it sets for itself, it need not wholly be rejected. On the contrary, it needs to be preserved, or, more precisely, the undeniable extent to which it is profoundly true requires acknowledgment. Indeed, despite his rejection of the line of argument which constitutes the letter of the position, Hegel accepts in general terms the spirit inherent in it. For he specifically endorses the concern with independent thought that marks the onset of modern philosophy, and hence separates this part of the Western philosophical tradition from its prior moments; and he endorses as well the concern with the problem of the unity of thought and being as the central difficulty to whose solution this instrument must be applied.

If this interpretation of Hegel's reception of Descartes's is correct, two inferences immediately can be drawn; each of them has the effect of calling attention to the signal importance of Descartes, more so even than Kant, for Hegel's reading of modern philosophy, and, in consequence, for his mature view of circularity.

In the first place, it is important to notice a subtle, but significant, shift in Hegel's interpretation of modern philosophy. Interestingly, this shift does not lie in a difference in appreciation between the early, immature, and later, mature phases of Hegel's thought. The early view of the *Differenschrift* and the later one of the *Encyclopedia* agree, as noted, in a nearly identical stress on the Kantian position as the central view in contemporary thought. But in the lectures on the *History of Philosophy,* which cover the entire period of Hegel's academic career and hence both precede and succeed the official version of the position in the *Encyclopedia,* with the extension of the discussion to philosophy as a whole, the stress shifts noticeably towards Descartes. Here the entire modern period is treated as a further development of the Cartesian framework, including both the principle of thought and the problem of the demonstration of the unity (from this angle of vision) of thought and being.

This shift in perspective is less a change in Hegel's basic understanding of the critical philosophy than a widening of perspective to include it within a larger conceptual context. There are several advantages which derive from this shift in perspective, especially as concerns Kant. An obvious advantage is that the opposition between the precritical and critical forms of thought is now relativized through its insertion in a broader background provided by the unfolding of the consequences of the Cartesian principle of thought.

Although Kant's position retains its status relative to others in the modern tradition, an immediate result is to redeem in part the promissory note implicit in the frequent claim for the unity of the history of philosophy. For Hegel indicates that just as the critical philosophy continues in the thought of Fichte and Schelling, so also does it prolong the attack on a new formulation, from the perspective of modern thought, of a problem already on the intellectual agenda at the origin of Greek philosophy. Kant's position, and its sequel in the views of Fichte and Schelling, should be measured not in terms of isolated positions to which they respond, but rather from the perspective of thought alone to demonstrate the unity of subjectivity and objectivity. To state this point differently, had Kant succeeded, his position would have resolved not only Hume's difficulty concerning causality but also Descartes's reformulation of the deeper problem of the relation of thought and being.

Second, we can infer that the mature Hegel regards his ultimate task as the resolution of the Cartesian problem in terms of the Cartesian principle of thought. This statement should not be taken to mean that Hegel desires to retrace Descartes's steps, either through the appropriation of his line of argument or through reliance on basic Cartesian distinctions. Nor is it sufficient to suggest that he desires only to be more critical than the critical philosophy, that is, self-critical, although that is certainly part of his intention. His wider goal is to accomplish, as Descartes cannot, a philosophical transition from certainty to truth which is aware of the conditions of the transition but makes no assumptions concerning it. It is this same undertaking which Hegel identifies as the task of modern philosophy itself, which he describes as proceeding from "the standpoint of actual self-consciousness" (HCP III, 159; XX, 63).

There is an important corollary as concerns the interpretation of Hegel's position. For Hegel's endeavor is not an attempt to transcend previous philosophy, except insofar as it is the latest version of the undertaking, everywhere present in the modern philosophical moment from Descartes onwards, to bring philosophy to a close through the successful resolution of its central problem. Hegel's own understanding of his thought would seem to imply that it is conditioned by the goal of succeeding where Descartes and later thinkers either had failed or at most had been only partially successful. This goal lies in the philosophical demonstration of the unity of thought and being, which as yet merely had been asserted on empirical, nonphilosophical grounds.

It further results that the turn to circularity is in the final analysis to be regarded both as a presuppositionless demonstration of the unity of thought and being, as Hegel says, and as the fulfillment of the Cartesian epistemological form of the ancient problem of knowledge. In other words, even if the concept of circularity is invoked initially in reaction to Reinhold's desire to systematize the critical philosophy, the deeper significance of that move, which Hegel only later realizes, is in the concern neither with Reinhold nor with Kant as such; it is, rather, in the concern with Descartes, or more precisely in the concern to resolve the Cartesian restatement of an enduring philosophy problem, that is, the demonstration of the unity of thought and being upon which knowledge depends.

This point should now be sharpened, since it provides a standard internal to Hegel's position in terms of which it can be evaluated. Study of the fate of the doctrine of circularity in Hegel's mature thought reveals three major changes. There is, to begin with, a significant elaboration of the mature view of circularity in comparison to its initial formulation. As noted, the major change in this respect is to understand circularity as following from the normative view of philosophy as a necessarily presuppositionless science. The doctrine of circularity is, then, an unavoidable result of the quasi-Platonic view of philosophy dominant in the philosophical tradition.

Second, there is a revision of Hegel's reading of modern philosophy, as a result of which Kant's position is understood in relation to Descartes's. In the present context, that means that although Hegel's position initially was intended to complete the critical philosophy, he came to understand that this task could occur only within the framework of the Cartesian philosophical moment.

Third, the problem with which Hegel ultimately is concerned in his mature position is the relation of thought and being from within the Cartesian perspective of subjectivity. It is, then, as a solution for this problem that the mature doctrine of circularity can be evaluated.

Since Hegel's analysis of modern philosophy is formulated largely in terms of the Cartesian position, it seems justified to appeal to it in order to provide the framework for an assessment of Hegel's thought. Even if Descartes's view legitimately can be seen from different angles of vision, from whatever perspective one chooses, there are two basic stages in the epistemological argument: 1) to discover a foundation, or Archimedean point, which will yield certain knowledge; and 2) to provide for the transition from certainty to truth. In other words, Descartes's problem, as Hegel reads the former's position, is an endeavor to resolve, from the perspective of subjectivity, the traditional problem of the unity of thought and being in the face of the diversity generated by the distinction in kind between two forms of substance.

Hegel's mature doctrine of circularity can be understood as a solution to the Cartesian formulation of the problem of knowledge through a theoretical analysis in which an appeal is made, in antirationalist fashion, to practice. For although Hegel accepts the need to resolve the problem of modern philosophy, and of philosophy itself, from the Cartesian perspective, he rejects the rationalist approach. In his doctrine of circularity, the stress shifts from theory to practice as the way to provide for a demonstration of knowledge.

Considered from the perspective of the Cartesian position, which Hegel adopts, the mature doctrine of circularity is adequate to provide for certainty, but not to provide for the transition from certainty to truth. The inadequacy lies in the ability to make out the claim for reason to know being, which must be the case in order to make the transition from certainty to truth. Hegel's endeavor to provide a philosophical demonstration of the unity of thought and being does not succeed, since he cannot show that reason is self-subsistent through its separation from faith.

Hegel's appeal to circularity can be understood against the Cartesian background. As concerns the demand for certainty, the doctrine of circularity can be regarded from two perspectives: either as a rejection of the original Cartesian view of a foundation, or indubitable first principle; or as a defense of one strand of the Cartesian position against another, better-known but incompatible strand. The difference of perspective depends on the manner in which Descartes's position is interpreted.

Study of Descartes's writings yields two distinct views of the justification of claims to know. The Cartesian position almost always is understood as based on the concept of the cogito, which functions as an absolute foundation, or *fundamentum inconcussum,* which can be demonstrated without presuppositions and which provides for the deduction of the remainder of the theory. It is this foundationalist view of knowledge which is in evidence in part 2 of the *Discourse* and in the second of the *Meditations.* But there is another, very different view of knowledge in Descartes's writings. In the sixth part of the *Discourse,* he unexpectedly presents a broadly pragmatic model, similar to the Hegelian doctrine of circularity. Speaking of two prior texts, the *Dioptrics* and the *Meteors,* Descartes writes:[4]

> For it appears to me that the reasonings are so mutually interwoven, that as the later ones are demonstrated by the earlier, which are their causes, the earlier are reciprocally demonstrated by the later, which are their effects. And it must not be imagined that in this I commit the fallacy which logicians name arguing in a circle, for, since experience renders the greater part of these effects very certain, the causes from which I deduce them do not so much serve to prove their existence as to explain them; on the other hand, the causes are explained by the effects.

These two doctrines not only are different but are further incompatible. The former doctrine justifies the truth of theory based upon it through an appeal not to experience but to the deductive relation to premises from which it follows and which have been established as true; in the latter doctrine, on the contrary, the claim is made that although principles do explain what follows from them, they themselves are established as true only through an appeal to their results in experience.[5] The initial doctrine is concerned wholly with the a priori, as based on an absolute foundation independent of possible experience. The second doctrine offers a merely relative justification, whose claim to truth is dependent on an appeal to experience. The better-known foundationalist approach would, if correct, yield apodictic, or unrevisable, claims to know. The lesser-known nonfoundationalist approach at best can yield the relative conviction provided by experience, but not apodicticity.[6]

Hegel's mature view of circularity can be regarded either as an inversion of the more widely known Cartesian foundationalism or as a further elaboration of the less well-known Cartesian appeal to experience. With respect to the former, Hegel substitutes for Cartesian apriorism an a posteriori approach. This approach bases the claim to know upon the relation of theory to experience, and accordingly relativizes its permissible strength. With respect to the latter, Hegel elaborates the consequence of an appeal to experience through a more developed understanding of the relation of circularity to all forms of justification and of the interrelation of forms of circularity.

The Hegelian doctrine of circularity is adequate to resolve the initial stage of the Cartesian form of the problem of knowledge. For at the price of a relativization of the claims to know, Hegel demonstrates how knowledge in fact arises out of experience. The limitation of the mature doctrine of circularity is its inability to account for the second phase of the problem of knowledge, that is, to effect the transition from certainty to truth, or, in Hegel's own terms, to demonstrate the unity of thought and being.

Although the need to provide a philosophic demonstration of this unity is indicated clearly in the *History of Philosophy,* Hegel's own positive view is most available in the *Encyclopedia.* The problem itself is discussed most prominently in the account of the Kantian view of the theological idea of reason (in pars. 49–52), in the context of the "Second Attitude of Thought to Objectivity." Hegel comments here on Kant's inability to offer a genuine identity, which would require reason to surpass the limits of experience (par. 49). According to Hegel, who here follows the argument developed by Fichte in the *First Introduction to the Science of Knowledge,* the desired unification can be carried out in only two ways (par. 50): from the perspective of being, or from the perspective of thought in the form of an ontological proof (par. 51; see also par. 52).

Hegel's own solution to the problem, through a positive concept of reason distinct from the Kantian view, is indicated, but never developed, in a number of passages. Of interest here is the constant association of the positive concept of reason and belief. From this perspective, three distinct claims for the positive form of reason can be distinguished.

One such relation is the assertion of the cognitive, or rational, content of religious belief, a doctrine already asserted in the last chapter of the *Phenomenology.* For instance, in the discussion of immediate knowledge in the context of the "Third Attitude of Thought to Objectivity," Hegel describes "truth for spirit" as *"reason* alone" before adding that although mediated knowledge should be limited to finite content, "thus is reason *immediate knowledge, belief* [Glaube]" (E 123; VIII, par. 63, 150). A similar association of religion and cognitive, or rational, truth is also stated in various ways in other paragraphs in this work, e.g., paragraphs 445, 554, and 573.

A second, related doctrine is found in the analysis of social ethics [Sittlichkeit], in the discussion of objective spirit. Hegel here identifies knowing and trusting [Vertrauen], which is the ethical equivalent of believing [Glauben], when he writes:

> The *social disposition* [Gesinnung] of individuals is the *knowing* of substance and of the identity of all their interests with the whole, and that the other individuals on the other side know themselves only in this identity and are actual is trusting [Vertrauen],—the true ethical disposition. [PM254; X, par. 515, 318–9]

Third, specifically epistemological relation between reason and belief apparently is identified only in the following passage, in the account of cognizing [Erkennen], under the wider rubric of the idea.

Here Hegel insists on the inseparability of belief and reason due to the constitutive role of belief for reason:

> Reason comes to the world with the absolute belief of postulating the identity and being able to raise its certainty to *truth,* and with the drive to postulate the *for-itself* futile [nichtig] contradiction as futile. [E 363; VIII, par. 224, 378]

Of the various relations between reason and belief, only the third one is directly relevant to the present discussion. This passage is of extraordinary importance for an understanding of how Hegel holds that the transition from certainty to truth, which is explicitly evoked here, can be effected through the capacity of a form of thought, or reason, to know being. Hegel's answer as to how that is possible, which nowhere is stated more clearly in his corpus, is that belief is necessary for, indeed constitutive of, reason's capacity to know. In other words, Hegel's solution for the problems of the unity of thought and being, and hence his proposed transition from certainty to truth, lies in the assertion that we inevitably must believe that thought can indeed know being.

Since it might be objected that this doctrine is not characteristic of Hegel's position, it is not without interest that this point is stated equally clearly on occasion elsewhere. An example is provided in the following passage in the preface to the *Phenomenology,* where, after a brief discussion of phenomenology as the science of the experience of consciousness, Hegel remarks: "The beginning of philosophy makes the presupposition or demand [Forderung], that consciousness be [sich befinde] in this *element*" (P 14; III, 29). In other words, the assumption which conditions the process of the unfolding of science is precisely that the unity to be described is already present at the beginning.

It is important to be clear about the claim which is ascribed here to Hegel. He is not making a traditional, quasi-Thomistic point about the nonconflictual relation of faith and reason. Nor is he, like Kant, asserting that belief can continue to hold sway in the conceptual interstices of reason, where it cannot legitimately penetrate and where knowledge is impossible. If there is an anticipation of Hegel's understanding of reason in the history of philosophy, it is perhaps in the Augustinian doctrine of *fides quaerens intellectum,* even if it would be incorrect to consider Augustine as other than a theologian with philosophical tendencies. More precisely, Hegel's view can be stated as the anti-Enlightenment claim that faith and reason are inseparable, since reason requires, and indeed rests on, faith, that is, faith in reason.

Several general conclusions can now be formulated. As concerns the problem of the unity of thought and being, it is apparent that Hegel's solution can count as one only in a quasi-Kantian, transcendental sense. It is well known that in his moral philosophy, Kant indicates the need for, but the impossibility to provide, a demonstration of freedom, or, in Kantian terms, the transition from pure practical reason to practical reason. Similarly, Hegel shows that if thought is to know being, we must presuppose a prior unity between thought and being. Hegel's philosophical solution to this enduring problem hence is based on the need to have faith in the ability of reason to know, although that is neither demonstrated nor demonstrable, but merely necessary. Accordingly, in an important sense Hegel can be held in fact to reject, or rather to show the inadequacy of, the belief in self-subsistent reason, which he regards as typical of modern times, since reason no longer is recognized by him as wholly self-sustaining.

To put this same point in the context of the Cartesian view, Hegel is not able to do more than point to the conditions of the transition from certainty to truth, as distinguished from a demonstration that the conditions are met in practice. Although Hegel thinks the problem through to the end and shows the way to escape from subjectivity through a transition to objectivity, because this escape is based on a mere presupposition it is unacceptable. He is, like his predecessors, still trapped within subjectivity. In Kantian terms, the scandal of philosophy's inability to prove the existence of the external world remains a scandal.

As concerns the concept of circularity, Hegel's need to assume that thought can know being violates the basic stricture that philosophy differs from all other sciences in that it can assume nothing. But since the appeal to circularity follows only from the need to make no presuppositions, the examination of the concept of circularity gives rise to a curious result: although philosophy is indeed presuppositionless, and hence circular, its ability to provide knowledge is based on the presupposition that it does so. For reason cannot ground itself in circular science, although no other strategy is possible, since we never can know that we know. Or, to put the point in other words, although we know the theoretical conditions of knowledge, we do not know that in practice they are met in and through the circular development of the object of knowledge in consciousness; and we hence cannot conclude positively as to the epistemic value of the ever-greater closure of the circle of philosophical science.

This chapter indicates that the function of circularity is to demonstrate the unity of thought and being within the general framework provided by the Cartesian principles of independent reason and subjectivity. But the discussion has further revealed that the concept of reason cannot be divorced from the belief in reason, upon which it depends, and which hence functions as a necessary presupposition. It follows that although Hegel is indeed correct to suggest that theory is presuppositionless, and therefore circular, he is not able, within the context of his own position, to justify the claim that as the circle closes, the theory progressively justifies itself. He is unable to prove, but must merely suppose, that thought can know being. In other words, although in virtue of the fact that it can presuppose nothing philosophy is necessarily circular, in virtue of its circularity it at best can justify the certainty of certainty, but not the transition to truth. But since circular philosophy is inadequate to demonstrate the unity of thought and being, it is inadequate to provide the solution of the problem which is its central task.

VII

BEYOND HEGEL
CIRCULAR EPISTEMOLOGY, PRESUPPOSITIONLESSNESS, AND KNOWLEDGE

It remains to provide an assessment of Hegel's doctrine of circular epistemology for philosophy in general. General evaluation of this doctrine must go beyond the genesis, mature form, and aim of Hegel's position to a comparison with other views.

An inquiry into the general philosophical significance of one or another idea cannot itself be wholly general. There is no possibility of an inquiry into the absolute importance of one or another concept in isolation from the philosophical tradition. And merely because a study of that kind, a historical evaluation of a given perspective, is undertaken so frequently is no reason to believe that it can be carried out successfully. No view is absolutely relevant, and none is absolutely true; at best, an idea is relevant to a given goal, in terms of which its significance can be measured, in comparison with others which share that end in view. To deny this point would not only be to deny a central Hegelian thesis and to choose a non-Hegelian standard for the evaluation of his position; it would further be to misunderstand the nature of philosophy and of philosophical argument.

If Hegel's own view must be judged against its conceptual competitors, the end in view is easily ascertained. It is the concern with objective knowledge that is as old as, if not older than, philosophy itself, in particular its modern form. Hegel's claim that if philosophy is presuppositionless it must be circular is a form of what recently has come to be known as the "antifoundationalist theory of knowledge." The concept of an epistemological foundation is specifically modern. It was neither formulated nor necessary in Greek thought, at least not in the modern sense of the term *foundation*. In Greek philosophy, the

claim to know, however formulated, did not require further justification than an appeal to an intuitive grasp of being, as distinguished
from appearance. This view, which presupposes for its validity the
presence of a subjacent ontological plane, effectively was untouched
by the ancient skeptical tropes, which concerned not being as such but
mere appearance.

For Greek philosophy, knowledge in the full sense meant "presuppositionless science." But the decline of the naive Greek ontology
transformed the problem of knowledge in general into that of knowledge derived from experience, and raised anew the question as to how
philosophy could maintain its claim to presuppositionless status. The
novelty of the modern portion of the philosophical tradition lies not
in the particular claim for knowledge, which itself is not new, but in
the need to make out that claim from the perspective of the subject.
For the claim to know in any absolute sense no longer can be justified
in terms of the object alone in the absence of the underlying ancient
ontology.

From this perspective, recent developments in phenomenology and
analytic philosophy, although arguably novel with respect to those
phases of the discussion in which they emerge, are merely the latest
forms of the belief that knowledge can in fact be had by carefully
attending either to the contents of consciousness or to the object as
given in experience.

Certainly, the strategy of what recently has become known as the
foundationalist approach in analytic epistemology is intended to show
how a theory of knowledge is possible which admits no presuppositions in terms of a ground, or foundation, which escapes that designation. The central point of the foundationalist approach to knowledge,
understood here in a closely Cartesian sense, is to advance a proposition whose truth is demonstrable without assumptions of any kind
and from which the remainder of the theory can be strictly derived.
In different ways, this goal is common to the Cartesian view and to all
later forms of foundationalist epistemology, whether or not it employs
this recent term.

If we take as the focus of this phase of the discussion the problem of
whether knowledge can have foundations, it cannot be doubted that
Hegel's position is fundamentally antifoundationalist. For Hegel does
not defend, in fact explicitly eschews, the approach to epistemology in
terms of an initial principle from which the justification for all claims
to know can be said to follow. To evaluate the present significance of
the Hegelian position, it will be appropriate, then, to review it against
the background provided by the post-Hegelian phase of the con-

tinuing dispute between those who hold that knowledge must have foundations and those who deny this view.

Such comparison obviously is rendered difficult by numerous factors, including our chronological proximity to the post-Hegelian moment and the sheer proliferation of contemporary philosophy as an academic cottage industry. It is doubtful that there is more philosophy today, although at no time in history have there been more philosophers. And we lack the historical perspective necessary to select those views which have enduring significance from those which eventually will recede into the historical past. Nor is the ability to transcend a historical moment a guarantee of intrinsic worth. Indeed, neither prominence nor the lack thereof is sufficient warrant for inherent value. For philosophy as for history, the significance of the past is constantly subject to reevaluation as a result of further occurrence.

If we are to compare Hegel's view to other, later ones, then these candidates for comparison must be selected from a large and diverse field in terms of some principle. There is no obvious way in which this selection must be carried out, since there is no evident principle of selection. Even were we to confine our attention to those views, or more generally even tendencies or movements, of arguably greatest importance, there is no unambiguous manner in which to identify them. There is no reason to believe that what counts as important for a philosophical position conceivably could be agreed upon by all, or even most, observers. Nor would such agreement be of significance if what we seek is the truth, and not merely what appears to be true. But the lack of agreement is noteworthy. There is a wide and apparently irreducible sweep of opinion as to whether figures in the history of philosophy that some hold to be pivotal are worthy of study at all, much less worthy of careful inquiry into aspects of their respective views.

An appropriate procedure is suggested by Hegel's own practice. Despite his enormous knowledge of the prior history of philosophy, in his account of the "Attitudes of Thought to Objectivity" Hegel properly studied not individual positions, with the important exception of Kant's view, which he considered in detail. Rather, he undertook to canvass general epistemological strategies, which he regarded as a series of dialectical contraries, each of which advanced the claim of thought to know objectivity.

A similar strategy will be followed here in order to assess the continued relevance of Hegel's own strategy. But it should be noted immediately that the present discussion will differ from Hegel's in several ways. On the one hand, whereas Hegel's discussion was prospective, prior to the elaboration of his own position, this discussion is necessarily retrospective; its aim is to contribute not to an understanding of what still needs to be accomplished but to an evaluation of what already has been done.

On the other hand, Hegel could omit without embarassment specific reference to particular theories which he considered in general form, since for the most part these positions were well known to his readers. Although not strictly necessary, it seems useful to provide some direct reference to particular examples of the general strategies to be canvassed here. But it should be stressed that the present review, like Hegel's, does not depend upon its precise relation to particular views; that is not its objective, which is, rather, the general study of typical post-Hegelian epistemological strategies.

The discussion differs in another way from Hegel's. He desired to take into account all preceding thought; but if that was ever possible, it is certainly more difficult at this late date in view of the post-Hegelian proliferation of philosophical views. With that in mind, it seems useful here to forego any attempt at completeness and to confine this phase of the discussion to consideration of some major forms of phenomenological and analytic epistemological strategies. Three reasons can be cited in favor of this kind of limitation.

To begin with, by any comparative standard, phenomenology and analytic thought are two of the most significant tendencies to emerge in this century; and they are widely regarded, whatever the final judgment to be rendered by history, as intrinsically significant. Second, in different ways consistent with their specific approaches, both these tendencies are centrally concerned with the problem of the justification of claims to know, which is the focus of the present inquiry into Hegel's position. The depth of concern with this issue separates these two movements from American pragmatism, another obvious candidate for this kind of review. Third, as will become clear, both phenomenology and analytic thought exhibit, although not in the same way, major alternative approaches to the problem of the justification of claims to know.

Despite their differences, which should be neither overlooked nor minimized, there are important similarities between phenomenology and analytic thought. These similarities can be expressed in different ways and from different perspectives. From a historical perspective, there is a similarity: both tendencies arose as part of the ongoing effort to be scientific in a manner which constitutes a viable alternative to the idealist concern with speculation, on the one hand, and natural science, on the other. The revolt against speculation shows itself in a

common concern with scientific rigor, in new beginnings, in a preoccupation with incorrigible knowledge, and in attention to the justification of claims to know.

It is, of course, easier to distinguish between phenomenology and
analytic philosophy than it is to characterize either movement. Speaking generally, phenomenology is continuous with the continental philosophical tradition from which it arose and to which it owes many
basic insights. In fact, there are many fundamental points of agreement between Hegel's position and post-Hegelian phenomenology, a
point which is recognized more widely in French circles than in either
the German or American discussions. In particular, post-Hegelian
forms of phenomenology tend to conserve the emphasis on consciousness characteristic of Hegel's thought and the post-Kantian
German philosophical tradition in general.

Despite the evident similarities and points of continuity between
Hegelian and post-Hegelian phenomenology, phenomenology is frequently, although incorrectly, held to originate in Husserl's thought.[1]
But it is clear that Husserl is the central figure in the post-Hegelian
development of phenomenology. And central to Husserl's position is a
profound meditation of the problem of methodology, extending from
one end to another of his corpus. It often has been pointed out that
for Husserl, in an important sense, phenomenology is not a philosophical theory but a method. In virtue of the key role played by
Husserl in the post-Hegelian phenomenological movement, one way
in which the evolution of post-Hegelian phenomenological epistemological strategy can be considered is as a series of views of methodology.

Anglo-American analytic thought, on the contrary, despite some
distant relation to Hegel's position,[2] originally was intended to mark a
complete break with its British restatement. Analytic thought arose as
a revolt by some British thinkers, especially Moore and Russell,
against the coherentist views of Bradley and other British idealists.[3]
In its initial phase, the revolt against idealism took shape as the claim
that there must be foundations for knowledge. With respect to earlier
British empiricism, this claim can be regarded as an endeavor to
overcome the skepticism with which it had terminated in Hume's
thought through empirical foundations, much as Hume had sought
to provide foundations for morality.

The reaction against idealism in a later phase of analytic philosophy
took the form of a neoidealist counterrevolution directed against the
view that knowledge can have absolute foundations, together with a
renewed interest in coherentism. Since the problem of founda-

tionalism is a main theme in analytic thought, it is one way in which the evolution of analytic epistemological strategy can be considered.

I. Presuppositionless Knowledge

The concern with presuppositionless knowledge, in evidence in both the phenomenological and analytic sides of the post-Hegelian epistemological discussion, represents the latest phase of the continuing endeavor, already initiated by Plato, to achieve knowledge in the fullest sense.

a) Presuppositionless Methodology

A basic theme of post-Hegelian phenomenology, as noted, is the concern with the problem of method adequate for knowledge in the traditional sense. From the phenomenological perspective, the attempt to arrive at presuppositionless knowledge is undertaken through the progressive clarification of the presuppositions of theory as a result of their examination within the theory. This strategy rests on the conviction that for normative reasons concerning the nature of philosophy, widely accepted since Plato, nothing merely can be accepted; and on the associated belief that if assumptions are candidly admitted, examined, and accounted for, the result will be a theory which is absolutely bereft of all presuppositions.[4]

Although the goal of this approach is familiar, the strategy for attaining it is novel. It differs from other quasi-rationalist approaches to philosophy as a science in the full sense, since the presuppositionless status is not held to be an original characteristic of the theory. Unlike rationalist forms of theory, this approach includes no initial proposition which can be known to be true in independence of all presuppositions and from which the remainder of the theory, consisting of indubitably true propositions, can be deduced. Presuppositionlessness rather is understood as a result at which the theory arrives through its internal self-examination.[5]

The value of this approach lies in the recognition of the point, implicitly denied by classical rationalists, that all thought must begin somewhere, so that presuppositions cannot be avoided at the start of the theory. The strategy, then, is to exclude presuppositions not at the beginning but in the course of the development of the theory. This concern to purify the theory and to attain presuppositionless status through the development of the theory represents progress with respect to the earlier, Cartesian form of presuppositionlessness, in which further clarification is unnecessary, since it already is accomplished through what can be regarded only as philosophizing prior to beginning to philosophize.

Although clarification of the assumptions of a theory is indeed useful, it is insufficient to reach the goal of presuppositionlessness if that goal is interpreted not as a regulative ideal but as constitutive of a fully scientific position, that is, as a method without presuppositions. The limitation of this epistemological strategy lies in the inability to carry out the self-clarification of the theory in a manner which provides total transparency, although that requirement is clearly raised. For the theory itself is necessarily dependent upon the presuppositions which it hopes to clarify as the condition of its claim to fully scientific status. Nor would it be possible to clarify the presuppositions of the theory on a prior theoretical plane, since the resultant, purified theory then would not be self-contained but would necessarily presuppose a prior theory. Although this strategy is correct to suggest that presuppositionless status cannot be obtained for the theory prior to its onset, neither can it result from the development of the theory in the course of its attempt at self-clarification.

b) Analytic Foundationalism

Analytic thought shares with other forms of empiricism the belief that knowledge is possible only on the basis of experience. The traditional goal of absolute knowledge at which phenomenology aims through the strategy of presuppositionless methodology is pursued within analytic thought through the concept of foundationalist theory. According to this strategy, knowledge is understood in a rationalist sense as an edifice or structure having foundations, in terms of which the claim to know can and indeed must be justified. The foundation consists in one or more propositions which can be known to be true in independence of any assumptions and which permit the justification of other propositions following from them.

This form of epistemological strategy has obvious historical antecedents. One of them is Reinhold's introduction of a quasi-rationalist theoretical model for the purpose of reconstructing the critical philosophy in the form of a rigorous system. Analytic foundationalist strategy further shares with Reinhold's strategy the insistence on the establishment of the absolute truth of the beginning point from an empirical perspective. But within the analytic discussion, the foundationalist strategy most often is associated with two other points of historical reference: resolution of the problem of justified true belief raised by Plato in the *Theaetetus,* and the concern to evade the consequences of the diallelus argument.

The greatest advantage of the foundationalist approach to epistemology lies in the proposed justification of the foundations of the knowing process. Previous thinkers had studied the question of empirically certain propositions on which to base claims to know. The novelty of the recent analytic strategy for foundationalism lies in the expressed concern to specify criteria for such propositions, instead of relying merely on the dogmatic claim for immediate experiential knowledge of them. Through its attempted justification of the foundations of knowledge, analytic foundationalism advances beyond the familiar claims that propositions can be specified which cannot be denied, or which are indemonstrable but empirically true, through the specification of criteria for such claims.[6]

The limitation of analytic foundationalist strategy lies in part in the way in which it differs from previous foundationalist strategy, and in part in the strategy of empirical foundationalism as such. For the suggestion that it is necessary to justify the certainty of empirical propositions through an appeal to criteria merely postpones the problem of justification but does not resolve it, since the criteria for such propositions themselves require justification. The problem of the justification of the empirical foundations for knowledge is not resolved through an appeal to criteriology, but merely displaced to another level. And although it has been known at least since Descartes that some observational statements are in fact incorrigible, and hence necessarily true, it so far has not been demonstrated that any such statement is sufficient to permit the deduction of other true statements.

II. Nonpresuppositionless Knowledge

The motivation for the interest in presuppositionless theory, whether in the phenomenological concern with method devoid of presuppositions or in the analytic concern with foundationalism, clearly is related to the influential Platonic belief that presuppositions and knowledge are incompatible. Within the post-Hegelian discussion, the evident difficulty in constructing a theory of justification devoid of presuppositions has led in a further stage of the evolution of epistomological strategy to its dialectical opposite. In this further form of epistemological strategy, the possibility of knowledge is dependent no longer on the exclusion of presuppositions but rather on their inclusion, or at least is consistent with their presence. This second form of post-Hegelian epistemological strategy is the aspect of the later discussion which most closely approximates Hegel's own form of antifoundationalism.

a) Nonpresuppositionless Phenomenology

It has been noted that in its initial post-Hegelian phase, phenomenology tended to approach the problem of knowledge in terms of a strategy for presuppositionless methodology. In that initial post-Hegelian form of phenomenological epistemological strategy, the claim for knowledge depends on fully rigorous, or scientific, philosophy, understood as the realization of the goal of methodological presuppositionlessness. In a later form of phenomenological strategy, which arose as a reaction to its predecessor, the interest in method is not abandoned. Rather, the concept of method is rethought in a manner which leads to changes in the views of philosophy and knowledge.

In this later form of phenomenological epistemological strategy, the earlier emphasis on presuppositionlessness as the condition of knowledge is transformed into the dialectically opposite view that presuppositions are necessary conditions of knowledge. The concept of a presupposition is not understood here in the Enlightenment sense of an impediment for the correct functioning of the intellect, associated with Francis Bacon, and later with the French sensualists (e.g., Condillac, Destutt de Tracy) or materialists (e.g., Helvétius, Holbach). It is understood as an anticipation of the object to be known as a necessary condition of its interpretation within understanding. According to this approach, an object cannot be grasped directly through an immediate intuition, but is disclosed only as the result of a process of interpretation of a necessary anticipation of what is to be known.

This later phenomenological strategy for knowledge conserves the earlier phenomenological interest in method and the concern for things in themselves as revealed directly in consciousness on a prepredicative level. In one prominent form of this strategy, phenomenology is understood as the concern to study the logos of the phenomenon, considered as the appearance of an autonomous entity, independent of the subject, but which discloses itself to us in experience through interpretation.

The result of this approach, which also requires a refusal of transcendental reduction associated as a fundamental methodological requirement with the strategy for presuppositionless methodology, is to shift the emphasis from the transcendental elucidation of general essences to the study of individual objects as given in experience.[7] From the perspective of epistemological strategy, the most interesting feature of this approach is the closely Hegelian claim that there is a necessarily circular relation between the object as known and the presupposition, or anticipation of it, which is the basis of the interpretation that constitutes phenomenological knowledge.[8]

The strategy which consists in the transfer of the study of the problem of knowledge from a transcendental analysis of its necessary conditions to a phenomenological description of how we in fact know the objects given in experience offers the general advantage of a practical solution to a theoretical question. With respect to the strategy for presuppositionless methodology, at the price of an obvious weakening of the permissible strength of the claim to know, two specific comparative advantages are further created by this new phenomenological approach. In the first place, it is possible to avoid the need to make good on the traditional claim for presuppositionlessness, specifically as concerns methodology, since presuppositions are incorporated as a necessary feature of the theory. Second, the question of the transition from a theoretical norm of what theory must be to a description of practical possibility is avoided in the restriction of the discussion to a phenomenological account of epistemological practice.

The basic epistemological claim raised in this strategy is that knowledge can tolerate presuppositions, since knowledge is necessarily the result of a circular relation in the understanding. Fortunately, it is unnecessary here to provide a complete discussion of this complicated epistemological strategy, many of whose details are as yet unclear. Here it will be sufficient to point to its relation to Hegel's own epistemological analysis. Speaking generally, post-Hegelian phenomenological strategy which tolerates presuppositions in view of the circular relation between thought and being provides a restricted restatement of the Hegelian position, as concerns knowledge of a given object only. This form of post-Hegelian epistemological strategy accordingly does not surpass Hegel's own view, which it also does not equal in virtue of the lack of a wider account of the relation of thought to objectivity.

b) Analytic Antifoundationalism

The general difficulty in providing a presuppositionless theory of knowledge, which within phenomenology led to the elaboration of nonpresuppositionless epistemological strategy, results within analytic thought in the turn to an antifoundationalist approach to knowledge.

This later form of analytic epistemological strategy is similar in general to the nonpresuppositionless form of epistemology, as well as to the antifoundationalist epistemological approach which originates in the German tradition within Fichte's thought. As relates to phenomenology, a relevant difference is that analytic antifoundationalism is concerned less with knowledge of single objects through a description of how they come to be known than with the wider problem of the relation of thought to objectivity, even if that language is not employed, through a noncorrespondence theory of truth.

It is obvious that analytic antifoundationalism is the dialectical opposite of analytic foundationalism. Analytic antifoundationalism starts from the conviction that since empirical claims for factual truth cannot be established by demonstrating that they are, in fact, satisfied, we must abandon the attempt to justify our criteria for knowledge, which in turn entails the abandonment of empirical foundationalism. In effect, this approach concedes that the diallelus argument is in principle correct, as a result of which any claim for knowledge must dispense with the insistence on an absolute foundation, although it denies the corresponding skeptical conclusion. But this approach is less extreme than the corresponding form of phenomenology, since it eschews the further step of incorporating presuppositions within the theory as a necessary condition of the claim to know.

The strategy of analytic antifoundationalism lies in the attempt to demonstrate the possibility of knowledge in the absence of the foundations required for analytic foundationalism, upon whose indemonstrability it is predicated. In analytic antifoundationalism, the interrelation of items of knowledge to form a systematic interpretation of experience functions as the criterion of presumptive knowledge in place of the indemonstrable correspondence between the idea of a particular object and that object. Analytic antifoundationalism shares this characteristic with nonpresuppositionless forms of phenomenology, differing mainly in the concern to know not a single object but a series of items within the aegis of a single theory (for instance, a scientific theory intended to describe possible future experience).

In practice, one way in which the argument for knowledge without foundations has been made within analytic thought is through a shift from a correspondence to a coherentist view of truth. In accordance with this approach, the claim to know no longer is to be defended in the traditional manner, which depends on a demonstrable correspondence between an idea of the object and the object. Rather, claims to know are to be defended through their systematic interrelation.[9] The resultant approach sometimes is characterized misleadingly as a quasi-

Hegelian inversion, since whereas for Kant system is the criterion of science, in this strategy systematicity has become the criterion of presumptive truth.

As with the nonpresuppositionless form of phenomenology, the parallel is clear between analytic antifoundationalism and Hegel's own analysis of the relation of thought to objectivity. Analytic antifoundationalist epistemological strategy, as noted, presupposes that the diallelus argument suffices to impeach the possibility of foundationalism, although not of knowledge, as the condition of the turn to a strategy which will provide knowledge without empirical foundations. If we recall that the fourth skeptical trope concerns presuppositions, and the fifth trope raises the question of the diallelus, or wheel, then one way of looking at Hegel's own form of antifoundationalism is as a view in which the justification of claims to know is provided by the model of the wheel, or circular relation.

The limitation of the parallel between the views of justification is indicative of the limits of the analytic antifoundationalist epistemological strategy. For a proper understanding of Hegel's view, it is important to note that his strategy combines both coherentist and correspondence features within his concept of circularity. His strategy is coherentist in the relation within the theory of the parts to the whole, and relies on correspondence in the relation of the theory to experience. On the contrary, within analytic antifoundationalism the inability to demonstrate a correspondence between thought and objectivity is taken as the ground for the interest in the coherentist approach.

The one-sided nature of the analytic antifoundationalist strategy for knowledge is evident in the exclusive reliance on the coherentist approach, in terms of which it differs from Hegel's own strategy, since it is unable to provide for the transition from presumptive truth to truth. A theory can easily be coherent but untrue if it fails to correspond to objectivity. The only manner in which to show that a given view, coherent or otherwise, is correct is through a demonstration of its correspondence to objectivity. At the limit, the coherence theory of truth necessarily presupposes the correspondence view, for knowledge of objectivity cannot be acquired solely on the level of thought.

III. Postepistemology

So far we have considered post-Hegelian epistemological strategies, which differ primarily as to whether presuppositions are excluded from, or admitted by, the respective theories of knowledge. Both of these epistemological strategies are supported by epistemological analyses which permit positive claims to know. We now have to consider a more extreme form of epistemological strategy, in which the claim to know cannot be supported on epistemological grounds.

This approach, which accordingly ventures beyond epistemology, presents itself to us in two forms, yielding widely disparate conclusions: from the phenomenological perspective as the attempt to draw the conclusion of the irrelevance of epistemology, and from the analytic perspective as the conclusion which follows from the failure of epistemology to provide a viable analysis of knowledge. Taken together, these two variations on a common theme represent a novel form of epistemological skepticism, that is, skepticism about the possibility of knowledge based on epistemology, although not necessarily skepticism about the possibility of knowledge.

a) Postepistemological Phenomenology

Both of the phenomenological approaches considered so far respond to the problem of justification of claims to know through methodological considerations, either in the concern to exclude presuppositions from theory as inconsistent with knowledge or in their necessary inclusion as a precondition of it. More recently, a third strategy has arisen on the periphery of post-Hegelian phenomenology, whose defining characteristic is the denial of the need to justify the claim to know other than through itself. This new approach to the problem of knowledge from the phenomenological perspective accordingly abandons method entirely, since it no longer has a role to play in the defense of claims to know. The result is an extreme form of phenomenology, which is opposed by its absence of concern with method to the central epistemological tenet of post-Hegelian phenomenology. That is the negation and decline of the original post-Hegelian phenomenological impulse, which here has been transformed into an entirely different and opposing view.

As formulated by a leading exponent, epistemology is replaced by historical discussion.[10] The point seems to be that epistemological considerations are not relevant, since we in effect can surpass epistemology through phenomenology. In particular, we do not require a justification of the beginning point of a theory, which in turn dispenses us from the need to engage in the usual methodological considerations, characteristic of post-Hegelian phenomenology. For at a certain point, presumably when one is confronted with the object as known, it is impossible in good faith to deny that one knows.

This strategy is not entirely unprecedented. It is not a return to the dogmatism of the old metaphysics, but rather a reversion to a form of the concept of direct knowledge studied by Hegel as the third of the "Attitudes of Thought to Objectivity." With respect to its post-Hegelian phenomenological predecessors, this strategy aims for a strategic advantage through the avoidance of methodological considerations, which are replaced by a moral claim about immediate evidence. The intent, then, is to transfer to the moral plane the epistemological question of the justification of claims for the relation of thought to objectivity.

This approach is one-sided, however, since it lacks any theory of justification. This lack is manifested in two ways. On the one hand, as Hegel notes in his own discussion of immediate knowledge, in this kind of approach it is impossible to exclude any belief whatsoever. On the other hand, it is unjustified merely to dispense with justification, as if the problem could be disposed of through turning away from the means for its solution. For although we can literally believe anything at all, our beliefs require demonstration before they can be admitted as knowledge. We cannot, therefore, go beyond epistemology, as this form of postepistemological phenomenological strategy would suggest. In fact, even the claim that we can dispense with epistemology, or more precisely with methodology, is itself an epistemological assertion which requires demonstration.

b) Analytic Postepistemology

A third analytic alternative recently has been proposed. This alternative both represents an attempted mediation between views of analytic foundationalism and analytic antifoundationalism, and constitutes the dialectical opposite to phenomenological postepistemology. Analytic postepistemology is the result of the denial of the central premise of analytic antifoundationalism, that is, that knowledge without foundations is possible. This new perspective accepts both the original analytic insight that knowledge requires foundations and the analytic antifoundationalist point that no foundations can be provided, in order to draw the skeptical conclusion that knowledge is not possible. Accordingly, this latest analytic attitude represents a strategy whose purpose is to show the validity of the traditional skeptical claim that we can know only that we cannot know within the context of the recent analytic epistemological discussion. More generally, this perspective constitutes the dialectical negation and decline of the analytic search for knowledge in the form of an argument against the possibility of knowing following from the failure of analytic epistemology.

It is obvious that this strategy has important historical roots in classical forms of skeptical argumentation. This new strategy can be regarded as the claim that since the diallelus argument is valid, as can be shown by a review of the failure of analytic attempts to construct a valid form of foundationalism, there can be no knowledge. The difference with respect to the associated phenomenological form is that this particular analytic strategy presupposes not the undemonstrated irrelevance of epistemology but rather the demonstrability of its failure. In at least one formulation of this argument, a review of the recent analytic epistemological discussion is held to show that since knowledge cannot be founded, only continued conversation, but no knowledge, is possible.[11]

The advantage of this strategy, that the argument for skepticism is made entirely within the confines of the analytic approach to knowledge through foundations, is also its limitation. The presupposition underlying this approach to epistemology is that foundationalism is the only possible manner in which to make out the claim to knowledge, so that the failure of foundationalism permits the skeptical conclusion to be drawn.

This presupposition is unwarranted; the purported insufficiency of prior analytic discussion of foundationalism does not suffice to demonstrate that an argument for foundationalism cannot be formulated satisfactorily. And it must further be shown that no other epistemological strategy could possibly be satisfactory, which is here merely assumed, in order for the failure of analytic foundationalism to yield a skeptical conclusion with regard to the possibility of knowledge. But this point is indemonstrable, since there are other, nonfounded forms of knowledge, as a glance at the history of philosophy will show. These forms of knowledge include that kind advanced by Aristotle in the *Nicomachean Ethics,* which precisely eschews the demand for apodicticity and hence does not require foundations, and the entire later pragmatist tradition following from Aristotle's view of practical theory.

The intent of this selective review of some major post-Hegelian epistemological strategies is to provide a background for the assessment of the continued relevance of Hegel's own view of the relation of thought to objectivity. Hegel's basic point is that although this relation cannot be founded, claims to know are justified in practice through the circularity of this relation. This point could be undermined in at least two obvious ways: either through a successful demonstration of foundationalism, or through a demonstration of the impossibility of knowledge without foundations.

Both of these epistemological strategies clearly are represented within the post-Hegelian epistemological discussion surveyed here. But although these arguments are made in new ways in the post-Hegelian period, they are not in themselves new; nor are they fatal to Hegel's position. On the whole, the post-Hegelian debate tends to restate different forms of the main varieties of the epistemological discussion preceding Hegel's thought, known to him, and discussed in his writings.

It is unnecessary here to repeat Hegel's arguments, since they already have been examined. The point that needs to be stressed is that the major post-Hegelian epistemological strategies canvassed here were already in evidence when Hegel wrote. For instance, in the debate concerning the reformulation of the critical philosophy in rigorous form Reinhold stands for foundationalism, Fichte represents antifoundationalism, and Aenesidemus and Maimon advance skeptical views subsequent to the failure of foundationalism. Despite the interest of later variations on these main epistemological themes, there is no reason to believe that the post-Hegelian epistemological discussion, which is elaborated mainly in ignorance of Hegel's thought, contains strategies basically novel and hence unlike those considered in detail by Hegel. If his arguments against the forms of these strategies which appeared in his predecessors' views were valid, they are also valid, mutatis mutandis, against the views of his successors.

There is a further point to be made about the nature of the post-Hegelian epistemological discussion in comparison to Hegel's own. A significant difference between the Kantian and the Hegelian approaches lies in Kant's concern, inconsistent with his own practice, to isolate systematic considerations from any historical contamination as a necessary condition of transcendental argument, whereas Hegel strives to combine them. An extraordinary aspect of Hegel's position, not duplicated in the later discussion, is the desire to build upon, to carry further, and to complete in this manner the work of previous thinkers concerned with the relation of thought to objectivity.

The tenor of the post-Hegelian epistemological discussion surveyed here unfortunately resembles Kant's approach more than Hegel's. It is not the case, despite appearances, that later thought has turned away from knowledge of the historical tradition. Even if a truly Hegelian grasp of historical sources is rarely, if ever again, encountered, there are outstanding counterexamples to the widespread historical ignorance prevalent in the post-Hegelian discussion.

Even more striking is the restricted use made of historical knowledge in this period, in which it is mainly, indeed nearly exclusively, devoted to the identification of the inadequacies of earlier views. There is almost no concern to carry forward previous efforts to justify claims to know in a broadly constructive manner. In this sense, Hegel's position, as the review of later epistemological strategies indicates not only is unsurpassed but is unique. For the kind of effort he undertook to combine historical and systematic dimensions within a position that is both aware of and builds upon previous efforts in the broadest possible manner seems never again to have been attempted in the later discussion.

The overall insight which emerges from the present selective review of some main post-Hegelian epistemological strategies is that Hegel's view of knowledge has not been surpassed, or in some ways even equalled by later discussion. As concerns the analysis of the relation of thought to objectivity, there has indeed been change, but the problem remains almost where it was when Hegel wrote. While it is obvious that the later discussion has brought forth different epistemological strategies, there is no reason to hold that they differ in fundamental ways, despite their novelty, from those already considered by Hegel. Accordingly, the development of the post-Hegelian epistemological discussion does not diminish the intrinsic interest of Hegel's own view. Indeed, as a result, the general post-Hegelian disinterest in Hegel's desire to build upon other, earlier views tends to increase rather than to decrease the appeal of Hegel's own endeavor.

CONCLUSION

Unsere philosophische Revolution ist
beeindigt. Hegel hat ihren grossen Kreis
geschlossen. Wir sehen seitdem nur
Entwicklung und Ausbildung der
naturphilosophischen Lehre.

—Heinrich Heine[1]

The concern of this book has been to call attention to, analyze, and
evaluate the significance of Hegel's centrally important but little-
studied doctrine of epistemological circularity. In the course of this
discussion, stress has been placed on a number of themes, including
the significance of the *Differenzschrift* for an understanding of Hegel's
thought, the importance of the difference in his approach in that text
to the views of Reinhold and Fichte concerning the further development of the critical philosophy, the systematic and historical aspects of
the doctrine of circularity in Hegel's mature thought, and the link in
Hegel's mature thought between the doctrine of circularity and the
problem of the relation of thought and being.

As concerns the *Differenzschrift,* the suggestion has been made that
this neglected text is indeed central to an appreciation of Hegel's
mature thought. For one finds here the initial statement of the position from which the mature view only later emerges, not through
basic change but through a deepening of the leading ideas. That is
especially the case for the doctrine of circularity, which in later texts is
indeed developed but not fundamentally altered. It was further
shown that Hegel here views the essential philosophical task as the
completion of the critical philosophy in the direction taken by Fichte.
That is an indication that the origins of Hegel's position lie not in his
meditation on ancient philosophy, which came only later, in the further development of his thought, but rather in the attempt to come to
grips with the contemporary discussion. And it is further an indication that, despite efforts to understand Hegel's view as simply in

opposition to Kant's, Hegel's objections are directed to the letter, but not to the spirit, of the critical philosophy.

This text further demonstrates the origin of Hegel's interest in circularity as a positive epistemological doctrine. As concerns the proposed reconstruction of the critical philosophy, Hegel follows Fichte's antifoundationalism in opposition to Reinhold's quasi-rationalist, grounded system. But whereas the early Fichte employs the concept of circularity to question the possibility of knowledge in the full, or traditional, philosophic sense, Hegel makes use of the identical concept to suggest that theory justifies itself despite the lack of a foundation.

Within the context of the *Differenzschrift,* the doctrine of circularity is eccentric to the main themes, which are the normative concept of philosophy and its relation to the contemporary discussion. But in Hegel's mature thought, this doctrine becomes central to the position and is expanded significantly. What was initially merely a response in the context of the post-Kantian reformulation of the critical philosophy to a contemporary form of nonphilosophy now is generalized as the result of the Platonic view of philosophy as intrinsically presuppositionless, and therefore circular. At the same time, the initial thesis of circular justification is expanded to include claims for the circularity of the epistemological object, the various sciences, and philosophy, as well as a necessarily circular relation between theory and experience.

Hegel's mature expansion of the original doctrine of circularity is clearly linked to his mature, wider reading of the history of philosophy. Even in the mature thought, the central emphasis remains fixed on the modern tradition and Kant's role within it. But that reading is now doubly expanded: in the view of the critical philosophy as a further development of the Cartesian discovery of independent thought, which Hegel holds is the basic insight in modern philosophy, and in the further view that these and other positions are successive approaches to the ancient problem, which traverses the entire philosophical tradition, of the relation of thought and being.

Insight into the link in Hegel's mature position between the doctrine of circularity and the problem of the relation of thought and being opens the way for an evaluation of that doctrine within Hegel's position and for philosophy in general. Hegel is correct to hold that thought can have no foundation, but that theory can justify itself in a nonlinear, circular manner through the relation of the results obtained to its beginning. And although it is usual to regard Hegel's thought as dependent on the selective appropriation of Aristotelian themes, as concerns circularity we can note a denial of the widely influential Aristotelian stress on linearity in the form of a qualified return to a pre-Socratic doctrine. In this way, Hegel thinks through to the end the problem of the possibility of a fully critical philosophy, which unavoidably must address the question of the relation of thought and being. And since later thought immediately forgot this central insight, Hegel in this respect remains in advance of those who followed, and for whom the problem of knowledge no longer concerns this relation.

Hegel's triumph is, however, incomplete in a significant sense. It is not enough, as he points out, to focus on the relation of thought and being, since their identity must be demonstrated, although he is manifestly unable to do so. For if, as Fichte and others before him already knew, thought is necessarily circular, then knowledge in the fully traditional sense, which Descartes correctly identifies as in principle unrevisable, cannot be had. Hegel's failure to provide the required demonstration further undermines his critique of Fichte and Kant, inspired by Schelling, as philosophers of subjectivity, since the implied transition from subjectivity to objectivity, which is the basis of the objection, cannot be carried out. In other words, knowledge of objectivity from the perspective of subjectivity, but not of objectivity as such, is revealed as the outer epistemological limit.

Hegel's inability to demonstrate the required unity of thought and being in terms of circularity, and hence his failure to solve the problem of knowledge, does not diminish the interest of that doctrine. Although that is not his intention, his discussion of circularity reveals a profound tension between the normative concept of philosophy as devoid of presuppositions and its goal of knowledge. For if philosophy is presuppositionless, it cannot yield knowledge in the full sense. Yet if knowledge is apodictic, it cannot result from presuppositionless theory.

The result is neither to surpass nor to abandon epistemology, except in an uncritical sense; it is rather to acknowledge, in a quasi-Kantian manner, intrinsic epistemological limits. Idealism has often been mistakenly equated with rationalism as holding that knowledge is infinite in scope, since there are no bounds which cannot be surpassed. Yet that is merely a simplistic caricature, since even for Kant the stress on knowledge as unlimited is inextricably related to an equal stress on its bounded character.

That Hegel may have been held to deny any form of this Kantian claim rests on a misunderstanding of his view of reason. For although knowledge arises in the relation between thought and being, thought is not sovereign but dependent upon being. That is not to assert a form of Pythagorean relativism, or to argue for a kind of epistemological anarchy. Nor is it to suggest the propriety of skepticism about knowledge in view of its impossibility. It is, rather, to say that knowledge in the full, or traditional, sense, which is completely unconstrained, cannot be had in the relation between thought and being. For the relation itself is inherently circular. Even if the rest of Hegel's thought were to be swept away by the later history of philosophy, which seems unlikely, this point would remain as an essential insight.

But there is no reason to believe that later epistemological discussion has negated or weakened Hegel's point. Indeed, in so many ways, as philosophy has taken leave from conscious consideration of its past, the problem with which Hegel was concerned, the relation of thought and being, no longer is even directly raised. Philosophy was never a tragedy; but it indeed becomes a comedy when it ceases to acknowledge the historical nature of its enterprise.

Despite the relation of philosophy to time, on occasion insights of permanent value emerge within the philosophical tradition. Hegel's merit is to have shown, although unintentionally, the inevitable tension between the inherent circularity of philosophy, indeed all forms of knowledge, and the need to demonstrate the unity of thought and being. It is indeed the case that thought must assume a self-reflective, systematic form and test itself against being, as revealed in experience, the standard for any knowledge claim. Conversely, this standard is not absolute but relative, since through the confrontation of thought with the experience of being it never can be shown that being is known by thought.

Interpreted in this way, Hegel's result can be expressed in a negative manner. For it is not only after idealism that there could only be pragmatism. Rather, idealism in Hegel's case, and others, as well, is form of pragmatism. Since, as the doctrine of circularity shows, the demand for total justification cannot be satisfied a priori, we must turn for knowledge to the uneasy relation between thought and being as revealed in experience. Neither element can be renounced, since knowledge can come only from their relation. But at the same time it must be stressed that this relation itself cannot be shown to yield knowledge of being in thought, since it must be presupposed to do so as the condition of experiential knowledge. That is indeed an absolute limitation of what can be known, as Hegel was clearly aware.

Yet if, as Hegel says, philosophy is presuppositionless, and therefore circular, the age-old dream of the demonstration that thought knows being, indeed the resolution of the problem of knowledge, ends in Hegel's position in an awareness that that is merely a dream, the dream of reason which would be self-subsistent in emancipating itself. Although epistemology has as its task the demonstration of the claim of reason to know, Hegel demonstrates that we can know only that reason ends in belief or hope. Epistemology, Hegel shows us, terminates either in morality, the claim that reason must know, or in religion, the hope that it can.

This point can be sharpened in terms of the problem of the end of philosophy, frequently evoked since Hegel's death in relation to his thought. Hegel's position often has been held—by both its enthusiasts and its critics, but for different reasons—to mark the end of philosophy.[2] Obviously, the claim admits of more than one interpretation. Heine, who provided a classic formulation of it, had in mind the completion of the movement of independent thought set in motion by Luther's revolt against religious dogmatism and continued in Kantian and post-Kantian thought. Heine's intention was to note that philosophy stagnated and failed to advance after Hegel's death. Marxists, on the contrary, since Engels, have held that philosophy in any meaningful sense actually ends in the Hegelian synthesis.

This latter view is inconsistent, to say the least, since it presupposes that Hegel is successful in taking up in his thought all that is of value in the preceding tradition at the same time as it negates the claim for philosophy to be meaningful. Indeed, neither of these claims can be accepted as formulated. It is not correct that all later views are forms of *Naturphilosophie;* nor can it accurately be held that philosophy as a whole has continued to stagnate, even if it has not often reached a Hegelian level since Hegel; nor again is it the case that philosophy as such terminates in Hegel's thought, since there are numerous later philosophers, including (as Marxists for their own reasons fail to acknowledge) Marx. But it seems possible to formulate the claim that Hegel brings philosophy to an end in another perhaps more persuasive, manner.

Hegel clearly does not bring to an end philosophy in all its forms; nor is there reason to believe that that was his intention. The perhaps unwitting lesson of his discussion of knowledge as necessarily circular is to reveal the limit intrinsic to any form of epistemology based on reason. The assumption of the inquiry into knowledge has always been that thought knows being, although as Hegel knew, this assumption never has been demonstrated. Hegel's own attempt to provide this demonstration fails, since as we have seen, it is in tension with his view that philosophy is necessarily presuppositionless, therefore circular, and accordingly unable to escape from the circle of thought and being.

It is perhaps paradoxical, but unquestionably the case, that a striking consequence of Hegel's endeavor to demonstrate that reason can be self-subsistent, that thought is identical with being, is to show that this result cannot be established through reason. Hegel, the archrationalist, unwittingly but definitively puts an end to the rationalist form of the epistemological enterprise as concerns the full emancipation of reason. For he shows the necessity of assuming the indemonstrable validity of the claim of thought to know being as an unavoidable presupposition of all epistemology.

NOTES

Introduction

1. See Richard Rorty, *Consequences of Pragmatism* (Minneapolis: University of Minnesota Press, 1982), p. 211.

I Circularity as a Problem in Hegel's Thought

1. See W. N. A. Klever, "Circulaire Bewijsvoering," in *Tijdschrift voor Filosofie* 44, no. 4 (December 1982): 603–642.

2. See Dietrich Mahnke, *Unendliche Sphäre und Allmittelpunkt* (Stuttgart/Bad Canstatt: Fr. Frommann Verlag, 1966 rpt.).

3. See H. Diels, *Fragmente der Vorsokratiker* (Berlin: Weidmann Verlag, 1922), Vol. 1, p. 89.

4. Ibid., p. 98.

5. For a discussion of this parallel, see Lynne Ballew, "Straight and Circular in Parmenides and the 'Timaeus,'" in *Phronesis* 19, no. 3: 189–209.

6. De. An. I, 3, 407a. For a discussion of this passage, see Harold Cherniss, *Aristotle's Criticism of Plato and the Academy* (Baltimore: Johns Hopkins University Press, 1944), App. 9, pp. 571–72; see also Sir David Ross, ed. and trans. *De Anima* (Oxford: Oxford University Press, 1961), pp. 188–91.

7. See W. N. A. Klever, *Carneades. Reconstructie en evaluatie van zijn kennistheoretische positie* (Rotterdam: Erasmus Universiteit, 1982).

8. See *Institutiones Theologicae, c.* 15.

9. See *Summa Contra Gentiles,* II, 46; *De. Ver.* 22.12.1, and 1.2.c.

10. See *La scienza nuova,* par. 331.

11. See *Critique of Pure Reason,* B xiii.

12. For a reading of Marx's theory of knowledge in this sense, see Leszek Kolakowski, "Karl Marx and the Classical Definition of Truth," in *Toward a Marxist Humanism,* trans. Jane Zielonko Peel (New York: Grove Press, 1968), pp. 38–66.

13. See the article on "circolarità" in *Enciclopedia filosofica* (Rome/Venice: Instituto per la collaborazione filosofica, 1957), vol. 1, pp. 1064–66.

14. *Georg Wilhelm Friedrich Hegel. Sämtliche Werke,* ed. Hermann Glockner (Stuttgart: Fr. Frommanns Verlag, 1927–1939), vol. 1, p. 27. See also ibid., pp. 25, 26, 27.

15. See Hans-Friedrich Fulda, *Das Problem einer Einleitung in Hegels Wissenschaft der Logik* (Frankfurt a.M.: V. Klostermann, 1965).

16. See *Hegel-Bibliographie,* ed. F. N. Steinhauer, *mit Stichwortregister,* ed. Gitta Hansen (Munich: H. G. Saur, 1980).

17. Berlin: W. de Gruyter, 1929.

18. See, for example. J. N. Findlay, *Hegel: A Re-examination* (New York: Collier, 1962); Werner Marx, *Hegel's Phenomenology of Spirit: A Commentary on the Preface and Introduction* (New York: Harper and Row, 1965); Jean Hyppolite, *Génèse et Structure de la Phénoménologie de l'Esprit de Hegel* (Paris: Gallimard, 1946); W. T. Stace, *The Philosophy of Hegel* (New York: Dover, 1955); Merold Westphal, *History and Truth* (Atlantic Highlands: Humanities, 1979); Michael Theunissen, *Sein und Schein. Die kritische Funktion der Hegelschen Logik* (Frankfurt a.M.: Suhrkamp, 1980).

19. Walter Kaufmann, *Hegel: A Reinterpretation* (Garden City, N.J.: Doubleday Anchor, 1966).

20. Charles Taylor, *Hegel* (Cambridge: Cambridge University Press, 1977).

21. Stanley Rosen, *G. W. F. Hegel: An Introduction to the Science of Wisdom* (New Haven: Yale University Press, 1974).

22. See *Etudes sur Marx et Hegel* (Paris: Marcel Rivière, 1955), p. 198.

23. See *Introduction à la lecture de Hegel. Leçons sur la Phénoménologie de l'Esprit professées de 1933 à 1939 à l'Ecole des Hautes-Etudes* (Paris: Gallimard, 1947).

24. See *Structures et mouvement dans la Phénoménologie de l'Esprit de Hegel* (Paris: Aubier-Montaigne, 1968), p. 247.

25. See *Versuch einer kritischen Erneuerung* (Heidelberg: Quelle und Meyer, 1953).

26. See *Das Problem der absoluten Reflexion* (Frankfurt a.M.: V. Klostermann, 1981), and "Hegel und das Problem der Aufhebung der Metaphysik," in *M. Heidegger zum 70. Geburtstag* (Pfullingen: G. Neske, 1959), pp. 67–92.

27. See *Absolute Subjektivitat und kategoriale Anschauung. Eine Untersuchung der Systemstruktur bei Hegel* (Meisenheim am Glan: Anton Hein, 1969).

28. See *Das Scheitern einer Einleitung in Hegels Philosophie. Eine Analyse der Phänomenologie des Geistes* (Munich/Salzburg: Verlag Anton Pustet, 1973).

29. See *Denkformen* (Berlin: W. de Gruyter, 1951), esp. pp. 176, 178, 180–81.

30. See *Das Problem der Subjektivität in Hegels Logik* (Bonn: Bouvier, 1976).

31. See *Das Sinnbild des Kreises im Denken Hegels und Lenins* (Meisenheim am Glan: Anton Hein, 1971).

32. See *Platon und Hegel. Zur ontologischen Begründung des Zirkels in der Erkenntnis* (Tübingen: Max Niemeyer V., 1968).

33. Ibid., p. 165.

II Epistemological Justification

1. But see Otto Ritschl, "System und systematische Methode in der Geschichte des wissenschaftlichen Sprachgebrauchs und der philosophischen Methodologie," in *Programm zur Feier des Gedächtnisses des Stifters der Universität König Friedrich Wilhelm III* (Bonn: Carl Georgi, 1906); see also Alois von der Stein, "Der Systembegriff in seiner geschichtlichen Entwicklung," in *System und Klassifikation in Wissenschaft und Dokumentation,* ed. A. Diemer (Meisenheim am Glan: Verlag Anton Hein, 1968).

2. See *Philosophia Moralis sive Ethica,* vol. 12, par. 285, in *Gesammelte Werke,* ed. J. Ecole, J. E. Hoffman, M. Thomann, and H. W. Arndt, Pt. 2, Lateinische Schriften (Hildesheim: Georg Olms Verlag, 1970).

3. Ibid., 889.

4. Cited in Diemer, ed., *System und Klassifikation,* p. 164.

5. *Philosophia Moralis,* par. 284.

6. See Ritschl, "System und systematische Methode," p. 68.

7. For a discussion of the "Nova Dilucidatio" in relation to Leibniz, Wolff, and Crusius, see Ernst Cassirer, *Kant's Life and Thought,* trans. James Haden (New Haven, Yale University Press, 1981), pp. 73f.

8. *Akad. Ausgabe,* vol. 5, p. 91.

9. See ibid., vol. 4, p. 391.

10. See ibid., vol. 5, p. 91.

11. See ibid., pp. 170, 171, 176.

12. Cassirer reminds us that reviewers saw in this work only the expression of personal views and dogma. See Cassirer, *Kant's Life,* p. 219.

13. See "Uber die Möglichkeit einer Form der Philosophie überhaupt," in *Schellings Werke,* ed. M. Schröter (Munich: Beck und Oldenbourg, 1927), vol. I, pp. 47–48: "Der Verfasser glaubte bald zu finden, dass gerade diejenigen Einwürfe dieses Skeptikers, die sich auf diesen Mangel mittelbar oder unmittelbar bezögen, die wichtigsten und bisher am wenigsten beantwortlichen sehen: er wurde überzeugt, dass auch die Theorie des Vorstellungsvermögens, so wie Reinhold bis jetzt gegeben hatte, noch nicht sich selbst gegen sie gesichert habe, dass sie aber am Ende nothwendig zu einer Philosophie führen müsse, die, auf tiefere Fundamente gegründet, durch dies Einwürfe des neuen Skeptikers nicht mehr erreicht würde. Durch die Reinholdische Elementarphilosophie sollte nämlich zunächst nur eine von den beiden Fragen beantwortet werden, die aller Wissenschaft vorangehen müssen, und deren Trennung voneinander bisher der Philosophie ausserordentlich viel geschadet hatte—die Frage nämlich, wie der Inhalt einer Philosophie möglich sey, während dass die Frage über die Möglichkeit der Form einer Philosophie durch sie im Ganzen genommen nur so beantwortet wurde, wie sie schon durch die Kritik der reinen Vernunft beantwortet war, d.h. ohne dass die Untersuchung auf ein letztes Prinzip aller Form zurückgefuhrt worden wäre."

14. "Mit einem Worte, ich war wie im Zirkel herumgetrieben und konnte nirgends festen Fuss fassen." "An die Freunde Lessings," in *Spinoza-Buchlein,* ed. Fritz Mauthner (Munich: Müller, 1912), p. 240.

15. See Schröter, ed., *Schellings Werke,* p. 54: "Hier befinden wir uns in einem magischen Kreise, aus dem wir offenbar nicht anders, denn durch die Annahme, auf die wir schon durch blosse Entwicklung des Begriffes eines obersten Grundsatzes gekommen waren, herauskommen können, die Annahme nämlich, dass es Ein oberstes absolutes Princip gebe. . . ." On the "Zirkel" in Schelling's thought, see Karl Jaspers, *Schelling. Grösse and Verhängnis* (Munich: Piper, 1955), pp. 91–93.

16. See F. Nietzsche, *Gesammelte Werke,* Grossoktavausgabe (Leipzig: C. G. Naumann, 1901–1913), vol. 6, p. 317. *Also sprach Zarathustra:* "Alles geht, Alles kommt zurück; ewig rollt das Rad des Seins. Alles stirbt, Alles blüht wieder auf; ewig läuft das Jahr des Seins. Alles bricht, Alles wird neu gefügt; ewig baut sich das gleiche Haus des Seins. Alles scheidet, Alles grüsst sich wieder; ewig bleibt sich treu der Ring des Seins."

17. See *Die Geburt der Tragödie,* in *Werke,* ed. K. Schlechta, vol. 1, pp. 86–87: "Denn die Peripherie des Kreises der Wissenschaft hat unendlich viele Punkte, und während noch gar nicht abzusehen ist, wie jemals der Kreis völlig ausgemessen werden könnte, so trifft der edle und begabte Mensch,

noch vor der Mitte seines Daseins und unvermeidlich, auf solche Grenzpunkte der Peripherie: wo er in das Unaufhellbare starrt."

18. See *Verstand und Erfahrung. Eine Metakritik zur Kritik der reinen Vernunft,* in *Herders sämmtliche Werke,* ed. B. L. Suphan (Berlin: Weidmann, 1877–1913), vol. 21, p. 18: "Wenn aber Vernunft kritisiert werden soll; von wem kann es werden? Nicht anders als von ihr selbst; mithin ist sie Parthei und Richter. Und wonach kann sie gerichtet werden? Nicht anders als nach sich selbst; mithin ist sie auch Gesetz und Zeuge. Sofort erblickt man die Schwierigkeit dieses Richteramtes." Herder was strongly influenced in his *Metakritik* by Hamann's views. See esp. J. G. Hamann, *Metakritik über den Purismum der reinen Verhunft,* 1788, rpt., in *Hammann's Schriften,* ed. F. Roth (Berlin: G. Reimer, 1821–1843), vol. 7.

19. See, e.g., Nicolai Hartmann, *Die Philosophie des deutschen Idealismus* (Berlin: de Gruyter, 1974), pp. 14–15.

20. Letter of October 12, 1787, quoted in K. Vorländer, *Kants Leben* (Leipzig: F. Meiner, 1921), p. 148.

21. Kant's letter of December 18, 1787 to Reinhold, in *Immanuel Kants Werke,* ed. Ernst Cassirer (Hamburg: B. Cassirer, 1921–23), vol. 9, pp. 343–44: "Ich habe, vortrefflicher, liebenswürdiger Mann, die schönen Briefe gelesen, womit Sie meine Philosophie beehrt haben, und die an mit Gründlichkeit verbundener Anmut nichts übertreffen kann, die auch nicht ermangelt haben, in unserer Gegend alle erwünschte Wirkung zu tun. Desto mehr habe ich gewünscht, die genaue Übereinkünft Ihrer Idee mit den meinigen und zugleich meinen Dank für das Verdienst, welches Sie um deren fassliche Darstellung haben, in irgendeinem Blatte, vornehmlich dem Deutschen Merkur, wenigstens mit einigen Zeilen bekanntzumachen. . . ."

22. *Beyträge zur Berichtigung bisheriger Missverständnisse der Philosophen* (Jena: Manke, 1790), vol. 1, p. 267.

23. See his "Rezension von Fichtes zur Wissenschaftlehre gehörenden Schriften," in M. Selling, *Studien zur Geschichte der Transzendentalphilosophie* (Uppsala: Dissertation, 1938), pp. 317ff.

24. For an account, see Reinhold Lauth, "Fichtes und Reinholds Verhältnis vom Anfange ihrer Bekanntschaft bis zu Reinholds Beitritt zum Standpunkt der Wissenschaftslehre Anfang 1797," in Reinhold Lauth, ed., *Philosophie aus einem Prinzip* (Bonn: Bouvier, 1974), pp. 137ff.

25. See Reinhold's "Sendschreiben an Lavater und Fichte über den Glauben an Gott," 1799 (Hamburg: K. Perthes, 1799).

26. See *C. G. Bardilis und C. L. Reinholds Briefwechsel über das Wesen der Philosophie und das Unwesen der Spekulation,* ed. C. L. Reinhold (Munich: J. Lentner, 1804); see also Reinhold's *Beyträge zur leichteren Übersicht des Zustandes der Philosophie bei dem Anfange des 19. Jahrhunderts,* 1801–1803 (Hamburg: K. Perthes, 1801–1803).

27. *Über das Fundament des philosophischen Wissens* (Hamburg: Meiner Verlag, 1978), p. xiii.

28. Ibid., p. xiv.

29. Ibid., p. 69.

30. See Letter to Markus Herz, Königsberg, March 26, 1789, in E. Cassirer, ed., *Immanuel Kants Werke* (Berlin: Bruno Cassirer, 1912–1922), vol. 4, p. 415. In reference to Maimon's manuscript, Kant writes that "allein ein Blick den ich darauf warf, gab mir bald die Vorzüglichkeit desselben zu erkennen und,

dass nicht allein niemand von meinen Gegnern mich und die Hauptfrage so wohl verstanden, sondern nur wenige zu dergleichen tiefen Untersuchungen soviel Scharfsinn besitzen möchten, als Herr MAIMON. . . ."

31. See *Philosophischer Briefwechsel nebst einem demselben vorangeschickten Manifest*, in *Salomon Maimon. Gesammelte Werke*, ed. Valerio Verra (Hildesheim: Georg Olms, 1970), vol. 4, pp. 204–205.

32. Ibid., p. 209: "Meiner Überzeugung nach, ist die kritische Philosophie durch Kant schon vollendet, und die Verbesserungen, die man darin vornehmen kann, bestehen nicht darin, dass man von ihr zu höheren Prinzipien hinauf steigt, sondern vielmehr dass man zu niedrigern Prinzipien herunter steigt. . . ."

33. See ibid., p. 202.

34. See ibid., p. 224: "Prinzipien an sich brauchen und können nicht bewiesen werden. Denn eben darum sind sie Principien, weil alles in einer Wissenschaft sich aus ihnen beweisen (auf sie zurückführen) lässt, sie aber sich aus nichts beweisen lassen, sondern an sich evident sind. Wohl! aber können und müssen Prinzipien als Prinzipien, d.h. in Ansehung ihres Gebrauchs, bewiesen werden." For Kant's similar view, see *Critique of Pure Reason*, B 797–810.

35. *Aenesidemus oder über die Fundamente der von dem Herrn Professor Reinhold in Jena gelieferten Elementar-Philosophie. Nebst einer Vertheidigung des Skepticismus gegen die Anmassmungen der Vernunftkritik*, 1792, rpt. ed. Arthur Liebert (Berlin: Verlag von Reuther und Reichard, 1911).

36. See ibid., p. 2.

37. See ibid., p. 15.

38. See ibid., pp. 306–307: "Allerdings scheint derienige Satz, den Sie für das Hauptresultat des theoretischen Teils der kritischen Philosophie erklären, dass nämlich nur in unserer Erfahrungserkenntnis Wahrheit anzutreffen sey, und dass diese weder aus den Eindrücke der Aussendinge auf das Gemüth allein bestehe, noch auch bloss durch die selbstthätige Wirkung des Gemüths entstanden sey, sondern aus beyden zugleich herrühre, manche Beschaffenheiten der menschlichen Erkenntnis aufzuklären und begreiflich zu machen; und als eine Hypothese genommen, möge derselbe sich wohl gegen die Behauptungen des Empirismus und Rationalismus recht gut vertheidigen lassen. Allein iener Satz der kritischen Philosophie soll nach der Erklärung ihres Erjinders und ihren Anhänger nicht bloss eine Hypothese seyn, die wegen ihrer Brauchbarkeit bey der Erklärung der Eigenschaften der menschlichen Erkenntnis auf Wahrheit Ansprüche macht; sondern er soll vielmehr in ihr völlig erwiesen und unbestreitbar gewiss dargethan worden seyn, und eben deswegen auch alle Nachforschung über die Macht und Ohnmacht des ganzen menschlichen Erkenntnisvermögens als das Allersicherste zum Grunde gelegt werden können. Nun sind aber die Gründe, welche die Vernunftkritik und die Elementar-Philosophie für die apodiktische Evidenz ienes Satzes geliefert haben, solchen Gründe, die, wie ich in meinen Bemerkungen dargethan haben, genau genommen, gar nichts bewiesen, und selbst von der Vernunftkritik und von der Elementar-Philosophie in keinem andern Falle für gültig gehalten werden."

40. See Ibid., p. 47: "Als der oberste Grundsatz alles Denkens wird der Satz des Widerspruchs in Ansehung dessen, wodurch er die Würde erhält, an der Spitze aller Urtheile zu stehen, aus einem andern Satze, wenn man nicht

einem Zirkel im Ableiten zu begehen will, nie abgeleitet werden dürfen."

41. Ibid., p. 61: "Wenn die Vorstellung als blosse Vorstellung gedacht werden soll; muss sie nicht, in wieferne sie wirklich auf Objekt und Subjekt bezogen wird, sondern nur in wieferne sie auf beyde bezogen werden kann, gedacht werden."

42. See Letter to Reinhold of May 24, 1794, Berlin, in Maimon's *Gesammelte Schriften*, vol. 6, p. 447: "Aus den Briefen an Aenesidemus besonders werden Sie sehn, wie mein Skepticismus von dem seinigen himmelweit verschieden ist." The letters were published as an appendix to a book which appeared in the same year, entitled *Versuch einer neuen Logik oder Theorie des Denkens. Nebst angehängten Briefen des Philateles an Aenesidemus* (Berlin, 1794).

43. In a draft of a letter to Reinhold, Fichte writes: "Eben so geht es mir mit Kant, dessen schriften verstanden zu haben ich jedoch mit grösserer Überzeugung glaube. Es wird immer wahrscheinlicher, dass er gerade aus meinen Grundsätzen gefolgert habe." Letter to Reinhold, March 1, 1794, Zürich, in *J. G. Fichte-Gesamtausgabe der Bayerischen Akademie der Wissenschaften*, ed. Reinhard Lauth and Hans Jacob (Stuttgart/Bad Canstatt, 1967ff.), pt. 3, vol. 2, p. 74.

44. This kind of claim was widespread in the German idealist tradition. Schelling, for instance, suggested that his own system explained Fichte's. See Schelling's *Grundlegung der positiven Philosophie. Münchener Vorlesung. Wintersemester 1832/1833 und Sommersemester 1833*, ed. H. Fuhrmanns (Turin: Bottega d'Erasmo, 1972), vol. 1, p. 175.

45. "Denn reine Wissenschaftslehre ist nicht mehr oder weniger als blosse Logik, welche mit ihren Principien sich nicht zum Materialen des Erkenntnisses versteigt, sondern vom Inhalte dessen als reine Logik abstrahirt, aus welche eine reales Objekt herauszuklauben vergebliche und daher auch nie versuchte Arbeit ist, sondern wo, wenn es die Transzendental-Philosophie gilt, allererst zur Metaphysik überschritten werden muss." *Intelligenzblatt No. 109*, reprinted in *Johann Gottlieb Fichte's Leben und litterarischem Briefwechsel*, ed. I. H. Fichte (Sulzbach: Seidel'sche Buchhandlung, 1831), pp. 175–76.

46. "*Wissenschaftslehre* sey nicht mehr und nicht minder als blosse Logik, welche, als *reine Logik*, von allem Inhalte des Erkenntnisses abstrahire. Über das letzere bin ich, wie sich versteht, mit *Kant* ganz einig, nur bezeichnet, *meinem Sprachgebrauch nach*, das Wort Wissenschaftslehre gar nicht die Logik, sondern die Transcendentalphilosophie oder Metaphysik selbst. Unser Streit wäre sonach ein blosser Wortstreit." See *Fichte-Schelling Briefwechsel*, ed. Walter Schulz (Frankfurt a.M.: Suhrkamp, 1968), p. 66.

47. Letter to Franz Volkmar Reinhard in Dresden, February 20, 1793, in *Fichte-Gesamtausgabe*, pt. 3, vol. 1, p. 373: "Ich habe die kritische Philosophie, nemlich ihrem Geiste nach, den weder Kant noch Reinhold dargestellt haben, u. der mir nur dämmert immer für eine unüberwindliche Festung gehalten."

48. Letter to Stephani, December 1793, in ibid., vol. 2, p. 28: "Kant hat überhaupt die richtige Philosophie; aber nur in ihren Resultaten, nicht nach ihren Gründen."

49. Letter to Reinhold of March 1, 1794, in ibid., p. 78: "Ich stimme mit dem, was Sie daselbst über das allgemeine Verfahren bei der philosophischen Reflexion, über die Erfordernisse einer Philosophie überhaupt, und insbesondere Ihres ersten Grundsatzes sagen, so sehr überein, dass ich nachweisen könnte, ohnegefähr das gleiche, noch ehe ich Ihre Schrift gelesen hatte,

niedergeschreiben zu haben. Um desto unerklärbarer ist mir es bis jetzo, woran es liegen möge, dass ich dem Satze des Bewusstseyn's—(dem Ihrigen)—die Merkmale eines ersten Grundsatzes, über die wir völlig einig sind, nicht zuerkennen kann. Nach mir ist er ein Lehrsatz, der durch höhere Sätze bewiesen, und bestimmt wird."

50. Plan for a Letter [Briefentwurf] to Flatt of November or December 1793, in ibid., pt. 2, vol. 2, p. 18: "Aenesidemus, den ich unter die merkwürdigsten Produkte unseres Jahrzehends zähle, hat mich von dem überzeugt, was ich vorher schon ahndete, dass selbst nach Kants, u. Reinholds Arbeiten die Philosophie noch nicht im Zustande einer Wissenschaft ist, hat mein eignes System in seinen Grundfesten erschüttert, u. hat mich, da sich's unter freiem Himmel nicht gut wohnt, genöthigt von neuem aufzubauen. Ich habe mich überzeugt, dass nur durch Entwicklung aus einem einzigen Grundsatze Philosophie Wissenschaft werden kann. . . ." See also Letter to Heinrich Stephani of December 1793, in ibid., pt. 3, vol. 2, p. 28.

51. See ibid., vol. 1, p. 29: "Der Verfasser dieser Abhandlung wurde durch das Lesen neuer Skeptiker, besonders durch *Aenesidemus,* und der vortrefflichen *Maimonischen* Schriften völlig von dem überzeugt, was ihm schon vorher höchst wahrscheinlich gewesen war: dass die Philosophie, selbst durch die neuesten Bemühungen der scharfsinnigsten Männer noch nicht zum Range einer evidenten Wissenschaft erhoben sei."

52. "Er glaubte, den Grund davon gefunden, und einen leichten Weg entdeckt zu haben, alle jene gar sehr gegründeten Anforderungen der Skeptiker an die kritische Philosophie vollkommen zu befriedigen" (ibid.). See also the letters in ibid., pt. 3, pp. 2, 18, and 28.

53. For a recent study of this point, see Wolfgang H. Schrader, "Philosophie als System—Reinhold und Fichte," in *Erneuerung der Transzendentalphilosophie im Anschluss an Kant und Fichte. Reinhard Lauth zum 60. Geburtstag,* ed. Klaus Hammacher und Albert Mues (Stuttgart/Bad Canstatt, 1979), pp. 331–44.

54. See Letter to Reinhold from end of March/beginning of April 1795, in *Fichte-Gesamtausgabe,* pt. 3, vol. 2, p. 282.

55. For a precise account of the impact of Maimon's thought on Fichte's, see Peter Baumanns, *Fichtes Wissenschaftslehre* (Bonn: Bouvier, 1974), pp. 55–56.

56. See "Aenesidemus-Rezension," in *Fichte-Gesamtausgabe,* pt. 1, vol. 2, pp. 31–68.

57. "die Vorstellung werde auf das Objekt bezogen, wie die Wirkung auf ihre Ursache, und auf das Subjekt, wie Accidens auf Substanz." Ibid., p. 60.

58. Philosophy's purpose, Fichte writes, is "dass alles, was in unserm Gemüthe vorkommt, aus ihm selbst vollständig zu erklären und zu begreifen ist. Es ist ihr nicht eingefallen, eine Frage zu beantworten, die, nach ihr, der Vernunft widerspricht. Sie zeigt uns den Zirkel, über den wir nicht hinausschreiten können; innerhalb desselben aber verschafft sie uns den innigsten Zusammerhang in unsrer ganzen Erkenntnis." Ibid., p. 55.

59. See ibid., vol. 1, p. 155.

60. See ibid., vol. 2, p. 51: "Das V.V. existirt für das V.V. und durch das V.V.; diess ist der nothwendige Zirkel, in welchem jeder endliche, und das heisst, jeder uns denkbare, Verstand eingeschlossen ist."

61. See ibid., pp. 61–62: "Und wenn nur seine Folgerung [i.e., Leibniz—

T.R.] nicht über den Zirkel hinausginge, in den der menschliche Geist eingeschlossen ist, und welcher er, der alles übrige sah, allein nicht sah; so wäre sie unstreitig richtig; *das Ding wäre an sich so beschaffen, wie es sich—sich selbst vorstellt.* Kant entdeckte diesen Zirkel."

62. See ibid., vol. 1, p. 277.
63. See ibid., pt. 2, vol. 3, p. 27n.
64. See ibid, p. 75n.
65. See ibid., p. 91.
66. See ibid., p. 110.
67. See ibid., p. 26.
68. See ibid.
69. See ibid., p. 21.
70. See ibid., p. 142.
71. See ibid., p. 111.
72. Ibid., pt. 1, vol. 2, pp. 255–256.
73. Ibid., p. 302.
74. Ibid., p. 402.
75. Ibid., p. 393.
76. Ibid., p. 402.
77. "Wir haben den absolut ersten, schlechthin unbedingten Grundsatz alles menschlichen Wissens *aufzusuchen.*" Ibid., p. 255.
78. "*Beweisen* oder *bestimmen* lässt er sich nicht, wenn er absolut erster Grundsatz seyn soll." Ibid.
79. "Merkwürdig aber ist es, dass seine Ideen auch der Fichteschen Spekulation zu Grunde liegen, dass Fichte eigentlich nur die Reinholdischen Ideen weiter fortgebildet hat." *Reinhold, Fichte, Schelling,* 2d ed., 1824, in *J. F. Fries Werke,* ed. Gert König and Lutz Goldsetzer, rpt. (Aalen, n.d.), vol. 24, p. 329. Fries further writes: "Fichte ist anfangs nur auf demselben Wege weiter fortgegangen, den Reinhold bezeichnet hatte; er folgte Reinholds Regeln und verwickelte sich noch tiefer in seine Fehler." (Ibid.)

III Circularity, System, and Antifoundationalism

1. Karl Leonhard Reinhold, ed., C. G. Bardilis und C. L. Reinholds Brief-wechsel über das Wesen der Philosophie und das Unwesen der Spekulation (Munich: J. Lentner, 1804), p. v.
2. Ibid., p. 1, Letter to Bardili in Kiel, December 1799: "Seit neun Wochen her studiere ich Ihren Grundriss der ersten Logik mit einem Interesse, womit ich noch nie ein Buch studirt habe. Fünfmal las ich bis isst schon das Ganze."
3. "welche Leibniz . . . zuerst aufgeregt hatte, das grosse Problem der Philosophie als Wissenschaft auszulösen." Ibid., p. 7.
4. Letter from Reinhold to Bardili in Kiel, January 1800, ibid., pp. 68–69: "Aber ich habe Sie seitdem durch mein täglich fortgesetztes Studium Ihres Grundrisses, und nun insbesondere, durch die in Ihrem Schreiben mit mitgetheilte neue Darstellung der Hauptmomente Ihres Systems. . . ."
5. See ibid., p. 82: "Meine neue Spekulation war nun die Coalition der Bardilischen Logik und der Transcendentalphilosophie."
6. Letter from Reinhold to Bardili of September 1, 1800, in ibid., p. 248: "Ich sehe nun auch ein, dass ich durch meine Behauptung, die Philosophie sey als Wissenschaft, eine durch die Worte bedingte Anwendung des Denkens mehr den Worten, als den Begriffen nach, mit Jacobi einig gewesen bin."

7. . . . eine völlig neue Darstellung Ihres [i.e., Fichte's—T.R.] transcendentalen Idealismus." Ibid., p. 83.

8. *Grundriss der ersten Logik, gereinigt von den Irrthümern bisheriger Logiker überhaupt, der kantischen insbesondere; keine Medicina mentis, brauchbar hauptsächlich für Deutschlands kritische Philosophie* (Stuttgart: Löflund, 1800).

9. Ibid., p. 45: "Aber alle beruhten auf Irrthümern, welche durch die Kantische Kritik vollends unabsehbar wurden."

10. Ibid., pp. 339–40: "Kant hat der spekulativen Vernunft noch Anschauungen als einzig mögliche Proben der Realität in ihren Aussagen, zugemuthet, nachdem er sie vorher selbst über die Grenzen der Möglichkeit irgend einer Anschauung hinweggerückt hatte, and in so fern er sie vorher selbst darüber hinweggerückt hatte; hat ihr also eine Leistung auferlegt, welcher zu entsprechen, durch seine selbsteigene Voraussetzung, unter welcher die Leistung geschehen sollte, von ihm in eigener Person unmöglich gemacht worden war, und hat dann das Höchste, was die Menschheit besitzt, als etwas bloss an und für sich betrachtetes, darüber verdammt, weil es nicht leisten könne, was er ihm gleichwohl durch seine eigene Voraussetzung, unter dieser Voraussetzung zu leisten, selbst und in eigener Person, zu leisten unmöglich gemacht hatte, hat aber dessen ungeachtet vor wie nach wieder behauptet. . . ."

11. Ibid., p. 4, par. 7: "A, als Einheit, in A, A, A u.s.w., mithin (schon diesfalls) im Vielen, oder in der Unbestimmtheit aller möglichen Fälle seines Gebrauchs, unendlichmal wiederholen können, nennen wir also unser Denken."

12. Ibid., p. 256: "Was in unserer Erkenntnis das Letzte ist, die reine Erkenntnis eines *Prius* kat' exochen, das ist im Wesen der Dinge selbst das Erste, ist der Wesen Wesen, ist A als A in A durch A."

13. *Beyträge zur leichteren Übersicht der Philosophie beym Anfange des 19. Jahrhunderts* (Hamburg: Friedrich Perthes, 1801).

14. Reinhold, *Bardilis und Reinhold Briefwechsel*, p. 2: "Ergründung der Realität der Erkenntnis."

15. Ibid., p. 67: "das Philosophieren wäre sonach das von der Liebe zur Wahrheit und Gewissheit ausgehende Bestreben, die Erkenntnis zu ergründen, oder, was dasselbe heisst, die Realität der Erkenntnis, als solche, zu bewähren und vergewissern."

16. Ibid., p. 72: "Sonach würde, wenn je Ableitung gelungen wäre, eine im strengsten Sinne bewährte Erkenntnis, ein Wissen statt finden, in welchem das Urwahre an dem Wahren durch das Urwahre erkannt wäre."

17. See ibid., p. 78.

18. See ibid., p. 82.

19. See ibid., p. 85.

20. Ibid., p. 87: "Der durchgeführte Idealismus führt auf Materialismus, und dieser auf jenen zürück. Beyde nemen dann auf den Skepticismus, inwieferne derselbe dogmatisch ist, d.h. inwieferne der die Realität des Unterschiedes zwischen dem Objektiven und Subjektiven in der Erkenntnis schlechthin läugnet, in sich auf. Sonach findet jedes bisherige verirrte Streben der Spekulation, was dasselbe auch sonst schon, wissentlich und unwissentlich, gesucht hat, in der blossen lautern—Ichheit."

21. Ibid., p. 91: "Die Analysis des Denkens als Denkens."

22. Ibid., p. 103: "Absolute Einheit des Identischen."

23. Ibid., p. 106: ". . . in dieser unendlichen Wiederholbarkeit, oder reinen Identität."

24. See ibid., p. 163.

25. See ibid., p. 133.

26. See ibid., p. 115.

27. See ibid., p. 141.

28. See ibid., p. 146.

29. See ibid., pp. 153–54: "Dass die eigene, individuelle Individualität—von welcher jene Herren abstrahirt zu haben glauben, und von der Sie glauben, dass nur wir anderen Unphilosophen nicht zu abstrahiren Kopf genug haben—jenes eigene Ich—nur die Individualität überhaupt, das wirkliche, reale, empirische Ich überhaupt ist, von dem Sie in der That hinweggesehen haben. Hinter diese hinweggesehene Individualität überhaupt—hat sich die Nichthinweggesehene, individuelle, Fichtesche, Schellingsche u.s.w. Individualität versteckt, um, ungesehen von sich selber, sich selber zuzusehen."

30. For Fichte's response, see Letter to Schelling of Nov. 15, 1800, in *Fichte-Schelling Briefwechsel,* ed. Walter Schulz (Frankfurt a M:, Suhrkamp, 1968), pp. 103–106.

31. Differenz des Fichte 'schen und Schelling 'scher Systems der Philosophie in Beziehung auf Reinhold's Beyträge zur leichteren Übersicht des Zustands der Philosophie zu Anfang des neunzehten Jahrhunderts, 1 Stes Heft.

32. See, e.g., Helmut Girndt, *Differenz des Fichteschen und Hegelschen Systems in der Hegelschen "Differenzschrift,"* (Bonn: Bouvier, 1965), p. 11. On Girndt, See H. Braun, "Differenzen. Bemerkungen von einem Buch von Helmut Girndt," in *Hegel-Studien* 4 (1967): 288–99.

33. See further Ludwig Siep, *Hegels Fichtekritik und die Wissenschaftslehre von 1804* (Freiburg/Munich: Albers Verlag, 1970).

34. In the recent Suhrkamp Verlag edition of Hegel's writings, the editors indicate that although the text probably was written in early 1801, the ideas go back to the last months of Hegel's stay in Frankfurt, prior to his taking up residence in Jena. See vol. 2, p. 586.

35. See Kant, *Critique of Pure Reason,* B xliv; see Fichte, "Über Geist und Buchstabe in der Philosophie," in *Fichtes Werke;* ed. I. H. Fichte, vol. 8, pp. 270–300.

36. *System of Transcendental Idealism,* trans. Peter Heath (Charlottesville: University of Virginia Press, 1978), p. 28.

37. See especially *Second Introduction to the Science of Knowledge,* sec. 5 and 6, in *Fichte: Science of Knowledge (Wissenschaftslehre) with the First and Second Introductions,*. trans. Peter Heath and John Lachs (New York: Appleton-Century-Crafts, 1970), pp. 12–20.

38. See *System of Transcendental Idealism,* p. 231.

39. Ibid., p. 27.

40. Ibid.

41. *Fichtes Werke,* vol. 11, p. 371: "Noch schlimmer ist oben, nicht zu sehen, dass die Eine und absolute Vernunft, ausser der Nichts sein soll, nicht die Indifferenz des Subjektiven und Objektiven sein kann, ohne zugleich und in derselben ungetheilten Weisheit auch die Differenz der beiden zu sein."

42. For Fichte's reaction to this text, see ibid., pp. 371–89: "Zur Darstellung von Schellings Identitätssysteme."

43. *Beyträge,* p. 12: ". . . beschäftigen sich ausdrücklich, und vor allen Dingen, mit der Aufstellung und Auflösung der ersten Aufgabe der Philosophie, und beginnen unmittelbar mit der Ergründung der Erkenntnis. . . . "

44. For Jacobi's reaction to Reinhold's reading of his thought, see Reinhold's *Beyträge,* Heft 3, 1802, Appendix.

45. See "Recension von Bardili's Grundriss der ersten Logik" (1800), in *Fichtes Werke,* vol. 2, pp. 490–503.

46. See "J. G. Fichte's Antwortsschreiben an Herrn Professor Reinhold" (1801), in ibid., pp. 504–534.

47. See *Fichtes Werke,* Vol. 2, p. 491.

48. See ibid., p. 521.

49. *Hegel, Werke,* vol. 2, p. 122: "Wenn die Philosophie als Ganzes sich und die Realität der Erkenntnisse ihrer Form und ihrem Inhalt nach in sich selbst begründet, so kommt dagegen das Begründen und Ergründen in seinem Gedränge des Bewährens und Analysierens und das Weil und Inwiefern und Dann und Insoferne—weder aus sich heraus noch in die Philosophie hinein. Für die haltungslose Angstlichkeit, die sich in ihrer Geschäftigkeit immer nur vermehrt, kommen alle Untersuchungen zu bald, und jeder Anfang ist ein Vorgreifen sowie jede Philosophie nur eine Vorübung. Die Wissenschaft behauptet, sich in sich dadurch zu begründen, dass sie jeden ihrer Teile absolut setzt und hierdurch in dem Anfang und in jedem einzelnen Punkt eine Identität und ein Wissen konstituiert; als objektive Totalität begründet das Wissen sich zugleich immer mehr, je mehr es sich bildet, und seine Teile sind nur gleichzeitig mit diesen Ganzen der Erkenntnisse begründet. Mittelpunkt und Kreis sind so aufeinander bezogen, dass der erste Anfang des Kreises schon eine Beziehung auf den Mittelpunktist, und dieser ist nicht ein vollständiger Mittelpunkt, wenn nicht alle seine Beziehungen, der ganze Kreis vollendet sind,—ein Ganzes, das sowenig einer besonderen Handhabe des Begründens bedarf als die Erde einer besonderen Handhabe, um von der Kraft, die sie um die Sonne führt und zugleich in der ganzen lebendigen Mannigfaltigkeit ihrer Gestalten hält, gefasst zu werden."

50. The source of this simile is probably in Lessing's statement "This wide and dreadful gulf over which I cannot pass, often and earnestly though I have attempted the leap." "Über den Beweis des Geistes und der Kraft," cited in H. Höffding, *A History of Modern Philosophy,* trans. B. E. Meyer (New York: Dover. 1955), vol. 2, p. 22; on Lessing, see also S. Kierkegaard, *Concluding Unscientific Postscript,* trans. David F. Swenson and Walter Lowrie (Princeton: Princeton University Press), pp. 59–67.

51. *Beyträge* (1801), p. vi: ". . . dass die ganze transcendentale Umfölgung durch sich selber auf die Kreislinie beschränkt, welche der fortschreitende Idealismus und die, als den einzig möglichen Mittelpunkt aller Wahrheit angenommene, Subjektivität herum,—und dass durch die Fichtesche, Schellingsche Sublimation des Kantianschen transcendentalen Idealismus jener Mittelpunkt entscheidend festgesetzt, und jener Kreislinie völlig vollendet sey."

IV Circular Epistemology

1. The difficulty is well described by Theodor Häring, who writes: "Es ist ein öffentliches Geheimnis, dass fast alle bisherigen Darstellungen Hegels oder Einführungen in ihn den Leser, der sich daraufhin an die Lektüre Hegels selbst machen will, gänzlich im Stiche lassen; ja, dass von diesen

Darstellern Hegels wohl wenige im Stande waren, eine Seite der Hegelschen Werke selbst restlos in ihrem Wortlaut zu erklären." *Hegel. Sein Wollen und sein Werk* (Leipzig/Bern: B. G. Teubner, 1929), vol. 1, p. vii.

2. The following passage expresses a widely entrenched view: "Seit geräumer Zeit hat sich immer mehr die Überzeugung durchgesetzt, dass man über den philosophischen und den wissenschaftlichen Wert der Hegelschen Theorie erst dann entscheiden kann, wenn man in der Lage ist, sich die in der Hegelschen Logik dargelegten Sachverhalte und die Verfahrung ihrer Plausibilisierung zu erschliessen." Hans Friedrich Fulda, Rolf-Peter Horstmann, and Michael Theunissen, *Kritische Darlegung der Metaphysik. Eine Diskussion über Hegels "Logik"* (Frankfurt a. M.: Suhrkamp, 1980), p. 8.

3. For these and similar comments by a long list of Hegel commentators, see Hans Rademaker, *Hegels Wissenschaft der Logik* (Wiesbaden: Fritz Steiner, 1979),foreword, pp.1–9.

4. See *G. W. F. Hegel: Werke in Zwanzig Banden*, vol. 8, p. 20: "Das Bedürfnis, meinen Zuhörern einen Leitfaden zu meinen philosophischen Vorlesungen in die Hände zu geben, ist die nächste Veranlassung, dass ich diese Übersicht des gesamten Umfanges der Philosophie früher ans Licht treten lassen, als sonst meine Gedanke gewesen wäre."

5. Ibid, p. 3: "Die gedrängte Kürze, welche ein Grundriss nötig macht . . . ."; see also ibid, p. 23: "Doch für den kompendischen Zweck des Lehrbuchs musste der Stil gedrängt, formell, und abstrakt gehalten werden."

6. See Letter to Victor Cousin, in *Briefe von und an Hegel*, ed. J. Hoffmeister (Hamburg: F. Meiner, 1952–1960) vol. 3, p. 169: "Ce livre n'est qu'une suite de thèses."

7. For details, see *Hegels Werke*, vol. 4, p. 604.

8. No systematic attention need be given to commentary by others, often printed with the text, collected by Leopold von Henning. On this point, see the foreword by J. N. Findlay to *The Logic of Hegel, Translated from the Encyclopedia of the Philosophical Sciences,* trans. William Wallace (London: Oxford University Press, 1969), p. v.

9. For an account of the controversy surrounding Plato's view of presupposition, see Richard Robinson, *Plato's Earlier Dialectic* (London: Oxford at the Clarendon Press, 1962), esp. chap. 7, pp. 93–114, and chap. 10, pp. 146–80.

10. *Plato's Republic,* trans. G. M. A. Grube (Indianapolis: Hackett, 1974), p. 165.

11. Ibid., p. 184.

12. The immense significance of Plato's distinction was seen, for instance, by Aristotle. In the *Nicomachean Ethics,* he comments on Plato's distinction in the *Republic* at 510 B in nearly identical language. See NE I, 4, 1095a.

13. Marxist writers who touch on this theme include G. Lukács, in *History and Class Consciousness,* and K. Kosik, in *Dialectic of the Concrete.* For a non-Marxist treatment of this theme, see E. Husserl, *Logische Untersuchungen,* vol. 2, p. 3: "Zur Lehre von den Ganzen und Teilen."

V Circular Epistemology and the History of Philosophy

1. For remarks on the genesis of Hegel's view of history and the publication of the manuscripts constituting this work, see *G. W. F. Hegel: Werke in Zwanzig Banden,* vol. 12, pp. 561f.

2. Ibid., vol. 20, p. 526: "Wer heute Hegels Vorlesungen liesst, tut dies sicher nicht in erster Linie, um etwas über Philosophiegeschichte zu erfahren,

sondern um zu erfahren, wie *Hegel* die Geschichte der Philosophie sah und deutete."

3. See, on this topic, Jean-Louis Vieillard-Baron, ed., *G. W. F. Hegel. Vorlesungen über Platon, 1825–1826. Unveröffentlicher Text* (Frankfurt a.M.: Ullstein Verlag, 1979).

4. For another classification of metaphysics, according to which Kant's basic divisions are determined by Suarez's systematic restatement of Aristotelian ontology, see M. Heidegger, *Basic Problems of Phenomenology*, ed. and trans. Alfred Hofstadter (Bloomington: Indiana University Press, 1982), p. 80.

5. See *La scienza nuova*, par. 331.

6. See below pars. 115 Anmerkung, 119 Anmerkung.

7. For an early study touching on this problem in Hegel, see F. A. Trendelenburg, *Die logische Frage in Hegel's System* (Leipzig: F. A. Brockhaus, 1843).

8. From this perspective, since we have Kant's explicit claim, spelled out in the *Prolegomena* but at best unclear in the *Critique of Pure Reason*, that his own position is in large part a reaction to Hume's, the critical philosophy can be said to fail to attain the objective it fixes for itself; in a word, it fails as evaluated by its own criterion.

9. For a similar view, see John E. Smith, "Hegel's Critique of Kant," in *Review of Metaphysics* 26, no. 3 (March 1973): 438–60.

10. See *Prolegomena*, par. 57, *Akad., Ausgabe*, vol. 4, pp. 354–55.

11. See *Introduction to Logic*, trans. Thomas Kingsmill Abbott (New York: Philosophical Library, 1963), p. 15; see also F. Van de Pitte, *Kant as Philosophical Anthropologist* (The Hague: Nijhoff, 1971).

12. For a non-Hegelian, neo-Kantian reading of Schelling, centered on the problem of freedom, and which refuses a central role to the stage of transcendental idealism, see Miklos Vetö, *Le fondement selon Schelling* (Paris: Beauchesnes, 1977).

13. *Jacobis Spinoza-Buchlein. Nebst Replik und Duplik*, ed. Fritz Mauthner (Munich: Georg Müller, 1912), p. 80: ". . . dass es an und für sich unmöglich sei, das Unendliche aus dem Endlichen zu entwickeln." This problem also bothered Moses Mendelssohn, who wrote: "Die grösste Schwierigkeit aber, die ich in dem System des Spinoza finde, liegt mir darin, dass er aus dem Zusammennehmen der Eingeschränkten das Uneingeschränkte will entstehen lassen" (ibid., p. 110).

14. Ibid., pp. 165–66: ". . . der Begriff einer unmittelbaren Gewissheit, welche nicht allein keinen Grund bedarf, sondern schlechterdings all Gründe ausschliesst und einzig und allein *die mit dem vorgestellten Dinge übereinstimmende Vorstellung selbst ist.*"

15. *Über die Religion. Reden an die Gebildeten unter ihrer Verächtern* (Hamburg: F. Meiner, 1958), p. 31: "Anschauen des Universums, ich bitte befreundet Euch mit diesem Begriff, er ist der Angel meiner ganzen Rede, er ist die allgemeinste und höchste Formel der Religion, woraus Ihr jeden Ort in derselben finden könnt, woraus sich ihr Wesen und ihre Grenzen aufs genaueste bestillen lassen."

16. Ibid., p. 29: "Ihr Wesen nach ist weder Denken noch Handeln, sondern Anschauung und Gefühl."

VI Thought, Being, and Circular Epistemology

1. *Akad. Ausgabe*, vol. 9, p. 50.

2. See Heinrich Heine, *Zur Religion und Philosophie in Deutschland.*

3. For an early objection of this kind, see Arnauld's criticism of Descartes's reasoning in the "Quatrièmes Objections," *Oeuvres de Descartes,* ed. F. Alquié (Paris: Garnier, 1963–1973), vol. 2, p. 652, and Descartes's response, ibid., p. 690.

4. Ibid., vol. 1, p. 647. "Car il me semble que les raisons s'y entre-suivent en telle sorte que, comme les dernières sont demontrées par les premières, qui sont leurs causes, ces premieres le sont réciproquement par les dernières, qui sont leurs effets. Et on ne doit pas imaginer que je commette en ceci la faute que les logiciens nomment un cercle; car l'expérience rendant la plupart de ces effets très certains, les causes dont je les déduis ne servent pas tant à les prouver qu'à les expliquer; mais, tout au contraire, ce sont elles qui sont prouvées par eux."

5. Indeed, it is interesting to note that the evident opposition between these doctrines has led to the curious hypothesis that the *Discourse* is not a single treatise, but rather is composed of a series of disparate texts. See ibid., pp. 550–52.

6. Descartes is usually held to insist on the form of absolute certainty implicit in his demand for a priori justification, although there is reason to believe that he intended his claim to have no more than subjective, or psychological, force. In response to a question put by Mersenne, he writes: "Car nous supposons une croyance et une persuasion si ferme qu'elle ne puisse être ôtée, laquelle par conséquent est en tout la même chose qu'une parfaite certitude." "Réponses aux secondes objections," ibid., vol. 2, pp. 569–70.

VII Beyond Hegel

1. For the view that phenomenology begins with Husserl and the sources of his thought, see John Wild, preface to *What Is Phenomenology and Other Essays* (Chicago: Quadrangle Books, 1962), p. 7: "Phenomenology originated with the profound and creative criticism of British empiricism inaugurated by Brentano and Husserl at the very end of the nineteenth century."

2. For some discussion of the relation of analytic thought to the continental tradition, especially as concerns Hegel, see Richard Bernstein, *Praxis and Action* (Philadelphia: University of Pennsylvania Press, 1971), esp. pt. 4.

3. For a brief description of the origins of analytic thought, see J. O. Urmson, *Philosophical Analysis: Its Development between the Two World Wars* (London: Oxford University Press, 1960), esp. chap. 1.

4. For a classic statement of this approach, see Edmund Husserl, *Ideas: General Introduction to Pure Phenomenology,* trans. W. R. Boyce Gibson (New York: Collier Books, 1962), p. 20: "Philosophy, as it moves towards its realization, is not a relatively incomplete science improving as it goes naturally forward. There lies embedded in its meaning as philosophy a radicalism in the matter of foundations, a securing for itself an absolute basis: the totality of presuppositions that can be 'taken for granted.' But that too must itself be first clarified through corresponding reflexions, and the absolutely binding quality of its requirements laid bare."

5. Among the commentators on Husserl, Maurice Natanson has clearly understood the meaning of Husserlian presuppositionlessness. He writes: "Phenomenology purports to be a 'presuppositionless' philosophy. What is meant is simply the principle that nothing can be accepted by the inquirer

unless he has scrutinized its character and implications and also recognized that it is a feature of experience. Strictly speaking, a presuppositionless philosophy is not a philosophy without assumptions. It is a philosophy in which assumptions are candidly admitted, examined, and accounted for." *Edmund Husserl: Philosopher of Infinite Tasks* (Evanston: Northwestern University Press, 1973), p. 12.

6. For a representative form of this view, see Roderick M. Chisholm, *The Foundations of Knowing*, esp. chap. 5: "The Problem of the Criterion." Michael Williams's suggestion that Chisholm's view is antifoundationalist seems clearly mistaken. See Michael Williams, *Groundless Belief* (Oxford: Blackwells, 1977), p. 84.

7. For a statement of this view, see Martin Heidegger, *Being and Time*, par. 7.

8. For the post-Hegelian evolution of the phenomenological view of what has become known as the hermeneutical circle, see Wilhelm Dilthey, "Die Entstehung der Hermeneutik," in *Gesammelte Schriften* (Stuttgart/Göttingen: B. G. Teubner/Vandenhoeck and Ruprecht, 1961), vol. 5, pp. 317–39; Heidegger, *Being and Time*, par. 32; Hans-Georg Gadamer, *Wahrheit und Methode* (Tübingen: J. C. B. Mohr, 1975), pt. 2, chap. 2, "Grundzüge einer Theorie der hermeneutischen Erfahrung," pp. 250–61.

9. This approach is developed by Nicholas Rescher. Although he writes in the analytic mode, and is widely regarded as a leading analytic thinker, he regards his position as "pragmatic idealism." For his trilogy on this topic, see *Conceptual Idealism* (Oxford: Blackwells, 1973), *The Primacy of Practice* (Oxford: Blackwells, 1973), and *Methodological Pragmatism* (New York: New York University Press, 1977).

10. For a phenomenological attempt to transcend epistemology, see Gadamer, *Wahrheit und Methode*, esp. pt. 2, chap. 1, sec. 3: "Überwindung der erkenntnistheoretischen Fragestellung durch die phänomenologische Forschung."

11. For a recent statement of this view, see Richard Rorty, *Philosophy and the Mirror of Nature* (Princeton: Princeton University Press, 1979) and *Consequences of Pragmatism* (Minneapolis: University of Minnesota Press, 1982).

Conclusion

1. *Zur Geschichte der Religion und Philosophie in Deutschland*, in *Werke und Briefe*, ed. Hans Kaufmann (Berlin: Aufbau Verlag, 1961), vol. 5, p. 303.

2. A recent example is provided by Derrida's revolt against "logocentrisme." In a passage on Hegel, he writes in part: ". . . il a sans doute *résumé* la totalité du logos." Jacques Derrida, *De la grammatologie* (Paris: Les Editions de Minuit, 1967), p. 39.

INDEX